The Frontier of Writing

The Frontier of Writing: A Study of Seamus Heaney's Prose is the first collection of essays solely focused on examining the Nobel prize-winning poet's prose. The collection offers ten different perspectives on this body of work which vary from sustained thematic analyses on poetic form, the construction of identity, and poetry as redress, to a series of close readings of prose writing on poetic exemplars such as Robert Lowell, Patrick Kavanagh, W.B. Yeats, Ted Hughes, Philip Larkin and Brian Friel. Seamus Heaney's prose is extensive in its literary depth, knowledge, critical awareness and its span. During the course of his life, he published six collections of prose entitled *Preoccupations: Selected Prose 1968–1978, Place and Displacement: Recent Poetry of Northern Ireland, The Government of the Tongue: The 1986 T.S. Eliot Memorial Lectures and Other Critical Writings, The Place of Writing, The Redress of Poetry: Oxford Lectures* and *Finders Keepers*. Each of these texts is addressed in the collection alongside occasional and specific essays such as 'Crediting Poetry', 'Writer and Righter' and 'Mossbawn via Mantua: Ireland in/and Europe, Cross-currents and Exchanges', among many others. This book is a comprehensive and timely study of Seamus Heaney's prose from leading international scholars in the field.

Ian Hickey has worked as a lecturer in the Department of English Language and Literature at Mary Immaculate College. His first monograph *Haunted Heaney: Spectres and the Poetry* was published by Routledge in 2021 and was a joint winner of the British Association for Contemporary Literary Studies Monograph Prize. He also co-edited, alongside Ellen Howley, *Seamus Heaney's Mythmaking* published by Routledge in 2023.

Eugene O'Brien is a professor of English Literature and Theory and head of the Department of English Language and Literature at Mary Immaculate College. He is also the director of the Mary Immaculate Institute for Irish Studies. He is the editor of the *Oxford University Press Online Bibliography* project in literary theory (Oxford Online Bibliographies: Literary and Cultural Theory) and of the *Routledge Studies in Irish Literature* series (Routledge Studies in Irish Literature).

Routledge Studies in Irish Literature
Editor: Eugene O'Brien
Mary Immaculate College, University of Limerick, Ireland

Reading Paul Howard
The Art of Ross O'Carroll-Kelly
Eugene O'Brien

Wallace Stevens and the Contemporary Irish Novel
Order, Form, and Creative Un-Doing
Ian Tan

The Art of Translation in Seamus Heaney's Poetry
Toward Heaven
Edward T. Duffy

Masculinity and Identity in Irish Literature
Heroes, Lads, and Fathers
Cassandra S. Tully de Lope

Modern Irish Literature and the Primitive Sublime
Maria McGarrity

Marina Carr and Greek Tragedy
Feminist Myths of Monstrosity
Salomé Paul

The Writings of Padraic Colum
'That Queer Thing, Genius'
Edited by Pádraic Whyte and Keith O'Sullivan

The Frontier of Writing
A Study of Seamus Heaney's Prose
Edited by Ian Hickey and Eugene O'Brien

For more information about this series, please visit: www.routledge.com/Routledge-Studies-in-Irish-Literature/book-series/RSIL

The Frontier of Writing
A Study of Seamus Heaney's Prose

Edited by
Ian Hickey and Eugene O'Brien

NEW YORK AND LONDON

First published 2024
by Routledge
605 Third Avenue, New York, NY 10158

and by Routledge
4 Park Square, Milton Park, Abingdon, Oxon, OX14 4RN

Routledge is an imprint of the Taylor & Francis Group, an informa business

© 2024 selection and editorial matter, Ian Hickey and Eugene O'Brien;
individual chapters, the contributors

The right of Ian Hickey and Eugene O'Brien to be identified as the authors
of the editorial material, and of the authors for their individual chapters,
has been asserted in accordance with sections 77 and 78 of the Copyright,
Designs and Patents Act 1988.

All rights reserved. No part of this book may be reprinted or reproduced or
utilised in any form or by any electronic, mechanical, or other means, now
known or hereafter invented, including photocopying and recording, or in
any information storage or retrieval system, without permission in writing
from the publishers.

Trademark notice: Product or corporate names may be trademarks or
registered trademarks, and are used only for identification and explanation
without intent to infringe.

ISBN: 978-1-032-5-97621 (hbk)
ISBN: 978-1-032-5-97652 (pbk)
ISBN: 978-1-003-4-56148 (ebk)

DOI: 10.4324/9781003456148

Typeset in Sabon
by codeMantra

Ian: To the memory of Matthew Hickey
Eugene: To Áine, Eoin Dara and Sinéad

Contents

Notes on Contributors		*ix*
Acknowledgements		*xiii*

Introduction: Coming to Poetic Terms with Himself and Others   1
EUGENE O'BRIEN AND IAN HICKEY

1 **'Things Founded Clean on Their Own Shapes': Seamus
Heaney and the Shape of Poetry**   14
EUGENE O'BRIEN

2 **Seamus Heaney's Uncanny Encounters**   35
HENRY HART

3 **Double Agent: The Redress of Seamus Heaney's Prose Poems**   51
WILLIAM FOGARTY

4 **Preoccupied with Redress: Heaney Meditates on Getting
his 'Feel into Words'**   71
RUTH MACKLIN

5 **'The Makings of a Music': Musicality and Seamus
Heaney's Prose**   89
IAN HICKEY

6 **The Limits of Redress: Heaney's Aesthetics of Grace
Confronts Larkin's Struggle with Gravity**   110
MAGDALENA KAY

7 **Different Animals: Heaney's Public and Poetic Ted Hughes**   130
CAOIMHE HIGGINS

viii   *Contents*

8 'Moving in Step': Seamus Heaney on Patrick Kavanagh   147
   GARY WADE

9 'The Push of the Whole Man': Heaney on Robert Lowell   168
   MEG TYLER

10 Seamus Heaney's Wordsworthian Prose Assessments
   of Brian Friel's Drama   179
   RICHARD RANKIN RUSSELL

   Index   *201*

Notes on Contributors

William Fogarty

Bill Fogarty is an assistant professor of English at the University of Central Florida. His book *The Politics of Speech in Later Twentieth-Century Poetry: Local Tongues in Heaney, Brooks, Harrison, and Clifton* was published in August. He has also published essays on modern and contemporary poetry in *The Wallace Stevens Journal*, *Twentieth-Century Literature*, *The Comparatist* and *The Journal of Working-Class Studies*.

Henry Hart

Henry Hart is the Mildred and J.B. Hickman Professor of Humanities at The College of William and Mary. His publications include several critical books on modern poets: *The Poetry of Geoffrey Hill* (1986), *Seamus Heaney: Poet of Contrary Progressions* (1991) and *Robert Lowell and the Sublime* (1995). His biography, *James Dickey: The World as a Lie* (2000), was runner-up for a Southern Book Critics' Circle Award. Wiley-Blackwell published his biography *The Life of Robert Frost* (2017). He has also published four books of poetry: *The Ghost Ship* (1990), *The Rooster Mask* (1998), *Background Radiation* (2007) and *Familiar Ghosts* (2014). From 1984 to 1994, he co-edited *VERSE*, an international poetry magazine. His essays and poems have appeared in *The New Yorker*, *Poetry*, *The Southern Review*, *Denver Quarterly*, *The Gettysburg Review*, *The Georgia Review*, *The Kenyon Review*, *Contemporary Literature*, *Twentieth Century Literature* and numerous other journals. From 2018 to 2020, he served as the poet laureate of Virginia.

Ian Hickey

Ian Hickey has worked as a lecturer in the Department of English Language and Literature at Mary Immaculate College. His first monograph *Haunted Heaney: Spectres and the Poetry* was published by Routledge in 2021 and was a joint winner of the British Association for Contemporary Literary Studies Monograph Prize. He also co-edited, alongside Ellen Howley, *Seamus Heaney's Mythmaking* published by Routledge in 2023. He has published numerous journal articles on the poetry of Seamus Heaney, Brendan Behan and twenty-first-century Irish writing, as well x *Notes on Contributors*

as on Benjamin Zephaniah in *Spoken Word in the UK*. He is currently writing his second monograph entitled *Fragmentation: Twenty-First Century Irish Poetry and Fiction*.

Caoimhe Higgins

Caoimhe Higgins is a PhD research student in the Department of English Language and Literature at Mary Immaculate College. She holds a BA in English from University College Dublin (2018) and an MA in Modern English Literature from Mary Immaculate College (2022). For her doctoral thesis, she is conducting a psychoanalytical reading of Ted Hughes's final collection of poems, *Birthday Letters*. Her research interests include twentieth-century poetry, contemporary Irish writing and psychoanalytical literary perspectives. She is currently writing a chapter for *The Routledge Companion to Sally Rooney* (2024).

Magdalena Kay

Magdalena Kay is a professor of English at the University of Victoria in Canada. She holds a BA in English (Harvard, 1999) and a PhD in Comparative Literature (Berkeley, 2007). Her research focuses on twentieth-century and twenty-first-century British and Irish poetry. She has written three books in this area: *Knowing One's Place in Contemporary Irish and Polish Poetry: Zagajewski, Mahon, Heaney, Hartwig* (Bloomsbury, 2012), *In Gratitude for All the Gifts: Seamus Heaney and Eastern Europe* (University of Toronto Press, 2012) and *Poetry Against the World: Philip Larkin and Charles Tomlinson in Contemporary Britain* (Routledge, 2018).

Ruth Macklin

Ruth Macklin studied English and Classics at the University of Otago, focusing on Latin and Greek. Her interest in Irish Literature led to research on Brendan Kennelly's Medea and on the poetry and prose of Seamus Heaney. She has published on Heaney's Latin translations in *Raids and Settlements: Seamus Heaney as Translator* (2021) and on Heaney's conceptions of redress, craft and technique in *Irish Studies Review*. She is currently writing on ritual and redress in Heaney's poetry.

Eugene O'Brien

Eugene O'Brien is a professor of English literature and theory and head of the Department of English Language and Literature at Mary Immaculate College and is also the director of the Mary Immaculate Institute for Irish Studies. He is the editor of the *Oxford University Press Online Bibliography* project in literary theory (Oxford Online Bibliographies: Literary and Cultural Theory) and of the *Routledge Studies in Irish Literature* series (Routledge Studies in Irish Literature). He has published a number of books on Seamus Heaney including *Seamus Heaney as Aesthetic Thinker: A Study of the Prose* (Syracuse University Press); *The Soul Exceeds its*

Circumstances: The Later Poetry of Seamus Heaney (University of Notre Dame Press); *Seamus Heaney: Creating Irelands of the Mind, Studies on Contemporary Ireland Series* (Liffey Press); *Seamus Heaney Searches for Answers* (Pluto Press) and *Seamus Heaney and the Place of Writing* (University Press of Florida). His latest book is *Reading Paul Howard: The Art of Ross O'Carroll-Kelly* (Routledge 2023); and he is working on a monograph of Micheal O'Siadhail (Routledge) and *A Companion to 21st Century Irish Writing* (with Anne Fogarty) (Routledge).

Richard Rankin Russell

Richard Rankin Russell is a professor of Modern and Contemporary British and Irish Literature at Baylor University in Texas where he directs the graduate program in English. He has written *Poetry and Peace: Michael Longley, Seamus Heaney, and Northern Ireland* (Notre Dame, 2010), which won both the 2011 South Central Modern Language Association Book Prize at the 2011 South Atlantic Modern Language Association Book Prize; *Seamus Heaney's Regions* (Notre Dame, 2014), which won the Robert Penn Warren/Cleanth Brooks Award for best book of literary criticism published in America that year; and *Seamus Heaney: An Introduction* (Edinburgh, 2016). He has also published *Modernity, Community, and Place in Brian Friel's Drama* (Syracuse, 2014; rev. ed., 2022), *Bernard MacLaverty* (Bucknell, 2009; pb. ed. forthcoming in 2024) and, most recently, *James Joyce and Samaritan Hospitality: Postcritical and Postsecular Readings in* Dubliners *and* Ulysses (Edinburgh, 2023). He has edited collections on MacLaverty (Bloomsbury, 2014), Peter Fallon (Irish Academic Press, 2013) and Martin McDonagh (Routledge, 2007), and in 2023, he edited a special issue of *Christianity and Literature* on Irish writers.

Meg Tyler

Meg Tyler was the 2016 Fulbright Professor of Anglophone Irish Writing at Queen's University in Belfast. She teaches Humanities at Boston University where she also directs a poetry series and directs the Institute for the Study of Irish Culture. Her book on Seamus Heaney, *A Singing Contest*, was published by Routledge in their series, Major Literary Authors. A new book of poems, *More Feathers in the Lake Than Swans,* is forthcoming from Finishing Line Press in 2025. Her poems and prose have appeared in *Agni, Literary Imagination, Kenyon Review, Harvard Review, Irish Review* and other journals. A chapter on Heaney and the Eclogue, 'Words that the rest of us can understand', recently appeared in *Heaney's Mythmaking*, edited by Ian Hickey and Ellen Howley (Routledge, 2023). An essay on 'The Plaints of Robert Lowell' will soon be published in *Robert Lowell in Context*, edited by Thomas Austenfeld and Grzegorz Kosc (Cambridge University Press, 2024).

xii *Notes on Contributors*

Gary Wade

Gary Wade attended St Columb's College, Derry (where Seamus Heaney boarded between 1951 and 1957) and later taught there from 1997 to 2008. Since then, he has taught Latin and religious studies at St John's School, Leatherhead, from 2010 to 2018. He is currently Assistant Chaplain at Haileybury College, Hertfordshire. He holds an MA in Theology from Rome and an MA in Classical Reception from University College London. He completed his PhD in Seamus Heaney and Catholicism at Durham University, where he was Warden of Trinity Hall between 2018 and 2021. He has just completed a monograph on *Seamus Heaney and Catholicism* to be published by CUP in 2024.

Acknowledgements

The editors would like to express their gratitude to all of the contributors for being a part of this book and for their professionalism in meeting deadlines. It was a pleasure to work with everyone. The editorial process was a joy from the beginning, and we must thank everyone involved in contributing what we feel are scholarly and caring essays on Seamus Heaney's prose writing.

We would like to thank members of the Department of English Language and Literature at Mary Immaculate College for their friendship and support: Thanks are due to John McDonagh, Marita Ryan, Deirdre Flynn, Eóin Flannery, Kathryn Laing, Ailbhe McDaid, Anne O'Keeffe, Joan O'Sullivan, Brian Clancy, Ilona Costello, Giana Hennigan, Justin McNamara, Chris Fitzgerald, Marie O'Brien, Tara Giddens and Linda McGrath.

Introduction
Coming to Poetic Terms
with Himself and Others

Eugene O'Brien and Ian Hickey

Seamus Heaney's prose has long been overlooked in academic criticism, which has tended to favour a discussion of the poetry. The prose has been subjected to only two major book-length studies that were undertaken by Michael Cavanagh and Eugene O'Brien. The attention that his poetry has received is certainly well-merited, and being awarded the Nobel Prize in 1995 has made such attention all the more sustained. Within public discourse, as well as in academic circles, the tendency towards an examination of the poetry is one that overshadows the prose. Very often, the prose seems to be reduced to a form of meta-commentary on the poetry, providing insights into the reasons behind certain poems or collections, and functioning as metatextual explanations which have the authority of authorship. To reduce the prose to such a simplified usage is to overlook its importance within the Heaney canon, but also to attenuate our understanding of literature more generally. Heaney's prose is much more important than this. It offers a scope for negotiating notions such as identity, place, politics, history, the function of poetry, literary critique and thinking in a discursive and more ample narrative form than the necessary brevity of lyric poetry. Thinking here may seem to be a simplified and generic term to what Heaney, and indeed all writers, are undertaking when writing. But, what Heaney is doing in his prose is teasing out and threading his thoughts through the multiple layers that underscore his way of visualising, reimagining and addressing the world.

One of the most interesting and unusual aspects of looking at Heaney's prose is finding out that there is so much of it. During his lifetime, he published six collections of prose:

Preoccupations: Selected Prose, 1968–1978;
Place and Displacement: Recent Poetry of Northern Ireland;
The Government of the Tongue: The 1986 T.S Eliot Memorial Lectures
*   and Other Critical Writings;*
The Place of Writing;
The Redress of Poetry: Oxford Lectures;
Finders Keepers.

DOI: 10.4324/9781003456148-1

2   Eugene O'Brien and Ian Hickey

This is by no means an exhaustive list; as there are also occasional and specific essays such as 'Among Schoolchildren', 'Crediting Poetry', 'Mossbawn via Mantua: Ireland in/and Europe, Cross-currents and Exchanges' and 'Writer and Righter' to name but a few. He has also prefaced some of his major works of translation with interesting introductions, as is the case with *Beowulf*, Jan Kochanowski's *Laments*, or edited volumes like *The Crane Bag*. This list merely points towards some of the main prose contributions that he has written; it is not an attempt to overlook or discount other writings that were not collected. However, what this list merely showcases from a generic standpoint is that to produce such a critical mass of prose in a lifetime would be highly commendable and noteworthy in itself, let alone to undertake this task alongside the process of writing high-quality poetry over a period of some forty-seven years. The volume of prose shines a light on how engaged Heaney was with the form of poetry, and that he is not just concerned with poetic form. He was keen to write about the aesthetic and ethical value of poetry as being a societal and cultural good, and not just offer a series of commentaries about his own work, or that of others. What is at stake here is a series of essays and chapters probing the very nature of poetry as a human activity.

That he would produce such a vast array of critical work on other writers, and on issues such as politics, identity, history, culture and society, is not surprising considering his background is in teaching and writing about poetry. He did not begin as a poet and then seek refuge in teaching, but rather began as a student and teacher of English literature and slowly became immersed in the creative output of poetry – without ever leaving the element of teaching behind. He has always taught, and thought about, poetry in one form or another either as critic and teacher or as practitioner. The critical eye that Heaney casts on other poets' works in collections like *The Redress of Poetry*, for example, was honed during his academic and teaching years. After receiving a scholarship to study English at Queen's University, Belfast between 1957 and 1961, Heaney went on to undertake a teaching diploma at Saint Joseph's College of Education. In essence, he never really left this profession as throughout his life he held many different positions in different institutions. After working as a teacher in Saint Thomas's Secondary School in Ballymurphy, in Belfast, he took up position as a lecturer in Saint Joseph's College in 1963, before taking up a position in 1966 in Queen's University. From 1970 to 1971, he was a visiting lecturer at Berkeley, before taking time to become a full-time writer, which was short lived. He ultimately returned to the teaching profession in 1975 when he secured a position as a lecturer in English at Carysfort College of Education, in Dublin, and taught there for a six-year period. In 1976, he took up the Beckham Professorship in Berkeley and worked for a semester in Harvard in 1979 before spending Spring there each year between 1982 and 1985. In 1983, he spent a summer at the College of Notre Dame, before taking up the position of Boylston Professor of Rhetoric and Oratory in 1984 at Harvard. In 1988, he delivered the Richard Ellmann Memorial Lectures at Emory University and went on to

Introduction 3

become Professor of Poetry at Oxford University in 1989. If anything, what this illustrates is not only a man who writes poetry, but one who does a lot of thinking and writing about it too. He is not only a practitioner of the artform but also someone who teaches it, criticises it for academic purposes, and who writes about it and its very nature as a specific mode of human discourse, which is of value in itself, and of value in many other ways 'for being itself and for being a help' as he put it in *Crediting Poetry* (Heaney 1995a, 11). While he will understandably be remembered as one of the greatest poets of the twentieth century, and possibly as one of Ireland's greatest-ever poets, his prose goes a long way towards demonstrating that he was also deeply involved and interested in thinking, critiquing and understanding poetry.

As has been already referenced from the outset, his prose has been about thinking and about understanding the poetic landscape. It is also most certainly about gauging the social, cultural, historical, critical and personal atmosphere of growing up and living in Northern Ireland. Beyond his critical writing on poets such as Yeats, Eliot, Hopkins and Bishop, or his collected Oxford lectures on Merriman, Dylan Thomas and John Clare, to mention but a few, the prose offers a meditative reasoning on poetry's social impetus, social responsibility and its power to see the world differently. It is at the frontier of writing that the interconnectedness of all of these elements combine. Writing is in itself a border form, created between the border of what is conscious and what is unconscious, and from as early as the first essay in the collected prose, *Preoccupations: Selected Prose 1968–1978*, we are rooted in the mindscape and landscape that is shot through the collections of poetry. In the 'Foreword' to the collection, Heaney admits us to his line of thought that carries through the book, and indeed, his prose writing more generally:

> I had a half-clarified desire to come to poetic terms with myself by considering the example of others, and to try to bring into focus the little I knew.... I hope it is clear that the essays selected here are held together by searches for answers to central preoccupying questions: how should a poet properly live and write? What is his relationship to be to his own voice, his own place, his literary heritage and his contemporary world?
> (Heaney 1980, 13)

From the beginning of his prose-writing, the matter of understanding his place, space and voice is a central tenet. In this quotation, Heaney outlines the *raison d'être* of the essays in the book, but also more generally of the place of the prose in his canon. Firstly, it demonstrates the centrality that Heaney ascribes to his prose, seeing it as a meditation on art and poetry, and as a coming to terms with his own voice through a consideration of other poets, what he terms, borrowing from Auden, 'breaking bread with the dead' (Heaney 1980, 14). From the outset, this is no piecemeal series of disparate essays and reviews; instead, it is a bringing 'into focus' his concerns about the

4 *Eugene O'Brien and Ian Hickey*

notion of 'art'; it is an enunciation of, what one might tentatively term, given its early placement in the Heaney canon, an aesthetic theory.

Secondly, this quotation attests to the teleology of his project, namely the 'searches for answers' to those central preoccupying questions which are cited above. This is foregrounded by the deictical *glissement* (sliding) in the above quotation, a *glissement* which is thematically significant in terms of his prose. He begins using the personal pronoun, first person singular: '[a]ll that *I* really knew about the art was derived from whatever poetry *I* had written and from those poets who had helped *me* to write it. *I* had a half-clarified desire to come to poetic terms with *myself*' [*our italics*]. It is clear that Heaney himself and his work are both the subject and object of this particular search for answers. His writing will focus on his own work, and on the work of others in terms of how they have helped him to come to poetic terms with himself. Interestingly, though, the second part of the quotation demonstrates the deictical progression from the personal to the general, with the teleological object of the searches for answers now becoming 'the *poet*', and *his* relationship with voice, place, literature and society: 'how should a *poet* properly live and write? What is *his* relationship to be to *his* own voice, *his* own place, *his* literary heritage and *his* contemporary world?' [*our italics*].

These concerns carry through the poetry, but what deserves attention is how these questions seem to crop up again and again in his prose. The first essay collected in *Preoccupations* is 'Mossbawn' which elucidates such issues in terms of the *omphalos*:

> I would begin with the Greek word, *omphalos*, meaning the navel, and hence the stone that marked the centre of the world, and repeat it, *omphalos, omphalos, omphalos*, until its blunt and falling music becomes the music of somebody pumping water at the pump outside our back door.
>
> (Heaney 1980, 17)

Heaney does not open with a search to understand poetry, nor does he open with a search to convey a poetic association with Greece. Instead, he aligns his own farm, Mossbawn, with the central stone at Delphi, the centre of the world in Greek thinking. He opens his prose *oeuvre* thinking about place and identity, and the sonic connections between the two, connections motivated by the associative thinking sanctioned by poetry. The physical pump and the stone at Delphi are connected through a noise, a sonorous connection between both places that is non-tangible, but at the same time that offers connectivity between the past and the present; the archaic and the contemporary; the local and the universal. This sort of thinking is what carries through *Preoccupations*, and the multiple prose collections that follow. If he is thinking about other poets, he is also invariably thinking about his own place and identity, his own lived realities and experiences and the connecting sonic

Introduction 5

rhythms between his experiences and those of other writers. Not only is the sound of the *omphalos* pump important to Heaney's poetic imagination, but it is also the nexus that connects him to his first place and experiences. At the end of the first section of 'Mossbawn', which had originally been broadcast on BBC Radio 4 in 1978, he connects the insertion of the pump in the ground at Mossbawn with the *omphalos*, we also get the digging metaphor being spelled out here, and then onwards to a connection with the Heaney name itself:

> I remember, too, men coming to sink the shaft of the pump and digging through that seam of sand down into the bronze riches of the gravel, that soon began to puddle with the spring water. That pump marked an original descent into earth, sand, gravel, water. It centred and staked the imagination, made its foundation the foundation of the *omphalos* itself. So I find it altogether appropriate that an old superstition ratifies this hankering for the underground side of things. It is a superstition associated with the Heaney name. In Gaelic times, the family were involved with ecclesiastical affairs in the diocese of Derry, and had some kind of rights to the stewardship of a monastic site at Banagher in the north of the county. There is a St. Muredach O'Heney associated with the old church at Banagher; and there is also a belief that sand lifted from the ground at Banagher has beneficent, even magical, properties, if it is lifted from the site by one of the Heaney family name. Throw sand that a Heaney has lifted after a man going into court, and he will win his case. Throw it after your team as they go out on the pitch, and they will win the game.
>
> (Heaney 1980, 20–21)

Here, he makes a literal connection between the land and his family name, spelling out a connection that was set in motion by the planting of the pump – which has literally offered him an imaginative, poetic flow. Heaney's poetry makes connections to his lived experiences in Northern Ireland, and his prose offers an illuminating connectivity to these routes and pathways as he probes and considers his own sense of identity in more detail. We see this sense of awareness in essays like 'The Sense of Place' and 'The Redress of Poetry'.

In the former, Heaney interrogates the local terrain of Northern Ireland as well as some of his key influences such as Patrick Kavanagh, W. B. Yeats, John Montague, William Wordsworth and Dante, who act as imaginative exemplars of how to write about space and place. However, most importantly, Heaney's frame of reference is not only literary but also deeply personal. His connectivity is affiliated with the surrounding areas of Bellaghy and Mossbawn, as well as the cultural and social vibrations of the local area. He extends this idea in 'The Sense of Place', when he suggests that when he was

6   Eugene O'Brien and Ian Hickey

exposed to places like Ben Bulben, Innisfree, Lissadell and Tory island, for example, these places and their reverberated feelings, became internalised in his imagination. He notes that:

> all of these places now live in the imagination, all of them stir us to responses other than the merely visual, all of them are instinct with the spirit of a poet and his poetry. Irrespective of our creed or politics, irrespective of what culture or subculture may have coloured our individual sensibilities, our imaginations assent to the stimulus of the names, our sense of the place is enhanced, our sense of ourselves as inhabitants not just of a geographical country but of a country of the mind is cemented.
>
> (Heaney 1980, 132)

Again, before Heaney thinks about poetry, or the inner workings of poetry on the imagination, he focuses on the landscape, the feelings of place, and connects the place to its sonic, imaginative rhythms. It is the feeling or mood of a place, just like the function of the pump and *omphalos*, that sets him on the trajectory of thinking. He goes on to note that it is 'this feeling, assenting, equable marriage between the geographical country and the country of the mind', that pulls from the oral or literary traditions that 'constitutes the sense of place in its richest possible manifestation' (Heaney 1980, 132). So, in essence, Heaney is consuming the imaginative conjuring of place and identity from the landscape and reinforcing it with his literary heritage.

If the poetry demonstrates these multivalent properties of the ties between the local imagination and his literary inheritances, then the prose articulates these connections in a manner that outlines a conscious effort on Heaney's part to produce poetry that reflects this. We might look towards 'The Frontiers of Writing', from *The Redress of Poetry*, to see how Heaney, as a prose writer, is consciously aware of the necessity of art, especially poetry, to offer a 'glimpsed alternative' (Heaney 1995b, 192) to the reality we encounter every day. In this lecture, delivered at Oxford University, Heaney is predominantly discussing notions of identity, culture and history in the context of the Troubles in Northern Ireland. He discusses the 1984 Hunger Strikes, the IRA, John Hume and the power of poetry to necessitate a shared space of two-mindedness. He treats poetry as an answering power against division and sectarianism, though he does recognise the reality of the British position in Ireland. What we can again see here is not only poetry being a 'source of truth and at the same time a vehicle of harmony' (Heaney 1995b, 193), but that it is again the sounds and musicality of the words that have as much of an impact as their implied meaning. He notes that even if poetry can be 'instrumental in adjusting and correcting imbalances in the world' (Heaney 1995b, 192), he is:

> intent upon treating poetry as an answer given in terms of metre and syntax, of tone and musical trueness; an answer given also by the

Introduction 7

unpredictability of its inventions and its need to go emotionally and artistically "above the brim", beyond the conventional bounds.

(Heaney 1995b, 192)

Alongside the poetry is a prose that intimately understands and articulates an intentionality towards the vibrations of culture, history, identity and the vibrations of words as they appear on the page. This is reinforced by his thoughts on writing poetry in 'The Makings of Music: Reflections on Wordsworth and Yeats', where he notes that:

the given line, the phrase or cadence which haunts the ear and the eager parts of the mind, this is the tuning fork to which the whole music of the poem is orchestrated, that out of which the overall melodies are worked for or calculated.

(Heaney 1980, 61)

Despite his awareness of this, his conscious manifesting of the music of poetry, Heaney is also fully aware of the complexities of creativity. It comes as a 'haunting ... arbitrarily, with a sense of promise, as an alertness, a hankering, a readiness' (Heaney 1980, 61).

On the one hand, Heaney is aware of the conscious motivations behind poetry and writing more generally, where we might consider the syntactical and sibyllic efforts that create a beat or emphasis. He is also conscious of the complications of rhyme, allusions and intertextuality that are major components of much of his poetry. However, the border between the conscious and the unconscious is the space where, what has been inherited in a literary, cultural, historical, social and personal sense, combines with the technicalities of poetry to engender a piece of art that is whole. In the prose, Heaney is aware on a conscious level of the power of the unconscious. The unconscious, the imaginative, what T. S. Eliot might call the 'dark embryo', is referenced consistently across all of the major collections of prose. While discussing Eliot's *The Waste Land*, he notes that it is born out of emotions and feelings, what Eliot would have termed the objective correlative, and that 'the poem does not disdain intellect, yet poetry, having to do with feelings and emotions, must not submit to the intellect's eagerness to foreclose. It must wait for a music to occur, an image to discover itself' (Heaney 1988, 92). Again, there is an eagerness on Heaney's behalf to equate the poem to a certain musicality, and he interestingly goes on to suggest that it is a 'process of dream and ... susceptible to gifts of the unconscious' (Heaney 1988, 92). Here, we see a certified combination of the auditory and sonic sense of the language of poetry with the unconscious wellspring of the content. This seems to be reinforced further in 'The Government of the Tongue', when he suggests that poetry is 'achieved not by dint of the moral and ethical exercise of mind but by the self-validating operations of what we call inspiration' (Heaney 1988, 92) which is in tune, Heaney adds, with Anna Swir's notion of poetry being

8 *Eugene O'Brien and Ian Hickey*

a 'psychosomatic phenomenon' (Heaney 1988, 93). As a poet, Heaney is engaging in this very phenomenon – actively accumulating and synthesising local and personal material, with that inherited, consumed and stored from literary sources. In simple terms, this is essentially poetry in action: a combination of the skillsets and knowledge attained from studying and reading other writers, but also the shaping influence of personal experience (the cultural unconscious).

On a conscious level, he is painfully aware of this, and he even writes about it in *Preoccupations*. This blending of the conscious and unconscious efforts afforded to the creative mind is in themselves unique, but the general theory which Heaney sounds out and thinks about in his prose is broadly universal in its understanding of this process. In 'Feeling into Words', he writes a passage on the importance of Gerard Manley Hopkins' poetry to him, and about the aural and thematic affect and effect that it has on his mind which becomes subsumed into the unconscious. The 'register', as he terms it, comes 'from somebody else, you hear something in another writer's sounds that flows in through your ear and enters the echo-chamber of your head and delights your whole nervous system in such a way that your reaction will be' (Heaney 1980, 44). He then extends his line of thought out towards a more broadly unconscious undertaking in terms of recalling his mother reciting affixes and suffixes, their etymology in a Latin sense, and rhymes she learned at school; he also recalls the foreign languages heard on the wireless radio from Stuttgart, Oslo, Leipzig and Hilversum; the BBC weather forecast; the words of the catechism; and the litany of the Blessed Virgin that was a central part of the rituals of the household (Heaney 1980, 45). Beyond the rituality of these events, the central feature that connects them all is language. Each emphasises a different phraseology and syntax, but in essence to the ear, they are all poetic in some way, in that he focuses on the sound and texture and connections of the words as ways of enhancing and amplifying their meaning. This is what, again, attracts Heaney to them. It is the certain musicality to the words, not necessarily their meaning, that attracts him. Each of them was internalised and compartmentalised in the unconscious for a number of years, but all, he admits in the essay, contributed in some way or another to the core of his poetry. He pointedly goes on to exhibit an understanding of what we have been tracing here, namely that poetry operates between the spheres of the conscious and the unconscious: 'that was the unconscious bedding, but poetry involves a conscious savouring of words also' (Heaney 1980, 46), and 'savouring', with its connotations of taste and the body, is a very apt word to encompass his sense that poetry expresses some combination of body and mind; of sensation and cerebrality. The prose demonstrates a complete understanding of the complexities of creativity and also articulates an awareness of the groundwork that goes in to becoming a Nobel laureate.

Prose, for Heaney then, is not journalistic or documentary-like: it is critical; critical in the sense of offering carefully thought-out critiques of other

Introduction 9

writers' works and it also critically thinks about the world in terms of space, place, culture, history and identity. The prose by no means offers a narrative approach towards articulating his own life; it may spring from the autobiographical, but it is beyond autobiographical, which makes it all the more powerful. The prose is a space to think out and elucidate an understanding of other writers and texts, his connection with them, their immediate context and how this all impacts and influences his own poetic sensibility. If digging is a metaphor that carries across the poetry, it is also one that sways across the prose as he becomes mired in, and inspired by, what he finds in critically thinking about art and humanity. Essays that may immediately spring to mind in this context are 'The Redress of Poetry', 'Crediting Poetry', 'Place and Displacement', 'Mossbawn via Mantua' and 'Thebes via Toomebridge'. Indeed, it may even be argued that any and all of his essays may fall under this remit, but the challenge that Heaney's work poses is not its direct connection to the poetry, but rather with its indirect associations. By this, we mean, that the prose is not there as a sort of footnote to the poetry, an explanatory by-product to accompany the poetry. The prose stands alone in its complexity to articulate an understanding of the world that is as multifaceted as the poetry and indeed shares many commonalities with it. If Heaney places himself within the pantheon of European poetry, he articulates this place in his prose writing. An essay that goes a long way to emphasise our point here is 'Mossbawn via Mantua: Ireland in/and Europe: Cross-Currents and Exchanges'.

Initially delivered as an opening speech at an EFACIS conference, the essay contributes to an overview of the poet's thinking about his poetic career. It develops a narrative that is a central part of the poetry, spanning multiple decades, and showing Heaney's awareness of the European contexts that inform so much of his own poetry and his own sense of intellectual development. It is no accident that a Greek word is so central to the early pages of *Preoccupations*. Of course, Europe is not the only important influence in his life, we think further beyond European borders here to Robert Lowell, Allen Ginsberg, Theodore Roethke, Robert Frost and Elizabeth Bishop here, but European identity and culture is a central tenet of upholding the roof which covers and shelters the ideological tapestry of his imagination. In 'Mossbawn via Mantua', Heaney suggests that there are five points that he draws upon in terms of a European constellation of literature and culture through which he is able to view Ireland from the outside like James Joyce. This, he argues, gives 'a closer view of that ground by standing back from it and help to establish a different focus, a more revealing angle of vision' (Heaney 2012, 19), offering a series of 'short cuts' (Heaney 2012, 19) to Irish destinations, ways to further understand and think about Ireland from an anamorphic angle. What is most interesting about these five points is that he relates them to provinces, much like that make-up of Ireland itself which is divided into four provinces that act in synecdoche for the country (with an original fifth province mythically located in the centre of the country). However, we may

10   *Eugene O'Brien and Ian Hickey*

also read these five separate imagined spaces as a series of fragments that are metonyms for Heaney's own thinking about poetry, the nation, identity and thinking more generally.

The first province relates to Greek, Roman and Judaeo-Christian inheritances that provide the 'co-ordinates of the western mind' and act as a guiding force through which 'the individual can locate himself or herself in culture and consciousness' (Heaney 2012, 20); the second province is that of a European poetic tradition where he cites Iron-Age people, the Vikings, Germanic tribes and the Anglo-Saxons as being exemplars of a 'barbarian element' in European thought and culture (Heaney 2012, 20); the third relates to as the 'Hyperborean' (Heaney 2012, 21), specifically the poets of Eastern Europe and Russia such as Mandelstam, Milosz and Brodsky, for example; the fourth province acknowledges the central role of Dante; and the fifth and final province of the mind is that of work in translation, mainly reserved here for the works of Virgil, Horace and *Beowulf*. While these provinces may be separate in terms of temporality and place, through the cast of Heaney's mind, they somehow act in synecdoche for an imagined whole that encapsulates Ireland and indeed places the conscious and unconscious stirrings of Heaney imagination in a wider European framework of culture.

Within this array of identities, vocabularies, languages, texts and cultures, Heaney places his own life and experiences as a central stone from which these webs of identity span out. They act as a 'common vocabulary' (Heaney 2012, 20) of a type of European cultural consciousness that chimes with his 'own personal territory, that is, in the fields around the townlands of Broagh and Anahorish and our farm at Mossbawn' (Heaney 2012, 22). Published in 2012, the essay merely reconfigures and expands upon the central idea expounded in 'Mossbawn' regarding the *omphalos* and water pump: the centrality of his first world matches with the central co-ordinates of his life. What changes in this later essay is that Heaney moves from thinking about points of connection through sound and sonic rhythms towards an articulated, thought-out negotiation of critique about European culture and identity. This journey, in many ways, is exemplary of poetry itself, combining the essence of feeling and rhythm with thought, both conscious and unconscious.

In the essays of his prose books, one finds ongoing parallel discussions of some of the central concerns of Heaney's poetry: the nature of Irish identity; the difficulty of writing about place, given the historical and cultural baggage that always accrues; the relationship of poetry with politics; the ethical questions that are intimately connected with aesthetic enterprises; the influence of European and world perspectives on his own work, and the whole notion of Irishness in general, the influences of other writers from different traditions on his work; the special relationship with the work of Yeats; and, finally, the attempt to set up a fluid spatial metaphor of an Irishness, which one might term negative dialectical, as it combines the multifarious traditions, cultures and ideologies that have been thrown together historically.

Introduction 11

Underwriting all of these concerns, or preoccupations, is the ongoing attempt to bring into focus some form of theorisation of the aesthetic, to take up some form of critical distance so as to better understand the mode of knowledge that is operative within art and which, by extension, is operative through poetry and prose in terms of the socio-political sphere. What emerges in these essays is a sophisticated approach to poetry, an approach which grants the internal laws of language and aesthetics which are applicable within the domain of poetry, but which at the same time demonstrates a growing awareness of the need to reconcile what he terms 'lyric celebration' (Heaney 1988, 12), and its concomitants 'the phrase or cadence which haunts the ear and the eager parts of the mind' (Heaney 1980, 61), with the demands of an ethical imperative which 'the poet may find as he exercises his free gift in the presence of the unfree and the hurt' (Heaney 1988, xviii).

The chapters in this book address a number of these concerns. Opening the book, Eugene O'Brien addresses the shaping dynamics behind the complexity of defining Seamus Heaney's political and cultural homes in Mossbawn, Northern Ireland and Ireland as a whole. For O'Brien, this is addressed through complex spatial metaphors – quincunxes – that are intrinsic to the prose. Heaney's thinking about such issues is envisioned through a European lens, one that offers a broader scope of vision through which to understand the national and the local. Drawing on his writing in *The Redress of Poetry* and 'Mossbawn via Mantua', O'Brien identifies the first quincunx, an imaginative arrangement of towers, as a symbolic trope that offers Heaney a visual representation that traces a far more nuanced interaction of Britishness and Irishness, as he uses a central image of ethnic Irishness, surrounded by, and interacting with, the thought of Yeats, Joyce, MacNeice, and Spenser. More significantly, it is not the towers *per se* that interest him, but rather their multiperspectival interaction with each other as processes from which different levels of meaning can be generated and through which different sub-relationships can be enunciated. The second quincunx is built upon the Greco-Roman and Judeo-Christian heritage; the northern 'barbarian' tradition; the Hyperborean perspective, which includes Eastern European influences; the influence of Dante Alighieri; and the influence of translation which offers a pluralistic and nuanced way of looking at Irish politics, identity, society, culture and history.

Chapter 2 sees Henry Hart address Heaney's uncanny encounters and experiences throughout his life. Focusing on Freud's notions of the *Heimlich* and the *Unheimlich*, Hart makes the point that, for Heaney, the repressed material that returns to the conscious mind can be a spiritual gift rather than a debilitating symptom. It is something which can offer a new vision or experience of the moment rather than one that is closed off and distorted. He then traces a series of examples of events from Heaney's own life, drawing on his prose, letters and interview materials, that enunciate a Freudian sensibility in his marriage into the Devlin family, his time at St. Columb's College, the family's move to Glanmore, and his time spent teaching in America.

12 Eugene O'Brien and Ian Hickey

In Chapter 3, William Fogarty argues that Seamus Heaney's prose poems illuminate some of the ways Heaney reckoned artistically with a lifelong quandary about the ethics of writing poetry in response to immediate social catastrophe. Particularly focusing on violence and the Troubles, Fogarty underscores these claims by focusing on Heaney's prose poems and his prose writing. He suggests that Heaney's strategy is not reliant on guilt as an animating force, because the prose poems take recourse against overt aestheticisation through the modulating elements of prose. The interconnectedness of the prose and prose poems demonstrates Heaney's prose as being in dialogue with the poetry and not merely being a meta-commentary to the poetry itself. Chapter 4 follows the theme of redress that is set out in Fogarty's chapter in terms of the prose poems, and sees Ruth Macklin contemplate similar notions of redress but from a different standpoint. Macklin emphasises that redress is a construct that allows Heaney to contemplate the process of writing. Though Heaney provisionally and tentatively names redress in the Oxford Lectures, his earlier prose is also an important locus for his contemplation of this nascent concept, providing a space in which he can explore his own process without being either too specific or definitive. His explorations of early exemplars such as Hopkins and Kavanagh reveal how redress as a corrective enables Heaney to negotiate the complexities of his literary and linguistic inheritances.

In Chapter 5, Ian Hickey focuses on Heaney's thought processes behind the formation of a poem, not in terms of word selection for meaning, but rather of word selection that emphasises a certain musical tone. Heaney's prose on Yeats, Hopkins, Wilde and Wordsworth, for example, demonstrates Heaney's interest in the musicality of poetry. He writes at length about the connections between the sonic rhythms of language and music. This chapter argues that these ideas can be traced across the collected prose, which shows a sense of coherence in terms of Heaney's approach to poetry throughout his life but also, more importantly, suggests that musicality lays at the very foundation of Heaney's thinking about what poetry is, and what it can achieve.

In Chapter 6, sees Magdalena Kay home in on notions of gravity and grace, as initially articulated by Simone Weil, in the context of Philip Larkin and Seamus Heaney. Again, the focus of this chapter is on redress and progresses the arguments set out in the previous two chapters, instead focusing on a single poet and Heaney's relationship to him. Heaney's belief in the counterweighing function of poetry as redress is admirable, in Kay's thinking, and she uses Larkin's work as a test case for Heaney's foundational concept, and the reading strategy allied with it. Heaney defends reparative reading and this defence, and concomitant critique of the gravity-bound Larkin, is an essential component of Heaney's aesthetic theory.

Heaney's relationship with Ted Hughes is examined in Chapter 7 by Caoimhe Higgins, where she tracks Heaney's mention of Hughes in *Preoccupations, The Government of the Tongue* and *Finders Keepers*. By deconstructing Heaney's portrayal of the public and poetic Ted Hughes, this chapter pays particular attention to Heaney's management of personal biography and poetic output. It offers a reading of Heaney and Hughes that asks the serious question of whether their friendship had a biased effect on their literary output. Carrying on from this discussion, in Chapter 8, Gary Wade focuses on a similarly monumental figure for Heaney, Patrick Kavanagh. Wade focuses on Heaney's two essays on Kavanagh from *Preoccupations* and *The Government of the Tongue*. He also addresses a 1972 essay from *the Listener*, where Heaney discusses Kavanagh's two lives, the one before Dublin and the one while living in Dublin. He argues that Kavanagh is a central component to Heaney's poetic thinking right up to the later poetry, especially in 'Clearances' from *The Haw Lantern*, and in the poems of *Seeing Things* (1991) which mark a visionary turn in Heaney's poetry, and which may owe something to Heaney's insights into Patrick Kavanagh in his prose.

Chapter 9 again focuses on the influence and impact of a singular poet on Heaney. Here, Meg Tyler discusses the place of Robert Lowell in Heaney's prose, and the specific essays and articles which Heaney dedicates to the American poet, especially his final collection of poetry *Day by Day*. Tyler makes the point that Heaney's perspective on Lowell exudes a tenderness and sharp-sightedness that are not at odds with one another. In writing about Lowell, Heaney was perhaps able to look from an oblique angle at his own work, which was so much under the magnifying glass of literary critics, his fellow poets and many others in Northern Ireland.

In the final chapter of this book Richard Rankin Russell addresses Heaney's long preoccupation with the short fiction and drama of Brian Friel through a Wordsworthian lens. He focuses on Heaney's reviews of productions of Friel's plays and essays on Friel by exploring how Heaney's often Wordsworthian prose engagements with Friel's drama and artistic persona reveal his deep debt to the great Irish playwright, who successfully kept faith with his truthful art, particularly in terms of its ability to conjure up an abiding love of his home ground, its mesmeric qualities and its ability to evoke powerful memories. Russell also focuses on their close relationship and similar cultural and social backgrounds in Northern Ireland.

Works Cited

Heaney, Seamus (1980) *Preoccupations: Selected Prose, 1968–1978*, London: Faber.

Heaney, Seamus (1988) *The Government of the Tongue: The 1986 T.S. Eliot Memorial Lectures and Other Critical Writings*, London: Faber.

Heaney, Seamus (1995a) *Crediting Poetry*, County Meath, Ireland: Gallery Press.

Heaney, Seamus (1995b) *The Redress of Poetry*, London: Faber.

Heaney, Seamus (2012) 'Mossbawn via Mantua: Ireland in/and Europe: Cross-Currents and Exchanges', in *Ireland In/And Europe: Cross-Currents and Exchanges*, volume 4, edited by Werner Huber, Sandra Mayer, and Julia Novak, Germany: Wissenschaftlicher Verlag Trier, 19–27.

1 'Things Founded Clean on Their Own Shapes'

Seamus Heaney and the Shape of Poetry

Eugene O'Brien

The title of this essay comes from Heaney's evocative poem 'The Peninsula', from *Door into the Dark*, his second volume of poetry. In this poem, it is clear that notions of shape are very important to him at an epistemological level. An early poem of this collection, 'The Forge', speaks of a blacksmith and his anvil:

> The anvil must be somewhere in the centre,
> Horned as a unicorn, at one end square,
> Set there immovable: an altar
> Where he expends himself in shape and music.
>   (Heaney 1969, 19)

When asked by Denis O'Driscoll about this, Heaney said that while in a way 'any one forge is all the forges', he was specifically thinking of 'Barney Devlin's forge at Hillhead, on the roadside, where you had the noise of myth in the anvil and the noise of the 1940s in the passing cars' (Heaney & O'Driscoll 2008, 91). The collocation of sounds from the anvil and the cars stands in synecdoche for the collocation, in Heaney's syncretic imagination, of the mundane and the mythic, of the world of cars and anvils and of the world of words and images. Throughout his prose, this encapsulating imperative is to be found, as he seldom sees anything from a single perspective, but is constantly looking for something else that connects and conjoins and brings different perspectives to bear on ideas, ideologies and events to offer a more comprehensive vision. In the same book of interviews, *Stepping Stones*, O'Driscoll asks the telling question 'What has poetry taught you?' and Heaney answers that it has taught him that 'there's such a thing as truth and it can be told—slant' (Heaney & O'Driscoll 2008, 467). This term is borrowed from Emily Dickinson's poem 'Tell the Truth but Tell It Slant' (Dickinson 1924, 506–507), and it summarises what might be termed a core aspect of his poetic thinking.

In Heaney's poetic thinking, access to truth needs to be oblique, as full understanding is very often beyond our capability, given that we are situated within language, thought and culture and that a transcendent position is all but impossible to achieve. Thus, 'slant' is the refracted manner in which

DOI: 10.4324/9781003456148-2

'*Things Founded Clean on Their Own Shapes*'   15

aspects of feeling and emotions and the unconscious are accessed by the self, and poetry is one of the vehicles that provides this access. Heaney suggests that knowledge and signification are transformational matrices of fluid and intersecting discourses as opposed to readily fixed, foundational pillars that can be passed on, whole and intact, from generation to generation. One of the unifying factors in this thinking is that text is modified by context, which is, in turn, further modified by the altered text.

In this chapter, I am going to look at some models that Heaney used to explain this very polysemic view of the kind of perspective and knowledge that is the provenance of poetry. I will look especially at his use of the notions of space and shape, and at some spatial models, to attempt to trace the complexity and multi-perspectival nature of the type of knowledge of the world that poetry can provide. For Heaney, this is always a process, an ongoing negotiation between here and there; between different nodes of meaning; between different perspectives; between different ideological perspectives; and between different linguistic discourses. I use the term 'negotiation' in a specific way, as it has been used by Jacques Derrida. He traces the etymology of 'negotiation' to the Latin *negotium*: 'not-ease, not-quiet ... no leisure' (Derrida & Rottenberg 2002, 11). He sees this '[no]-leisure' as the 'impossibility of stopping or settling in a position ... of establishing oneself anywhere'. This process is typified by the image of a shuttle, what he terms '*la navette*, and what the word conveys of to-and-fro between two positions, two places, two choices' in a process of 'going back and forth between different positions' (Derrida & Rottenberg 2002, 12). This is also how Heaney's thinking works, as he always looks for a liminal point between different perspectives, a point made overt in *The Haw Lantern*, in the poem 'Terminus', where he sees the complexity of his own identity in a number of images which focus on things:

> I was the march drain and the march drain's banks
> Suffering the limit of each claim.
> Two buckets were easier carried than one.
> I grew up in between.
>
> (Heaney 1987, 5)

It is interesting that it is a drain and two buckets that are used here to explain his sense of being pen to many different influences. In 'Something to Write Home About', he discusses this poem and expands on his sense of compound identity, recalling that as he crossed the river Sluggan every day on his way to and from school, his sense 'of living on two sides of a boundary was emphasized. I never felt the certitude of belonging completely in one place', and in a political sense, he was correct as all of the 'townlands and parishes and dioceses' that had once belonged 'within the old pre-plantation, ecclesiastical geography of Gaelic Ireland' had since been taken into 'another system and another jurisdiction' (Heaney 2002, 54). Here, his unconscious

16   Eugene O'Brien

feelings of being 'in-between' are replaced by the socio-political realities and contexts of his life, and this is a pattern that will become more overt in his writing about place and identity. As he puts it in *Preoccupations*, 'Mossbawn lies between the villages of Castledawson and Toome. I was symbolically placed between the marks of English influence and the lure of the native experience, between "the demesne" and "the bog"' (Heaney 1980, 34). So, the sense of being in-between that was an unconscious and felt emotion spreads out to become part of a stance towards his sociocultural and political placement in the divided community of Northern Ireland.

And looking at the language of the unconscious, of the somatic and of feeling and emotion, the work of Sigmund Freud will be of value, especially in terms of relating the world of things to the world of words, and of relating the noises of the cars in the opening paragraph to those of the mythic forge. In 'The Unconscious' (Freud 1981, 159–215), Freud writes about the connection (one might say negotiation), between the conscious and the unconscious. He distinguishes between two types of representation (*Vorstellung*), namely, 'word-presentations' (*Wortvorstellungen*) and 'thing-presentations' (*Sachvorstellungen*) (Freud 1981, 201). These are complex and contested terms (Freud changed his own mind about them over time), but they do offer us a way of seeing Heaney's negotiation between things, words and symbols through language. For Freud, consciousness brings together both 'the presentation of the thing plus the presentation of the word belonging to it, while the unconscious presentation is the presentation of the thing alone' (Freud 1981, 201); and it is the connections between the word-presentation and the thing-presentation that are of import to this discussion. Freud felt that dream formation made use of these two modes of *Vorstellung*:

> We have already in *The Interpretation of Dreams* described the way in which the regression of the preconscious day's residues takes place in dream-formation. In this process thoughts are transformed into images, mainly of a visual sort; that is to say, word-presentations are taken back to the thing-presentations which correspond to them, as if, in general, the process were dominated by considerations of representability.
>
> (Freud 1981, 228)

In poetry, focus on the materiality of the world is important, it is a process of 'thinking in things' and 'among things' (Deleuze & Parnet 1977, 26), and Freud himself saw the risks that when we think in abstractions 'there is a danger that we may neglect the relations of words to unconscious thing-presentations' (Freud 1981, 204).

There are, of course, dangers in transposing terms and concepts from a different discipline, but I think a case can be made that both psychoanalysis and poetry attempt, in their different ways, to access and to some extent, voice, aspects of the unconscious – indeed, it was a disciple of Freud, Jacques

'Things Founded Clean on Their Own Shapes' 17

Lacan, who coined the phrase that '*the unconscious is structured like a language*' [*italics original*] (Lacan 1977, 20). Poetry, with its focus on things is, I would argue, involved in an analogous process. As Simon Critchley, writing about Wallace Stevens, puts it, the poetic voice 'speaks of things, of things both in their unexceptional plainness and their peculiar gaudiness' (Critchley 2005, 5), and Heaney, in his writing about poetry, will develop this theory, as unconscious associations help to provide a form of cathexis as he looks at signification spatially through things, as opposed to ideas or more abstract discussion: 'thinking in thing-presentations is imagistic thinking' (Boothby 2001, 82). Heaney will explore this level of imagistic thinking in his prose, as well as in his poetry, especially through his use of spatial metaphors. These are ways of connecting the unconscious with the conscious, something that both psychoanalysts and poets have the ability to do, and to return to our initial poetic location of the forge, it is the blacksmith as shape-maker who attracts Heaney's attention because, as someone very much of the real world as he makes shoes for horses and mends shoes for horses, he is also a mythic figure standing in shadow amid the sparks and fire. He is also an emblematic figure, as he connects elemental metals with living animals, and as such is a locus of connection that Heaney recalls him in *Stepping Stones*:

> The phrase 'door into the dark' comes from the first line of a poem about a blacksmith, a shape maker, standing in the door of a forge; and, as a title, it picks up on the last line of *Death of a Naturalist,* where the neophyte sees a continuity between the effect he wants to achieve in his writing and the noise he made when he used to shout down a well shaft 'to set the darkness echoing'.
>
> (Heaney & O'Driscoll 2008, 91)

Representation in language is a journey between consciousness and the unconscious; between the thing and the word; between reality and language; and between 'word-presentations' (*Wortvorstellungen*) and 'thing-presentations' (*Sachvorstellungen*), and it is the oscillation and negotiation that is the important aspect of this process, a point that is made clear in our first spatial metaphor.

In *Among Schoolchildren*, a text to which we will return later in this chapter, Heaney spoke about a great-aunt of his, Catherine Bradley, and about an example of her school needlework, from 1843. This included the following verse, embroidered on her 'sampler':

> Ireland as she ought to be
> Great glorious and free
> First flower of the earth
> First gem of the sea.
> (Heaney 1984, 6)

18 *Eugene O'Brien*

The embroidery beneath this verse was of a shamrock, the traditional symbol of Ireland, but 'squeezed to the right of the verse' were the words 'God Save the Queen' (Heaney 1984a, 6). Here, the prevalence of binarisms in Heaney's thought is embodied spatially on a piece of Ulster linen. Is the message here meant to be seen as stressing how Ireland 'ought' to be, inclining to the notion of being free of British influence, as signified by the shamrock, or else of being free as part of the union between Great Britain and Ireland, as signified by the rubric 'God Save the Queen'? This is precisely what Heaney terms the notion of 'needing to accommodate two opposing notions of truthfulness simultaneously' (Heaney 1995a, 4), and indeed, it is the very condition which has been emblematically rendered in Catherine Bradley's embroidery sampler, where 'two value systems, which now explode daily, are lodged like dormant munitions' on one piece of Ulster linen (Heaney 1984, 6). The use of 'munitions' is proleptic and significant as the identitarian conflict on the sampler has the latent ability to become something far more violent in the real world of politics and ideology in Northern Ireland.

I would suggest that Heaney's writing aims to dislodge these positions in order to bring out the etymological sense of 'munition' as a fortification ('*munitio-onis*'), but also its cognate term '*muniment*', meaning a document entailing rights or privileges. Two sets of fortified rights and privileges are exactly what is signified by the shamrock and the slogan on the sampler, and both have munimental designs on the notion of 'Ulster' in that piece of Ulster linen. By dislodging these fortifications, Heaney is, symbolically, bringing these symbols into dialectical interaction and negotiation, with the reader's mind shuttling between the two. Looking at them side by side in the shape of the piece of material makes the connections between both thing-presentations and word-presentations, and the full complexity of what is being expressed can be taken in by a reader at a glance in their dialectical interaction. It is worth keeping in mind at this juncture that the term 'dialectic' originates from the Greek '*dialektos*', meaning discourse or conversation, and the sampler is a mimetic example of this process in Heaney's epistemology of writing, as he sets up an oscillation, a negotiation, between the two positions found on this piece of Ulster linen, an oscillation that parallels his own sense of being 'in-between', as he crossed the river Sluggan and carried the two buckets. As he put it in the aptly entitled *Place and Displacement*: 'the poet is stretched between politics and transcendence, and is often displaced from a confidence in a single position by his disposition to be affected by all positions, negatively rather than positively capable' (Heaney 1985a, 8).

The image of the poet being stretched is both uncomfortable and highly visual, as politics and transcendence exert forces on him that are unavoidable, and that change the nature of the space he is occupying as well as changing his own spatial presence by stretching it. The actual spatial form of poetry does the same thing, as the 'forms of English poetry lie along various continua', with the most important being 'the steady progression of beats,

'Things Founded Clean on Their Own Shapes' 19

like a single row of posts extending across the landscape' (Glaser & Culler 2019, 192). This spatial metaphor again underlines the sense of a linguistic and intellectual journey that goes on as we try to represent ideas, words and things in poetry in order to grasp as full a meaning as we can.

In psychoanalysis too, there has been a shift from the static to dynamic modes, as the connections between 'word-presentations' (*Wortvorstellungen*) and 'thing-presentations' (*Sachvorstellungen*) are now seen as dynamic and protean, as indeed are the connections between what Freud termed the manifest and latent content of our dreams. Furthermore, our sense of the value and our ability to interpret spatial metaphors has similarly transformed:

> As one outcome of these shifts in our spatial metaphors, we have moved from a static to a constantly shifting *dynamic* perspective on the relations between manifest and latent contents. Instead of regarding the clinical situation as composed of upper surfaces and lower depths, we employ to our advantage (knowingly or unknowingly) one of the principles of the fetishism strategy—the foreground-background relationship. We focus our attention on the *shifting surfaces* of foreground and background. We do not accept one surface or the other as the true and only meaning.
> [*italics original*] (Kaplan 2006, 125)

Heaney, across the range of his writing, engages dynamic images and symbols of shape in order to outline the complexity of the knowledge and wisdom that is to be found in poetry. In one of Heaney's translations from a poem by the Irish language poet Eoghan Rua Ó Súilleabháin, where the poet is asking a blacksmith to make him a spade, the poetic speaker talks of how:

> The plate and the edge of it not to be wrinkly or crooked –
> I see it well shaped from the anvil and sharp from the file;
> The grain of the wood and the line of the shaft nicely fitted,
> And best thing of all, the ring of it, sweet as a bell.
> (Sonzogni 2022, 90)

What is especially interesting here is how the shaping function is also a factor in the sound that the spade makes, as form and phonetics (both of which are core components of poetry) are intimately connected; and of course, the sound, 'the ring of it', can only be heard when the spade is interacting with the earth – another image of fluidity and movement. Also, in translating Constantine P. Cavafy's poem, 'Sculptor of Tyana', he imagines the sculptor wondering about 'Poseidon', and about 'how to shape/and fit the horses in', as he tries to capture the dynamism of the horses in the static shaping form of sculpture, as they have to 'to surge above the waves' (Sonzogni 2022, 137). In both translations, Heaney is concerned with the interaction of static form and dynamic content, and in both, he uses things to emphasise that

20   *Eugene O'Brien*

the dynamism and fluidity of form can never be allowed to attenuate the 'this-ness', the *haecceity*, of the real world.

The interactivity that can be brought about by presenting things in words allows for a deeper connection to the unconscious and conscious cathexes that can be associated with words, a process especially strong in poetry and in poetic thinking. Shapes within the mind are interacting with shapes in the world, as 'word-presentations' (*Wortvorstellungen*) and 'thing-presentations' (*Sachvorstellungen*) interact and interanimate each other, a point beautifully caught in Heaney's translation of Robert Henryson's *The Testament of Cresseid*:

> The image of a thing by chance may be
> So deeply printed in the memory
> That it deludes what's in the outer eye,
> Presenting a form similar and twinned
> To that which had been shaped within the mind.
> (Sonzogni 2022, 523)

The shapes of the mind both mirror and transform the shapes of the material world, just as those of the material world can change the valences and cathexes of the world of words and ideas. Indeed, Heaney can see poems themselves in spatial terms and as things whose shape and form add to their enunciative abilities. Speaking about Robert Frost's poem, 'To Earthward', he speaks about its power and its intense lyricism and goes on to see both the shape and the space of the poem as central to this lyrical quality 'the quatrains are like fossils, constrained within their shapes but minutely and energetically expressive of the life that gave them shape' (Brodsky, Heaney, & Walcott 1996, 80). Once again, the sense of shape is a very dynamic one, and it is this aporia of stasis and movement that seems to especially attract Heaney as a resonant image of how poetry interacts with the world through a mixture of word-presentation and thing-presentation.

In his book on Heaney, *The Makings of a Poet*, Michael Parker sees Gerard Manley Hopkins, Patrick Kavanagh, and Ted Hughes as seminal figures in Heaney's Bloomian anxiety of influence, and he sees strong connections between the language of Hopkins and that of Heaney. Tracing the provenance of Hopkins's language, he traces the influence of scholastic philosopher Duns Scotus, whose notion of *haecceity* would go on to be important to Heaney. Parker discusses the scholastic probing of how humans could know the universal from our own very immanent perspective, and he refers to Scotus's belief that this could come about by an apprehension of 'an individual object's essence, which he named its "this-ness" (*haecceitas*)' (Parker 1993, 19).

For Heaney, poetry is very much concerned with how the interaction of form and shape with the specific presentation of words and things, can uncover their 'this-ness', and their interaction in the poetic line. Writing about the composition of his translation of *Beowulf*, Heaney explains the hard

'Things Founded Clean on Their Own Shapes' 21

work necessary to do this to the standards, not interestingly of accessibility or modern language, but to the standards of poetry. He calls it 'labour-intensive work, scriptorium-slow', because what he was trying to do was get the meaning established in his head 'and then hope that the lines could be turned into metrical shape and raised to the power of verse' (Heaney 1999, xxii) – so it is the metrical shape that acts as the transformative index which will raise the line to the power of verse: the *Wortvorstellungen* needs to have about it some shaping aspects of the *Sachvorstellungen* so that the words in the poetic line themselves become part of a 'shape'; part of a spatial structure which has a satisfaction to the auditory imagination as well as to the sonic and phonetic expectation of the rhythmical shape that connects all of the lines to each other.

His reading of other poets also tends to be drawn to presentations of things in language, as he attempts to work through notions of shape and structure and *haecceity*. Hence, in his discussion of Ted Hughes's *Wodwo*, Heaney notes its epigraph from *Sir Gawain and the Green Knight*, the Middle-English poem, and makes the connection between the two works in terms of their sharing of 'a clear outline and an inner richness'. Again, that sense of negotiating between complexity and movement within a broader shape is repeated, and in a manner similar to his own sense of looking for a language that will be fluent but formal; that will embody the swerve and the shuttle of words and syntax and rhyme; and that will be surprising, but also contained in a loose but shaping structure. It is with these imperatives in mind, I would argue, that he comments on the value of Hughes's language, noting that his diction is 'consonantal', as it 'snicks through the air like an efficient blade, marking and carving out fast definite shapes; but within those shapes, mysteries and rituals' (Heaney 1980, 153). It is this fusion of the fluent and the formal that attracts him to Hughes's writing, as this is very much what he prizes himself as part of the power of poetry as he notes that these 'mysteries and rituals are circles within which he [*Hughes*] conjures up presences' (Heaney 1980, 154). Charles Bernstein, commenting on poetry as a specific genre of writing, sees this sense of thingness as central to poetry as a form of writing. He sees its importance as being 'its wordness, its physicality, its *haecceity* (this-ness) is, in its impulse, an investigation of human self-sameness, of the place of our connection: in the world, in the word, in ourselves' (Bernstein 2001, 32), and in this, he is paralleling Heaney's own views on the importance of both specificity and the concrete, but also of the connections between language and reality, of those between word and thing, and of those between the words and the shaping metrical pattern in the poem.

The sense of a thing-presentation becomes pervasive in Heaney's descriptions of poetic writing and thinking when it is looked for. For example, when describing the structure of *Finders Keepers*, Heaney notes that it has the same 'shape as *Preoccupations*', which he sees as having three sections: a topical and autobiographical one; one which discusses different authors; 'and the third section is a kind of kite-tail, a stringing out of miscellaneous pieces'

22 Eugene O'Brien

(Heaney 2002, x). Seeing a book as a kite is an interesting metaphor, though of course it allowed a different aspect of Heaney's writing, namely, his essays and prose pieces, to take flight in a manner similar to his poetry, and was the generative text that would give rise, some twenty-two years later, to the selected prose volume which ran to some 416 pages. In this light, the image of the book as kite-like is accurate and captures the sense of a broadening of Heaney's writing. The sense of a shape that manages to enfold both word and thing, both stasis and movement, is caught again and again in his lectures and essays. We can look at the image of ideas in a book taking fight, and flight is one of those tropes that Heaney assimilated more fully from his writing of *The Haw Lantern* onwards, as he looked less at the ground 'like some monk bowed over his *prie-dieu*' (Heaney 1995a, 19) and learned the 'luxury of walking on air' (Heaney 1995a, 11). He tends to write in binaries as a way of proto-deconstructing them so as to focus on the areas where they are not oppositional, but rather appositional, where they are not black or white but melding and melting into shades of grey. It is at the frontiers of thinking, as well as of writing, that Heaney finds his home. In Freudian terms, he is a thinker who looks at the *Heimlich* in the *Unheimlich* and the *Unheimlich* in the *Heimlich* (Freud 1955, 217–256).

So, when writing in *The Redress of Poetry* about the polysemic meaning that he sees in the word 'redress', Heaney's sense of dynamic and fluid shape interacting with some kind of static framework is behind every sentence. He speaks of the 'surprise of poetry':

> I want to profess the surprise of poetry as well as its reliability; I want to celebrate its given, unforeseeable thereness, the way it enters our field of vision and animates our physical and intelligent being in much the same way as those bird-shapes stencilled on the transparent surfaces of glass walls or windows must suddenly enter the vision and change the direction of the real birds' flight. In a flash the shapes register and transmit their unmistakable presence, so the birds veer off instinctively. An image of the living creatures has induced a totally salubrious swerve in the creatures themselves.
>
> (Heaney 1995b, 15)

Here again, like the kite, there is structure but also movement, and for Heaney, this is where poetry tends to cohere as a mode of writing, speaking, thinking and knowing: it is the structure of the metre and rhythm and stanza, but at the same time, the freedom of enjambment and association and rhyme, that allow for this movement in stasis; as he put it to Henri Cole, speaking of his early collections, 'those books wanted to be texture, to be all consonants, vowels and voicings, they wanted the sheer materiality of words' (Cole 1997, 106). This sense of the materiality, the thingness, the *haecceity* of language is central to Heaney's sense of what poetry can do, and how it works as an epistemological discourse. We are reminded of

'Things Founded Clean on Their Own Shapes' 23

his admiring comments on the language of Hughes in *Wodwo*, as he makes a very similar point, seeing Hughes's linguistic vigour as having to do with the 'matter of consonants that take the measure of his vowels like calipers, or stud the line like rivets' (Heaney 1980, 154). In both his own early books and in those of Hughes, it is this search for *Sachvorstellung*, for *haecceitas*, that he sees as being of value, as things allow for that sense of stasis and movement.

So, just as the stencilled birds can affect the real birds' flight, poetry can also affect real life, and the stencil influencing the actual birds is a telling symbol of this aspect of poetic thinking. It also suggests, rather than states, the power of poetry in the real world, and the suggestion is again embodied in a static shape of a stencilled flight of birds, which manages to convey movement and flight, and 'swerve' in its stasis: a symbol of poetic action denoted yet again by a spatial shape, and these shapes become more complex as Heaney's writing career progressed.

This was a carefully wrought process, and there are a number of different stages in it. As Heaney told Rand Brandes, speaking about *The Haw Lantern*, he wrote a poem called 'The Mud Vision', something which, in terms of aesthetic appeal, would seem far away from the stencil of a gradual flight of birds swooping and swerving, but which, nevertheless, gave Heaney a shaped 'thing' from which he derived 'an abstract poem which follows its own inventiveness' (Brandes 1988, 20). It is a poem about mud apparitions, and one that was written at a time in Ireland when there was a phenomenon of people seeing statues moving, and on first reading, it would seem that this poem was trying to utter something on that broad psycho-cultural issue, but in fact, its genesis was far more deliberate and far less mystical. Heaney explained that the poem derived from an artwork in the Guinness Hops store in Dublin, now a gallery, by an English artist called Richard Long, who made an artistic structure out of mud, one which juxtaposed the elemental material with quite a sophisticated spatial structure:

> Long had made a huge 'flower face' or rose window type of structure entirely by dipping his hand in mud and placing his hand-prints so as to begin with four handmarks in the shape of a cross or compass. When you put four more in the northeast, southwest and so on, so you have eight radiating from the centre – then you begin to move out from that. So there it was, this immense design made of mud.
>
> (Brandes 1988, 20)

The design, while static, has a fluid and circular shape, and it sparked Heaney into his poem about the mud vision; for some reason, possibly the structural one, it appealed to his 'shape-making impulse' (Cole 1997, 104), which always looked to have both a shape as a controlling structure and a form of freedom as part of that structure. The structure of the shape – one with an overall pattern but a significant amount of internal parts that can be in

24 Eugene O'Brien

differential relationships with each other and with the overall shape and containing form – is a pattern to which we will return.

Speaking about form, Heaney is very thoughtful and precise about the differences between shape and form, and this is because that difference is of great significance to his sense of what poetry is and what it can do. In *Stepping Stones*, he explains the common error of confusing shape with form, through a discussion of the sonnet as an example. He speaks of 'the sonnet shape' but makes the point that it is not just a matter of 'rhyming the eight lines and the other six; they happen to be set one on top of each other like two boxes, but they're more like a torso and pelvis', and again, we see the sense of shape, of thingness and of the need for some kind of negotiation within elements of the structure and some form of internal dynamism. Having anthropomorphised the structure of the octave and sestet into a torso and pelvis, Heaney goes on to extend the corporeal metaphor by adding 'there has to be a little bit of muscle movement, it has to be alive in some sort of way', so form, shape and life all cohere in what he sees as poetry. He adds to this that the term a 'moving poem' has a dual meaning: it is not just a poem that touches you in some way, it also:

> has to move itself along as a going linguistic concern. Form is not like a pastry cutter – the dough has to move and discover its own shape. I love to feel that my own voice is on track; that can happen within a metrical shape where you're stepping out to a set or it can happen in a less regulated way within a free shape.
>
> (Heaney & O'Driscoll 2008, 447)

Shape then has an organic relationship with language in Heaney's view of poetry: there is a shape that controls and gives form to the lines, but it is not a box into which the poetic lines must fit, no matter how much they are squeezed or squished in order to do so; nor is it a free association of words and ideas, where the poetic line ends with the margin of the page and has little formal or spatial internal coherence. Instead, there must be a fluid relationship, a negotiation between the 'this-ness' of the words chosen, the thing-presentations, the *Sachvorstellungen* that captures aspects of the *haecceitas* of the world and the form of the living poetic line.

In *Among Schoolchildren*, where we already analysed his discussion of Catherine Bradley's sampler, which is named after the great Yeatsian poem, Heaney again addresses this sense of a living *Gestalt* between all of these areas that go to make a living and vibrant poem: the sense, as he said in *Beowulf*, that words and images are 'turned into metrical shape and raised to the power of verse' (Heaney 1999, xxii). At the end of this essay, he quotes the great concluding stanza of the Yeatsian poem and then goes on to explain its significance for him, and to his sense of what poetry is, and what it can do:

'*Things Founded Clean on Their Own Shapes*' 25

Labour is blossoming and dancing where:

The body is not bruised to pleasure soul
Nor beauty born out of its own despair
Nor blear-eyed wisdom out of midnight oil.
O chestnut tree, great rooted blossomer,
Are you the leaf, the blossom or the bole?
O body swayed to music, O brightening glance,
How can we tell the dancer from the dance?
(Yeats 1996, 219)

Heaney rightly calls this 'one of the high watermarks of poetry' (Heaney 1984, 16) and offers a number of reasons for this. In terms of the argument of this chapter, the core point about the stanza is that it coheres around two shapes – the body and the tree, and the poem actually probes the relationship between static form and dynamic content just as this essay and Heaney's writings have been doing.

The first lines of the stanza offer a very positive description of a space where labour, the necessary toil that accrues with living in the world, is 'blossoming and dancing', and these participles will organically connect with their nouns ('blossomer ... dance') later in the stanza in another example of that shape that is inherent in poetry and which allows the *haecceitas* of the body and the chestnut tree to be themselves, but also to be part of a buoyant metrical shape. For labour to blossom and dance, body and soul, beauty and despair, and knowledge and study must be annealed in some way, and the triple-anaphoric 'nor' makes the connections between them overt. These three binary oppositions set out in the first four lines are sublated and synthesised in the two great images of the 'body swayed to music', and of the 'chestnut-tree, great-rooted blossomer', in the final lines, with the rhetorical apostrophic 'O' serving as the 'muscle' that joins the two halves of the stanza, and the two four-line sentences, together. The apostrophes signal two rhetorical questions, both asking about how the component parts of each shape can retain their 'this-ness', when they are both such fine examples of how the 'power of verse' can fuse shape, and dynamic context. Hence, the chestnut tree, while static in form is constantly organically growing as all the aspects – leaf, blossom and bole – are in an interanimating relationship, and the same is true of the dancer, who performs the movements of the dance so that it is difficult to see these movements as being in any way separate apart from their being embodied in the movements of the dancing body.

Heaney's description of the poetic force of this stanza is achieved, not through normative critical discourse, but through another image of another shape, which again speaks to his specific poetic thinking. He sees this stanza as having the energy and presence of a 'green breaking wave, deep and on the move, rising with thrilling self-propelling force, solid and mysterious at once,

26 *Eugene O'Brien*

gone just as it reveals its full crest of power, never fully apprehended but alluring with its suggestions' (Heaney 1984, 16). This sense of a shape that comes to a form of completion just before it disappears is a resonant image of Heaney's view of the kind of knowledge that poetry can embody and enunciate. It suggests 'an idea of transcendence, an impatience with the limitations of systems, a yearning to be completely fulfilled at all levels of our being' and a mode of linguistic being which involves 'the continuous realisation of all the activities of which we are capable' (Heaney 1984, 16). To quote Heaney about himself, this explanation is a high watermark of his own writing and thinking about poetry – both its ontology and its epistemology – as well as a high watermark of explaining the power of the aesthetic to fuse pattern and *haecceitas*.

The final paragraph of the essay is worth quoting in full, as it is a *summa* of the previous thoughts and arguments, and it brings them together in a way that is really clear and focused, while at the same time offering possibilities for extrapolation to so many other areas of poetry and writing:

> It is the mode of thinking which we should cultivate in ourselves and try to awaken in our pupils: munificent, non-sectarian, energetic and delightful. This is poetry escaping from the actual into the imagined, from external circumstance to internal penetration, from outer to inner space. The mode is the mode of dream and revelation. It does not refer for its validation to the routine facts and events of daily life but to the inner possibilities dormant in our nature. It alerts faculties that doze inertly as we go about our usual business, stirs capacities that are too seldom exercised. The walls of the world expand, the scope of our possibilities opens and widens for the duration of the stanza. We go beyond our normal cognitive bounds and sense a new element where we are not alien but liberated, more alive to ourselves, more drawn out, more educated.
>
> (Heaney 1984, 16)

There is so much one could say about this, but I will confine myself to looking at the importance of shape in this paragraph. The fact that poetry can allow 'the walls of the world' to 'expand' is significant to our discussion, as it shows that structural relationship again that is specific to writing that is 'raised to the power of verse'; like 'The Mud Vision', poetry can use structure not as a constraint but rather as a way of combining representations of thingness in a fluid and dynamic way.

All of the work of imagery and symbolism and transcendence and possibility is made possible by the 'duration of the stanza'; it is the fluid shape that allows all of these interactions because, bounded by the shape, our focus of attention is on how the terms 'blossom' and 'dance' actually flow through the eight lines: the shape of the stanza on the page is a way of ensuring that our

'Things Founded Clean on Their Own Shapes' 27

attention is focused on the stanzaic space bounded by words 'Labour' and 'dance', and the negotiations that take place in that stanza. The shape of the wave is important, even more so as it dissolves, and while we may remember the two great syncretic images of the organic tree and the dancing body, it is within the shape of the stanza that these images themselves take shape and have their being.

For Heaney, shape and the shaping aspects of poetry have a relevance that is unconscious and conscious; shape can allow poetry to achieve an aesthetic but also an ethical function in the society and culture within which it is written. Writing in *The Government of the Tongue*, about the symbolic import of the tongue itself, he notes how Osip Mandelstam, writing in the repressive Soviet Union, compared the tongue to the baton of the conductor of an orchestra. Heaney goes on to quote from this approvingly, noting that the analogy makes clear 'how deeply structured in all our thinking is this idea of imagination as a shaping spirit which it is wrong to disobey' (Heaney 1988, 95). He quotes a passage wherein Mandelstam explains how integral the baton is, calling it a 'dancing chemical formula', and concluding that, in a sense, the baton 'contains within itself all the elements in the orchestra' (Heaney 1988, 95). Heaney agrees with this sense that the baton is the giver of shape to the orchestra, and to the music being played, as it guides and integrates the different sections of the orchestra as it plays the musical piece, as it performs the chemical alchemy that poses us the same question as we saw in Yeats – how can we tell the music from the orchestra? Heaney likes the way that Mandelstam sees the world 'slant', to use his own term alluded to earlier, and uses his reading of Dante as an example. Dante has been a significant figure for Heaney throughout his own writing, both in terms of his poetry and in terms of his criticism, notably 'Envies and Identifications: Dante and the Modern Poet' (Heaney 1985b). What he likes about Mandelstam's revision of Dante is the avoidance of the obvious comments on his epic poem, its structure, its portrayal of a full society and the medieval worldview, or the sense that Dante is a 'mouthpiece of an orthodoxy'. Instead, Mandelstam sees Dante as 'the epitome of chemical suddenness, free biological play, a hive of bees, a hurry of pigeon flights, a flying machine whose function is to keep releasing other self-reproducing flying machines' (Heaney 1988, 95); here is a Dante who has more to say when we focus on the stanza as opposed to the *Commedia* as a whole, and who will repay attention to the text as opposed to the context. As Heaney notes, he is 'recanonized as the sponsor of impulse and instinct'; he is no longer an 'allegory-framer up to his old didactic tricks in the middle of the journey, but a lyric woodcutter singing in the dark wood of the larynx' (Heaney 1988, 95). Poetic thinking, when applied to other poets, can unveil some very different perspectives, slanted and anamorphic but which offer revelatory and original truths about work that seems to have been firmly positioned in its critical box. But of course, as we are seeing in this discussion, for Heaney, if boxes are to be effective, they must be permeable and moveable.

28   Eugene O'Brien

Mandelstam as a poetic thinker is a touchstone for the prose-writing Heaney, just as Hopkins, Hughes, Kavanagh and Yeats have been for the poet, and again, it is in terms of shape that he describes the latter's poetic power. He sees him as an emblem of 'the poet as potent sound-wave', and he uses the example of a musical note cracking a glass as a metaphor for how Mandelstam's own writing was able to 'put a crack into the officially moulded shape of truth in a totalitarian society' (Heaney 1988, xx). Writing as he was at a time of ongoing violence in Northern Ireland, and being expected to comment on it at different stages, Heaney is acutely alert to the need for the aesthetic not to become totally imbricated in the ethical or the political and certainly not to become subservient to either. There is a duty to comment and to be true to one's own instincts and beliefs, but at the same time, poetry is not politics, and Heaney's exemplars in Eastern Europe are all poets who have walked that tightrope between uttering artistic truth and at the same time, not being used by repressive regimes as a token artistic voice. In essence, what Heaney learned and practised was the sense that the voice of the poet is an individual voice, which is part of the reason why he is so supportive of the recanonization of Dante as an individual voice 'singing in the dark wood of the larynx', as opposed to a choral mouthpiece singing in the dark wood of a church and state-validated medieval ideology and eschatology. Thus in the context of poetry's relationship with politics, he looks at the work of Joseph Brodsky, and takes from him the idea that poetry is not 'in the business of mass education', that the poetic voice is not a megaphone or some form of mass media; instead it is attuned to the individual ear. In the kind of attention to the shape and plurality of meaning to which we have become accustomed in his work, he makes the point that, for Brodsky, poetry is heard by the individual's 'inner ear'; it is that which is 'truly h-e-a-r-d as opposed to that which is a mass produced message directed at the h-e-r-d' (Heaney 2010, 12). This sense of the literary and poetic as having an individual effect is important, and the difference that one letter can make in the shape of a word, and to its meaning, is not lost on him. In his later writings, Heaney will look to the shaping power of poetic thought as a way to offer a shape to the politics and history of Ireland. He is not looking to describe a possible solution, or to make vainglorious claims for poetry as a way of 'setting a statesman right'; rather is he offering a shape and fluid pattern within which to enfold the different, and sometimes antagonistic, literary traditions that exist in Ireland. It is for others to attempt to apply these to the political realm: he is looking to be 'h-e-a-r-d' at an individual level; he is not addressing the 'h-e-r-d', though it is fair to say that in an Irish context, he is aware that he has a broader audience when speaking and writing about issues of identity.

In his essay 'At the Frontiers of Writing', in *The Redress of Poetry*, Heaney set out an imagined shape – the quincunx – that offers a permeable context for these competing literary traditions and cultures in Ireland. I have dealt with this at some length in my *Seamus Heaney as Aesthetic Thinker* (O'Brien 2016), and it is an essay of his that has achieved some critical attention but not

'Things Founded Clean on Their Own Shapes' 29

a significant amount which is interesting. Possibly it is seen as an aberration, a broader swathe in his normally microcosmic focus on poems and writers, but I think in the context of this discussion, it is clear that shape and form have always been of significance, and this shape, and the final one with which I will deal, are really the climax of a life-ling thought-process. They are both developments from 'The Mud Vision', where we saw the permeable, containing shape with smaller shapes within. In what Neil Corcoran calls Heaney's own 'new geometry of modern Irish writing' (Corcoran 1999, 62), Heaney calls this shape the quincunx, a term with possible antecedents in Sir Thomas Browne's *The Garden of Cyrus* (Browne 2012 (1736), which traced the quincunx pattern in art, nature and mysticism, or from James Joyce's short story in *Dubliners* titled 'Grace', where the term described the seating patterns of five men at a church service (Joyce 1994, 172). Heaney is careful as he sets out this idea, noting that this was 'another attempt to bring the frontiers of the country into alignment with the frontiers of writing' and went on to explain that the focus was literary as opposed to political: it was 'an attempt to sketch the shape of an integrated literary tradition' (Heaney 1995b, 199).

In any case, it involves sketching a diagram of Irish literary identity in a way that transcends the simple Irish-English binary opposition. In a specifically Irish context, Heaney sets out the parameters as a five-point structure that would grant the plurality of what he terms an Irishness that 'would not prejudice the rights of others' Britishness (Heaney 1995b, 198). This structure is a 'diamond shape' of five towers, with each tower representing an aspect of Irish identity. In the centre was the 'tower of prior Irelandness, the round tower of original insular dwelling', located perhaps on what Louis MacNeice had termed 'the pre-natal mountain'. The southern part of the diamond shape was 'Kilcolman Castle, Edmund Spenser's tower', a symbol of English conquest and Anglicisation; to the west was William Butler Yeats's Thoor Ballylee, 'a deliberate symbol of *his* poetic effort' [*italics original*], which was to restore aspects of what Spenser's 'armies and language' had destroyed. The fourth tower, in the east, was James Joyce's 'Martello tower, on Dublin Bay', a symbol of Joyce's attempt to marginalise the imperium by Hellenizing the island through a range of 'Homeric correspondences, Dantesque scholasticism and a more or less Mediterranean, European, classically endorsed world-view'. The final tower in the diamond is 'Carrickfergus Castle', Louis MacNeice's 'keep', 'where William of Orange once landed on his way to secure the Protestant Settlement', and which had long been a garrison to British troops (Heaney 1995b, 199–200).

These five towers offer a thingness, a concrete *Sachvorstellung*, with each one standing for an element of tradition that is often inimical to, and in contestation with, the other elements. The fact that this shape is composed of towers would suggest a strong sense of *haecceitas*, of 'thing-ness' and of their being unmoveable, and as such could symbolise the entrenched attitude that has bedevilled Irish politics for generations. Heaney is not pretending his structure can uproot these towers; instead, they are an attempt to offer an

30   *Eugene O'Brien*

enabling shape and form within which they can interact. Indeed, Heaney is clear in his writing that for him, it is the dialectical interaction, the negotiation and the fluid interanimation between these towers that is important to his shaping of such an inclusive Irish literary tradition.

Each tower faces towards the other towers, and has imagined lines of communication between them; it is a shape full of dynamism and interchange. As he puts it, he imagines that MacNeice can look towards the 'visionary Ireland' of the central tower, while retaining strong connections with Spenser in terms of his 'English domicile', and having an affinity with Yeats through his 'ancestral and affectionate links with Connemara', and with Joyce through his 'mythic and European consciousness'. In short, MacNeice, looked at from the 'slant' perspective of the quincunx, can be regarded as an 'Irish Protestant writer with Anglocentric attitudes who managed to be faithful to his Ulster inheritance, his Irish affections and his English predilections' (Heaney 1995b, 200). Politically, this would not have huge import, nor does Heaney suggest that it should have: instead, this is an exercise in poetic thinking, it is an example, to refer back to *Among Schoolchildren*, of how such thinking can be 'munificent, non-sectarian, energetic and delightful', and how it can escape from 'the actual into the imagined, from external circumstance to internal penetration, from outer to inner space' (Heaney 1984, 16).

This perspectival structure allows for a range of views in its interactions. Heaney, taking Spenser and Yeats as examples, makes no attempt to sublate or synthesise their different ideological and cultural viewpoints. When Spenser looks at the tower of prior Irelandness, he sees 'popery, barbarism and the Dark Ages', whereas when Yeats looks, he sees a 'possible unity of being, an Irish nation retrieved and enabled by a repossession of its Gaelic heritage'. In Heaney's mind, Joyce would see the '*omphalos,* the navel of a reinvented order', or perhaps a symbol of Catholicism from which the country needed to be liberated (Heaney 1995b, 199–200). There are plural negotiations and movements to be had within this shape, a shape that is more dynamic with each interaction. For Heaney, it is the lines of interaction and negotiation between these towers that are creative of meaning, 'the lines of flight or of deterritorialization' (Deleuze & Guattari 1987, 32), and deterritorialization, in the sense of an Irish literary tradition, can really only be underscored in such a fluid shape where the territory is clearly defined in the *haecceitas* of the towers but where there is a sense that all belong and all have a voice. Such deterritorialization makes for an integrated, if contestatory tradition, which accepts the 'British dimension of Northern Irishness and the centrality of the English language but as part of a larger Irish reality' (Foster 1995, 94).

Heaney's quincunx has been commented on by a number of critics. Daniel Tobin notes that Heaney's 'Ireland of the mind incorporates the diversity of Ireland's complex history within its design' (Tobin 1998, 302), while Michael Cavanagh sees the structure as making a connection 'between Irish frontiers and different traditions of Irish writing' (Cavanagh 2009, 6). That so

'Things Founded Clean on Their Own Shapes' 31

complex an idea is outlined in just two pages from *The Redress of Poetry* means that it has not been fully worked out, but it does again underline the importance of shape and structure as a way of presenting the realities of Irish writing in the shadow of different ideologies. The *Sachvorstellung* of the five towers is important, as is the fact that all of the dwellings here are part of a military frame of reference – images of conquest and colonisation and defence are implied, as the Irish built round towers to defend themselves from the Vikings, while all of the other towers in the quincunx have been built by the British originally, so there is a *haecceitas* of colonisation at work here, despite the annealing attempts of poetry to encompass and negotiate between the different elements of language and literature and traditions. He is all too aware of the entrenched political realities and his quincunx makes no attempt to elide or attenuate these. His second quincunx will attempt to set up a new and broader context within which this integrated tradition can exist.

At the conference of the European Federation of Associations and Centres of Irish Studies, held at the University of Vienna in 2009, Heaney delivered a reading and a lecture based on the conference theme, which was 'Irish/European Cross-Currents and Exchanges'. The title of this lecture is germane to our discussion: '"Mossbawn via Mantua": Ireland in/and Europe, Cross-Currents and Exchanges', as it sets out a form of attunement between his own place, and the city in northern Italy and, by extension, between Irishness and European intellectual and cultural traditions. As he set out a framework wherein to read his poems, and again we note that structural and shaping imperative in his thinking, he outlined 'five main European starting points which gave me short cuts back into Irish destination' (Heaney 2012, 19).

He began with the 'Greek and Roman and Judaic past, all that came to Ireland from the fifth century onward with the arrival of Patrick and his Christian missionaries', before moving on to the 'barbarian element in European culture', which is symbolised by 'the runic Germanic letter or the Irish ogham stone' (Heaney 2012, 20). He also speaks of Eastern Europe as a third area, and of the poets who spoke within such repressed societies, poets like Zbigniew Herbert and the Czesław Miłosz, 'dual citizens of the republic of letters and the republic of conscience' (Heaney 2012, 21). The fourth province of this five-part structure is that of 'Dante Alighieri, and the Dante part of my work is inhabited by shades of the dead who tell their stories in a book called *Station Island*', while the fifth 'zone of European operations' is that of translation 'and my translation activity has been mainly carried out in three of the four provinces already mentioned' (Heaney 2012, 21).

The complexity of the shape and structure is again important, as is the fact that he does not actually sketch out a shape but leaves it to the reader to imagine it, and to also image the dynamic negotiations between the different areas. Of course, this shape also allows an Irish literary tradition to further deterritorialise itself by placing it within a European context. He is keen to retain aspects of his givens, and of the autochthonous tradition, but is reluctant to let it be the limit of his horizon of expectation. These five areas

32 Eugene O'Brien

all conspire to pluralise the Irish literary tradition through the European influence and experience, which can offer reflected and refracted light on Ireland, as each influence in some way illuminates an aspect of the Irish experience as part of a broader and changing European contextual framework. It offers a new shape within which we can reimagine ourselves, where we can see ourselves 'slant', as it were. Heaney's lecture begins by talking about two stalwarts of the English literary tradition, Samuel Taylor Coleridge and William Wordsworth, and he explains how Coleridge, in *Biographia Literaria*, and Wordsworth, in his *Preface to the Lyrical Ballads*, both make the case for a poetry of recuperation, of a poetry 'capable of refreshing perception', of poetry as a 'certain colouring of imagination, whereby ordinary things should be presented to the mind in an unusual way' (Heaney, 2012, p. 19). In other words, of a poetry where the thing becomes itself but more than itself in a new perspective and a new shape and structure.

To return to Barney Devlin's forge where this essay began, Heaney noted that on the last day of 1999, Barney showed that he was 'still capable of striking the epic out of the usual', as at 'midnight on the last day of 1999, he hit the anvil twelve times to ring in the millennium – and relayed the tune to his son in Edmonton by cellular phone' (Heaney & O'Driscoll 2008, 91). Here, shape, form and sound combine with technology to forge a connection between Heaney's past and present; between Hillhead and Edmonton; between utility and the aesthetic, as in his shaping imagination, the power of language to conjure up the *haecceitas*, the 'this-ness' of the anvil at a particular time, and then to somehow turn that into an aesthetic symbol, is something that is unique to Seamus Heaney's sense of things founded clean on their own shapes – the shapes of poetry.

Works Cited

Bernstein, Charles (2001) *Content's Dream Essays: 1975–1984*, Evanston: Northwestern University Press.

Boothby, Richard (2001) *Freud as Philosopher: Metapsychology after Lacan*, London: Routledge.

Brandes, Rand (1988) 'An Interview with Seamus Heaney', *Salmagundi*, 80: 4–21.

Brodsky, Joseph, Seamus Heaney & Derek Walcott (1996) *Homage to Robert Frost*, New York: Farrar, Straus and Giroux.

Browne, Thomas (2012) *Garden of Cyrus*, originally published in 1736, New York: Gale.

Cavanagh, Michael (2009) *Professing Poetry: Seamus Heaney's Poetics*, Washington, DC: Catholic University of America Press.

Cole, Henri (1997) 'Interview with Seamus Heaney', *The Paris Review: The Art of Poetry*, 75, 144, 89–138.

Corcoran, Neil (1999) *Poets of Modern Ireland: Text, Context, Intertext*, Cardiff: University of Wales Press.

Critchley, Simon (2005) *Things Merely Are: Philosophy in the Poetry of Wallace Stevens*, London: Routledge.

'Things Founded Clean on Their Own Shapes' 33

Deleuze, Gilles & Félix Guattari (1987) *A Thousand Plateaus: Capitalism and Schizophrenia*, Minneapolis: University of Minnesota Press.

Deleuze, Gilles & Claire Parnet (1977) *Dialogues*, translated by Hugh Tomlinson and Barbara Habberjam, Paris: Flammarion.

Derrida, Jacques & Elizabeth Rottenberg (2002) *Negotiations: Interventions and Interviews, 1971–2001*. Stanford, CA: Stanford University Press.

Dickinson, Emily (1924) *The Complete Poems of Emily Dickinson*, Boston, MA: Little, Brown, and Company.

Foster, John Wilson (1995) *The Achievement of Seamus Heaney*, Dublin: The Lilliput Press.

Freud, Sigmund (1955) 'The "Uncanny", Volume XVII (1917–1919)', in *The Standard Edition of the Complete Psychological Works of Sigmund Freud*, edited and translated by James Strachey, London: Hogarth Press and the Institute of Psycho-Analysis, 217–256.

Freud, Sigmund (1981) 'On the History of the Psycho-Analytic Movement Papers on Metapsychology and Other Works, Volume XIV (1914–1916)', in *The Standard Edition of the Complete Psychological Works of Sigmund Freud*, edited and translated by James Strachey, London: Hogarth Press and the Institute of Psycho-Analysis, 7–66.

Glaser, Ben & Jonathan Culler (2019) *Critical Rhythm: The Poetics of a Literary Life Form*, New York: Fordham University Press.

Heaney, Seamus (1969) *Door into the Dark*, London: Faber.

Heaney, Seamus (1980) *Preoccupations: Selected Prose, 1968–1978*, London: Faber.

Heaney, Seamus (1984) *Among Schoolchildren: A Public Lecture given by Seamus Heaney on 9 June 1983*, Belfast: Queen's University of Belfast.

Heaney, Seamus (1985a) 'Place and Displacement: Reflections on Some Recent Poetry from Northern Ireland', the Pete Laver memorial lecture delivered at Grasmere 2nd August 1984, Grasmere: Trustees of Dove Cottage.

Heaney, Seaus (1985b) 'Envies and Identifications: Dante and the Modern Poet', *Irish University Review*, 15, 1 (Spring, 1985), 5–19.

Heaney, Seamus (1987) *The Haw Lantern*, London: Faber.

Heaney, Seamus (1988) *The Government of the Tongue: The 1986 T.S. Eliot Memorial Lectures and Other Critical Writings*, London: Faber.

Heaney, Seamus (1995a) *Crediting Poetry*, County Meath, Ireland: Gallery Press.

Heaney, Seamus (1995b) *The Redress of Poetry*, London: Faber.

Heaney, Seamus (1999) *Beowulf*, London: Faber and Faber.

Heaney, Seamus (2002) *Finders Keepers: Selected Prose 1971–2001*, London: Faber.

Heaney, Seamus (2010) *Writer and Righter Fourth IHRC Annual Human Rights Lecture*, Dublin: Irish Human Rights Commission.

Heaney, Seamus (2012) 'Mossbawn via Mantua: Ireland in/and Europe: Cross-Currents and Exchanges', in *Ireland In/And Europe: Cross-Currents and Exchanges*, Volume 4, edited by Werner Huber, Sandra Mayer, and Julia Novak, Germany: Wissenschaftlicher Verlag Trier.

Heaney, Seamus & Denis O'Driscoll (2008) *Stepping Stones: Interviews with Seamus Heaney*, London: Faber.

Joyce, James (1994) *Dubliners*, London: Secker and Warburg.

Kaplan, Louise J. (2006) *Cultures of Fetishism*, London: Palgrave Macmillan.

Lacan, Jacques (1977) *The Four Fundamental Concepts of Psycho-Analysis*, translated by Alan Sheridan, London: Hogarth Press.

34 *Eugene O'Brien*

O'Brien, Eugene (2016) *Seamus Heaney as Aesthetic Thinker: A Study of the Prose*, Syracuse: Syracuse University Press.
Parker, Michael (1993) *Seamus Heaney: The Making of the Poet*, London: Macmillan.
Sonzogni, Marco (2022) *The Translations of Seamus Heaney*, London: Faber.
Tobin, Daniel (1998) *Passage to the Center: Imagination and the Sacred in the Poetry of Seamus Heaney*, Lexington: University Press of Kentucky.
Yeats, William Butler (1996) *The Collected Poems of W. B. Yeats*, edited by Richard Finneran, revised edition, Volume 1, New York: Scribner Paperback Poetry.

2 Seamus Heaney's Uncanny Encounters

Henry Hart

In 'Crediting the Poet: What Seamus Heaney Means to Me', the scholar Eugene O'Brien notes that the 'fusion of familiarity and strangeness, of the *Heimlich* and the *Unheimlich*, the canny and the uncanny' becomes 'almost a norm' (online) in Heaney's work after *Death of a Naturalist* (1966). O'Brien alludes to Sigmund Freud's essay 'The Uncanny' (1919), which uses the German word *Unheimlich* (meaning, among other things, 'unhomely', 'unhomelike') to describe disturbingly 'novel and unfamiliar' experiences that 'lead back to something long known to us, once very familiar' (Freud 1919, 219–220). According to Freud: 'An uncanny experience occurs either when repressed infantile complexes have been revived by some impression, or when the primitive beliefs we have surmounted seem once more to be confirmed' (Freud 2019, 248). Confusion, anxiety, and terror typically attend these uncanny experiences.

Freud contends that the paradoxical nature of the uncanny is embedded in the German language: 'The German word *Unheimlich* ["uncanny" in English translations] is obviously the opposite of *Heimlich, heimish*, meaning "familiar", "native", "belonging to the home"', but 'the usage of speech has extended *das Heimliche* into its opposite *das Unheimlich*' (Freud 1919, 219–220). These opposites merge because of the dynamic relationship between repression and expression. When something familiar has been repressed in the unconscious, but then is expressed—literally 'pressed out'—into consciousness, one experiences the uncanny. Freud writes:

> If psychoanalytic theory is correct in maintaining that every emotional affect, whatever its quality, is transformed by repression into morbid anxiety, then among such cases of anxiety there must be a class in which the anxiety can be shown to come from something repressed which *recurs*. This class of morbid anxiety would then be no other than what is uncanny, irrespective of whether it originally aroused dread or some other affect. In the second place, if this is indeed the secret nature of the uncanny, we can understand why the usage of speech has extended *das Heimlich* into its opposite *das Unheimlich*; for this

DOI: 10.4324/9781003456148-3

36 *Henry Hart*

uncanny is in reality nothing new or foreign, but something familiar and old—established in the mind that has been estranged only by the process of repression.

(Freud 2019, 241)

The feeling of *Unheimlich* occurs when a repressed *heimlich* experience recurs.

As a devout Catholic growing up on an isolated farm in Northern Ireland, Heaney was particularly susceptible to the feelings Freud associated with the uncanny. As a mature writer who adopted a Jungian, mythopoetic world-view, he tended to regard uncanny experiences less in terms of the etiology of neurosis, though, and more as beneficial rites of passage. His essay '"Apt Admonishment": Wordsworth as an Example', which appeared in *The Hudson Review* in 2008, summarizes his view of the uncanny as a restorative rite of passage in a poet's development. While Freud analyzes the way daemonic spirits, animated corpses, a homesickness for a mother's genitals, the castration-complex, and other 'figments of the imagination' (Freud 2019, 245) trigger uncanny anxieties and fears, Heaney dwells on the way the uncanny operates in 'poetic recognition scenes' that involve a 'close encounter between the poet and the muse' or between the poet and an inspiring precursor. 'In the modern era', he declares, 'the sense of visitation and rededication will often derive from meetings and occasions which are ... bathed in an uncanny light, occasions when the poet has been, as it were, unhomed, has experienced the *Unheimlich*'. The effect of these uncanny meetings, whether ancient or modern, is the same. After initial feelings of disorientation and distress, the poet enjoys a new influx of inspiration and renewed access to the source of his or her gifts:

> Even in the modern period ... the poet typically comes away from such encounters with a renewed sense of election, surer in his or her vocation. What is being enacted or recalled is usually an experience of confirmation, of the spirit coming into its own, a door being opened or a path being entered upon. Usually also the experience is unexpected and out of the ordinary, in spite of the fact that it occurs in the normal course of events, in the everyday world.
>
> (Heaney 2008, 21)

Heaney's references to 'visitation', 'rededication', 'election', 'confirmation', 'vocation', and 'the spirit' hark back to the Catholicism of his youth.

Throughout his career, Heaney examined *Unheimlich* moments in which *Heimlich* memories of his first home, Mossbawn, returned to him. In the essay 'Mossbawn', which he placed first in *Preoccupations: Selected Prose 1968–1978*, he called that home his '*omphalos*, meaning the navel, and hence the stone that marked the centre of the world' (Heaney 1980, 17). As his wife

Marie remarked near the end of his life: 'All he's ever wanted to do is go back [to Mossbawn] ... his paradise ... his Eden' (McCrum, online). The loss of Mossbawn, which occurred in 1954 after his younger brother Christopher died in a road accident, and his parents decided to move to a different farm, was one of Heaney's most traumatic experiences of *Unheimlich*. But leaving Mossbawn, whether to attend Anahorish Primary School or St. Columb's College, had always been traumatic. In each case, he prized *Unheimlich* encounters that reconnected him with the 'friendly, intimate, homelike ... sense of peaceful pleasure and security ... within the four walls of his house' (Freud 1919, 222), which is how Freud defined *Heimlich*.

For Heaney, Wordsworth's encounter with a leech-gatherer in 'Resolution and Independence' exemplifies the way the uncanny works. In Wordsworth's well-known poem, the solitary, stoical leech-gatherer depends on 'God's good help' for 'Housing' and 'did seem/Like one who I had met with in a dream/Or like a man from some far region sent/to give me human strength, by apt admonishment'. An unhomed, unhomelike wanderer, the leech-gatherer must search for free lodging because he makes so little money. Wordsworth assumes that this destitute old man on the moor must be depressed, so he's surprised by his 'vivid eyes', 'firm ... mind', and the way he 'cheerfully uttered' (Wordsworth 1965, 168–169) information about his work. The meeting is uncanny because it involves an unfamiliar figure evoking a familiar one and, in the process, transporting the poet to a 'gifted state' (Hyde 2007, 195). The leech-gatherer reminds Wordsworth of Christ, no doubt because he provides leeches for healers who cure people by bleeding them. Christ's sacrificial bleeding was also supposed to heal. If the leech-gatherer at first appears to be a sad, alien figure 'not all alive nor dead,/Nor all asleep', Wordsworth soon associates him with the Trinitarian Christian God. When Wordsworth exclaims at the end of his poem, 'God... be my help and stay secure' (Wordsworth 1965, 168–169), he is addressing the leech-gatherer as if he were God. The chance encounter between the poet and the ghostly man produces an epiphany that restores Wordsworth's spirit and faith. Literally and figuratively unhomed on the moor, the poet is transported back to his original Christian 'home' where God is his 'help and stay'. The equanimity of *Heimlich* replaces the fears, anxieties, and confusions of *Unheimlich*.

Heaney, in 'Apt Admonishment', compares Wordsworth's 'recognition scene' with similar scenes in poems by Hesiod, Dante, T.S. Eliot, and D.H. Lawrence:

> in each case, the poet arrives on the scene either abstracted or disoriented, and is then brought more fully alive to his or her obligations and capacities—is helped, in fact, to get back in touch with his or her proper poetic gifts.
>
> (Heaney 2008, 25)

38 Henry Hart

If muses were the enlivening agents for traditional poets, Heaney points out:

> in the age of Freud there was a far more fluid awareness of the sources of inspiration, a much greater readiness to locate the radiance of the gift in those very areas of the psyche that have been the most repressed.
>
> (Heaney 2008, 22)

As a Catholic youth, Heaney had located 'the radiance of the gift' in the divine realm. As an adult poet, he tended to locate the source of gifts in the unconscious realm of memory.

When Heaney says in 'Apt Admonishment' that Milton favored an 'identification of the muse with the Holy Spirit of his three-person Christian God' (Heaney 2008, 20), he could be speaking for himself as a young Catholic. Heaney may have stopped attending Mass regularly in his mid-20s, but he did not abandon his early Catholicism so much as revise it to explain his experiences as a mature poet. As he told John Haffenden in *Viewpoints*: 'I've never felt any need to rebel [against Catholicism] or do a casting-off of God or anything like that, because I think in this day anthropologists and mythologists have taught us ... to live with our myths' (Haffenden 1981, 60). As he developed a new religious vocabulary and mythology, he tended to represent the 'three-person Christian God' as an artistic gift-maker and gift-giver. And he repeatedly invoked the Christian rite of 'confirmation' (when a priest tells new Church members they are sealed with the gift of the Holy Spirit) to refer to those instances when a poet received in-spiriting 'gifts' from precursors, mentors, and other secular sources.

One of Heaney's earliest uncanny 'confirmations' came from the poet Ted Hughes. On May 24, 1979, Heaney acknowledged in a letter to Hughes: 'Since I opened *Lupercal* in the Belfast Public Library in November 1962, the lifeline to Hughesville has been in its emergent differing ways a confirmation' (SHP-EU May 24, 1979). Heaney's view of Hughes as a priestly gift-giver was encouraged by *Lupercal*'s title poem 'Lupercalia', which alludes to a Roman ritual in which young priests known as *luperci* offered sacrificial gifts to the fertility goddess Februus and then tried to pass on the goddess's gifts of fertility to nubile Roman women. This mythic gift exchange and the mesmerizing way Hughes presented it in *Lupercal* had a powerful effect on Heaney. In his essay about uncanny encounters, he claims that Hughes had bolstered his 'faith in the finality, wisdom and sufficiency of his gift' and confirmed his belief that the 'poet's first duty ... is to his gift'. Heaney cites D.H. Lawrence as a similar priest-like precursor whose writings admonished him to respect his gift and renounce those forces that tempted him to 'sin ... against his gift' (Heaney 2008, 23).

In his prose and poetry, Heaney obsessively retraces journeys from an unhomed state to one where he is rehomed at the omphalos of his gifts. One synecdoche for the original home of his gifts in 'Mossbawn' is the water pump outside his boyhood farmhouse. He says the pump is his '*omphalos*' at 'the centre of the world', but he also identifies it as an 'idol...marking the centre of another world' (Heaney 1980, 17). (In Greek mythology, the *omphalos* was a stone with magic powers that Zeus placed at the center of the world. It supposedly belonged to Antaeus's mother, Gaea—it was imagined to be her navel—and it rested in the temple at Delphi where a priestess uttered prophesies inspired by Apollo.) For Heaney, the pump's nourishing water from an underground source is a symbol for the poetic gift that rises from the mind's unconscious depths and that nourishes audiences. The pump is uncanny in the sense that it is both *Unheimlich* and *Heimlich*. It is outside the home, but close to the home. It is a familiar source of water that taps an unfamiliar, hidden source.

Heaney's essay about Mossbawn taps several uncanny experiences he had as a boy outside his first home. As in his prose poem 'Cauled', which he published in *Stations* (1975), one experience of *Unheimlich* occurred in his Aunt Mary's pea garden. Although he was familiar with the garden, it suddenly became unfamiliar when he managed to get lost among the plants. In his essay and prose poem, he envisions what happened in the pea garden as a regression into an Edenic womb where he was enclosed in a protective 'caul of veined light ... full of assuaging earth and leaf smell, a sunlit lair'. After losing himself in this other world, he began a rite of passage that led to a rebirth when he was 'wakened [as if] from a winter sleep' and 'gradually ... aware of voices' (Heaney 1980, 17). Like most births, this one was painful; he cried when he heard the familiar voices. Later, he realized that the voices were harbingers of literary voices that would waken and confirm his voice as a poet.

Another anecdote in 'Mossbawn' about uncanny withdrawals involves a 'secret nest' in a beech tree in front of his old house. He says that by climbing to a notch in the tree he could be 'at the heart of a different life, looking out on the familiar yard as if it were suddenly behind a pane of strangeness' (Heaney 1980, 17–18). His visionary perspective here resembles Robert Frost's vision in 'After Apple-Picking' when he holds up a 'pane of glass' (it's actually ice from a drinking trough) and sees his once-flourishing farm changed to a 'world of hoary grass'. Frost tries to 'rub the strangeness' (Frost 1972, 68) from his eyes, but he fails and subsequently dreams of multiple failures. Heaney's dream-like experience in the tree follows the more auspicious pattern outlined in his essay about Wordsworth. Rather than end in darkness, weakness, despair, and confusion, as Frost's apple-picker does, Heaney ends in an imaginary realm full of light and strength. 'In that tight place', he writes, he 'sensed the embrace of light' and felt like 'a little Atlas shouldering it all' (Heaney 1980, 18). Frost broods on death and human limitations; Heaney celebrates life and superhuman possibilities.

Most of the secret nests and womb-like Edens commemorated in 'Mossbawn' are outside Heaney's central nest—his farmhouse. In these exterior spaces, his feelings of *Unheimlich* re-establish bonds with the familiar space inside his house. In his Nobel Prize lecture, 'Crediting Poetry', he claims that

40 *Henry Hart*

he and his family during the 1940s lived 'a kind of den-life' that 'was more or less emotionally and intellectually proofed against the outside world'. It was 'an intimate, physical, creaturely existence ... in the doze of hibernation'. Speaking specifically of his boyhood, he says it was 'ahistorical, pre-sexual, in suspension between the archaic and the modern'. In this liminal state, he was as 'impressionable as the drinking water that stood in a bucket in our scullery' (Heaney 1988, 415). Water, in this case, is his symbol for the poet's quiet, meditative, keenly attentive sensibility that would later produce lines of verse like ripples in the bucket.

One of the most memorable of Heaney's uncanny rites of passage as a boy occurred in another liminal place outside Mossbawn—the marshy stretch of 'forbidden ground' near Lough Beg, a lake about three miles east of his farmhouse. Locals believed the area was haunted by bogeys, mystery men, and a recluse nicknamed Tom Tipping. It took courage for Heaney, who was only about nine at the time, to go there with a friend, strip off his clothes, and jump naked into a muddy bog hole. Both boys emerged, according to Heaney, 'initiated [and] ... betrothed ... [to] the watery ground' (Heaney 1980, 19). The vaguely sexual plunge seems to 'betroth' the boys to an Earth goddess like Gaea or the fertility goddess Nerthus in P.V. Glob's *The Bog People*, a book that would inspire some of Heaney's most remarkable poems. The suggestion in Heaney's anecdote is again that gifts of new life and new poems arise from an uncanny union of *Unheimlich* and *Heimlich*.

Heaney suffered some of his most painful unhomings as a boy in 1944 when he had to go to Anahorish Primary School. Because he was so frightened by the prospect of leaving home for school, his parents asked an older girl who lived across the street, Philomena McNicholl, to accompany him on the three-quarter-mile walk along Lagans Road to Anahorish. As it turned out, even the attractive, ginger-haired girl with the saintly name could not assuage Heaney's anxieties. His father, who was eager to get to a cattle fair on his son's first day of school, got angry as he sobbed and whined. Finally, after much parental prodding, Heaney joined Philomena and headed down the road.

Going to school proved to be another uncanny rite of passage, another instance of 'the spirit coming into its own, a door being opened or a path being entered upon', another initiation into the 'obligations and capacities' of gifts. In *Stepping Stones*, his book-length interview with Dennis O'Driscoll, Heaney indicated that his initial departure for Anahorish had all the *sturm und drang* of an epic journey. He felt this way partly because the school was housed in two zinc-roofed Nissen huts that Allied soldiers had left behind when they went to fight the Axis powers in Normandy. It was as if he were a soldier going off to war or, as he told O'Driscoll, a Native American journeying to 'the land of the dead' where he knew he would feel 'lost and homesick' (O'Driscoll 2008, 242). As he approached the small school, he was particularly concerned about his hand-made leather shoulder bag, which his Uncle Peter had used to carry money when he sold bread from a cart. The bag looked shabby and second class and reminded him of his family's poverty. This bag would later become the subject of a poem, 'The Schoolbag' in *Seeing Things*, that alludes to Dante's descent into the *Inferno*'s 'land of the dead'. As an adult, Heaney knew that Dante's path eventually led to a vision of blessings and gifts. In his poem, Heaney acknowledges that his second-hand schoolbag was 'a handsel' (Heaney 1991, 30), a gift intended to bring good luck to someone at the beginning of a new endeavor. Although he showed little gratitude for the bag as a boy, his poem treats the gift as a metonymy for all the gifts he would receive during his education as a poet.

Heaney overcame his fears of elementary school, but he continued to think of it as an *Unheimlich* or unhomelike place. This was especially true when he was assigned the job of getting water from a nearby stream to make ink for fountain pens used at the school. As soon as he was outside the Nissen-hut classrooms, he was reminded of fetching water at Mossbawn. It was as if he'd been transported from a relatively unfamiliar place—the schoolroom—to his familiar home:

> What was odd and memorable was the otherness of the school at that moment: you were only a few yards away from life in the classroom you'd just left, but you felt a world away. You were outside, you had the whole sky and land to yourself, yet there it was in front of you, the silent building. You saw it in all its uncanniness and had a taste of yourself in all of your own solitude and singularity.
>
> (O'Driscoll 2008, 244)

Heaney alludes here to an observation Gerard Manley Hopkins made in a commentary on *The Spiritual Exercises of St. Ignatius Loyola*: 'I consider my selfbeing, my consciousness and feeling of myself, that taste of myself ... [to be] more distinctive than the taste of ale or alum, more distinctive than the smell of walnutleaf or camphor' (Devlin 1959, 122–123). Heaney's 'distinctive' sense of 'solitude and singularity' would bear poetic fruit as he matured.

This intense self-consciousness arose in part from an awareness of being Catholic in a place dominated by British Protestants. As Heaney walked to school, he could see signs of his Catholic heritage wherever he looked. Slemish Mountain, where St. Patrick had reputedly herded sheep as a boy, formed part of the northeastern horizon. The steeple of a Catholic church rose above an island in Lough Beg a short distance to the east. Among these familiar surroundings, though, place-names and Protestant schoolmates reminded Heaney that the land he considered 'home' didn't really belong to him; it belonged to the British Empire that had conquered it and ruled it for centuries.

Another one of Heaney's experiences of *Unheimlich* occurred in 1951 when he left home for a private Catholic secondary school, St. Columb's College in Londonderry. Recalling this momentous trip decades later, he said

42 Henry Hart

he'd 'crossed some kind of psychic shadow line' (Madden & Bradley 2004, 72). His first day at the school had been especially traumatic:

> Everybody was lined up. I'd never seen such execution, such executive strapping as happened that day. That first day there was a definite sense of scare, really. You had come from a home and suddenly you were in an institution. I was homesick for weeks, and very vulnerable and didn't know the ropes. Weeping, internally weeping.
>
> (Fitzpatrick 2010, 60)

Elsewhere, he described his rites of initiation at the school as another Dantesque descent into an inferno.

Heaney believed his parents suffered a similar sense of *Unheimlich*—of being painfully unhomed—when they dropped him off at the school: 'I know the uncanny sense of their own individuality and responsibility that must have been with them that day. They were consigning me to an unknown and we were all growing up' (O'Driscoll 2008, 33). Heaney's sense of disorientation, though, was partly assuaged by the gift of a fountain pen that his parents bought for him shortly before dropping him off at the school. 'I always remember that twelve and sixpence [Conway Stewart] fountain pen', he told the school's historian, Maurice Fitzpatrick. 'That was a kind of initiation into the higher condition' (Fitzpatrick 2010, 59). From his early poem 'Digging' to one of his last poems, 'On the Gift of a Fountain Pen', he eulogized the material gift of the pen as if it embodied his gift for writing. During his ordeals at St. Columb's, he used that gift to write home and to restore bonds with his family. In his later poems, he would do the same.

During Heaney's years at St. Columb's, the brutality of the priests and the sectarian strife outside the school's walls convinced him that he had fallen from an Edenic home into a violently divided world. In 1951, the Royal Ulster Constabulary broke up a St. Patrick's Day parade in Londonderry with batons after the well-known nationalist politician Eddie McAteer raised an Irish flag in the city center. Angered by the police action, the IRA re-armed itself by raiding British military bases in England and Northern Ireland. Anti-Unionist IRA units from the Republic crossed the border in 1956 and attacked a BBC relay transmitter in Londonderry, a British army barracks in Enniskillen, and a courthouse in Magherafelt. More than 300 attacks took place in Northern Ireland during 1957, the year Heaney graduated from St. Columb's.

Heaney heard about the new IRA campaign from friends and family (the school prohibited radios and newspapers), and on one of his bus trips home, he saw the results of the bombing of the Magherafelt Courthouse. 'This was the first time outside of newsreels or books or photographs', he said, that he'd witnessed 'evidence of destructive intent' (Fitzpatrick 2010, 61) by sectarian groups. He later wrote in 'The Border Campaign' that news of the attack had left him feeling exposed and fearful. In fact, he was so haunted by the image of the destroyed courthouse roof that he felt as if the roof on his St. Columb's dormitory had been blown off: 'When I heard the word 'attack'/In St. Columb's College in nineteen fifty-six/It left me winded, left nothing between me/And the sky beyond my boarder's dormer' (Heaney 2001, 21). The bombed courthouse was memorable partly because it was so close to home and partly because he associated it with Mossbawn. The *bawn* in 'Mossbawn' referred to a fortified enclosure on the 'moss' or bogland, but, as Heaney was learning, *bawns* were vulnerable; they could be damaged or lost. After the spate of IRA attacks, he knew that Catholics would suffer reprisals in the form of unroofings and unhomings at the hands of Protestant citizens, paramilitary groups, and police officers.

During the summer of 1965, Heaney had another experience of *Unheimlich*, but this one had nothing to do with unroofed buildings, erotic bog holes, or punitive schools. It occurred at his wedding. Heaney had been dating Marie Devlin for almost three years, knew her family well, and looked forward to formalizing their relationship. As he remarked to Dennis O'Driscoll, the gathering of family and friends at the wedding was 'an unmysterious, ordinary get-together. Everybody in good form and in full cry. The families being themselves, even more themselves than usual, our friends enjoying the fling'. The aristocratic site of the wedding reception may have been unfamiliar (it was at Drumsill House, a posh eighteenth-century mansion surrounded by a park near Lough Neagh), but Heaney felt pangs of homesickness during what was supposed to be a festive occasion: 'there was necessarily a rare newness about the whole occasion', he recalled. 'It ... [was] in the literal sense *Unheimlich*, an unhoming ... [There were] moments of strangeness, sudden lancings or fissures in the fun..., intense intimations that the first circle...[had been] broken' (O'Driscoll 2008, 253–254). He was breaking away from his family to join another family. Once again, he was being unhomed.

Heaney, however, soon realized that his marriage compelled him 'to be renewed, transfigured, in another pattern' (O'Driscoll 2008, 253–254). There were losses, but also compensatory gains. 'See, now they vanish,/The faces and places, with the self which, as it could, loved them,/To become renewed, transfigured, in another pattern', T.S. Eliot had written in 'Little Gidding' (Eliot 1943, 55). The 'faces and places' may be lost, but they return in a new pattern in memories and poems, which is why Eliot ends his poem with a cheerful flourish: 'All shall be well, and/All manner of thing shall be well/When the tongues of flame are in-folded/Into the crowned knot of fire/And the fire and the rose are one' (Eliot 1943, 59). In retrospect, Heaney knew Eliot was right. 'There was definitely a new charge, a quicker flow', he said about his courtship and wedding in the early 1960s. 'Everything happened quickly and at the same time—the development of our relationship, the entry into poetry, the marriage itself. Inside three years. One excitement quickening the other' (O'Driscoll 2008, 63). During these rites of passage, he felt disoriented and unhomed, but also 'more fully alive to his ... obligations and capacities' and more 'in touch with his...proper

44   Henry Hart

poetic gifts' (Heaney 2008, 25). A year after he married, he published *Death of a Naturalist*, and before long he was recognized as one of the most gifted poets writing in English.

Another transfiguring incident occurred a few years later when Heaney bought P.V. Glob's *The Bog People* as a Christmas present for himself. In his essay on 'Resolution and Independence', he claimed that the book's photographs of Iron Age bodies sacrificed in fertility rituals and preserved in bogs 'had an effect on me comparable to the effect of the leech gatherer on Wordsworth' (Glob 1969, 28). Glob's book began with a chapter about the Tollund Man, the body discovered by two Danish men digging peat in 1950. Glob contended that the Tollund Man 'had been deposited in the bog as a sacrifice to the powers that ruled men's destinies' (Glob 1969, 20). A rope around his neck indicated that he'd been hanged. Glob speculated that his death had come in mid-winter or early spring during 'celebrations whose purpose was to hasten the coming of spring' with an offering 'to the deities who controlled the earth's increase' (Glob 1969, 57). The man's body was a gift to an Earth goddess, given with the expectation that she would reciprocate with bountiful crops and vegetation.

Glob's description of the Tollund Man's corpse is reminiscent of Freud's descriptions of uncanny phenomena related to 'death and dead bodies, to the return of the dead, and to spirits and ghosts ... which ought to have been kept concealed but which ... nevertheless come to light' (Freud 1919, 225). In Glob's account, the peat-diggers bring to light one of the living dead:

> Momentarily, the sun burst in, bright and yet subdued, through a gate in blue thunder-clouds in the west, bringing everything mysteriously to life. The evening stillness was only broken, now and again, by the grating love-call of the snipe. The dead man, too, deep down in the umber-brown peat, seemed to have come alive. He lay on his damp bed as though asleep, resting on his side, the head inclined a little forward, arms and legs bent. His face wore a gentle expression—the eyes lightly closed, the lips softly pursed, as if in silent prayer. It was as though the dead man's soul had for a moment returned from another world, through the gate in the eastern sky.
>
> (Glob 1969, 18)

Heaney also uses 'gate' imagery when he recalls perusing photos of the Tollund Man: 'Opening Glob's book was like opening a gate, crossing a line into a new field where the air was headier, the ground more mysteriously ancestral, the sense of scope altogether more ample' (Heaney 2008, 28). Heaney remembered being 'entranced' by the dead man who'd been 'betrothed to the goddess of the earth ... in a fertility rite' (Heaney 2008, 28–29). As he wrote in 'Mossbawn', he'd once felt 'betrothed' to an Earth goddess in a more familiar bog.

Seamus Heaney's Uncanny Encounters   45

After he got over the initial shock of seeing the unfamiliar, mummified Tollund Man, Heaney realized how familiar he was:

> He felt as close to me as a contemporary, as familiar as my Great Uncle Hughie [his father's Uncle Hugh Scullion], who had a similar bristle on his long upper lip and a similar weathered look that suggested both stoicism and a capacity for survival. At the same time, the head had the stillness and focus of a votive object. It did not appear like human remains. It invited contemplation, seemed capable of putting one in touch with the timeless.
>
> (Heaney 2008, 29)

Heaney composed his poem 'The Tollund Man' over Easter weekend in 1970, and, as he told the journalist Patrick Garland, he thought of the Tollund Man as 'a kind of Christ figure: sacrificed so that life will be brought back', as well as a 'symbol ... of sacrifice to the goddess of territory'. For Heaney, the Tollund Man was typologically related to the many Irish Catholic martyrs who'd died on behalf of Mother Ireland in the fight for independence from British rule. 'In many ways the political upheavals of Ireland, especially in the 20th century', he said, 'have been a renewal of that kind of religion' (Garland 1973, 629). At first as unfamiliar and off-putting as Wordsworth's leech-gatherer, the Tollund Man in the end had the inspirational qualities of Christ and his sacrificial followers.

When political upheavals worsened in Ulster shortly after Heaney wrote 'The Tollund Man', he left home to teach in Berkeley, California, and in 1972, he moved with his family to Glanmore Cottage in the Republic of Ireland. The anxieties that accompanied his move south were assuaged by his discovery that his new home, which he rented from the Canadian scholar Ann Saddlemyer, was uncannily similar to Mossbawn. In correspondence with friends, he hailed the cottage as his new farmhouse, his new bawn (he called it a 'garrison against ... [the] world' in a letter to the poet Medbh McGuckian) (SHP-EU September 12, 1988), his new womb of writing and source of gifts. Heaney's desire to sequester himself in Glanmore Cottage in County Wicklow arose in part from his nostalgia for the familiar security—the *Heimlich*—he'd enjoyed at Mossbawn as a boy. The deaths of his mother in 1984 and his father in 1986 had reminded him of previous unhomings. Sometimes in interviews, he characterized losing his parents in terms of losing parts of his physical home. His father's death, he said in *Stepping Stones*, was like a 'final 'unroofing' (O'Driscoll 2008, 322). In Glanmore, he hoped to reroof his original home.

At the beginning of 1988, while dining with Heaney at the University of Toronto where she taught, Saddlemyer gave him the opportunity to rehome himself when she offered to sell him the cottage:

> "I nearly fainted at the table," Heaney said afterwards. "She was prepared to give me access for a second time to the *locus amoenus* ['lovely

46 Henry Hart

place']. Nothing that had happened since we left Wicklow [in 1975 to live in Dublin] was more important in my writing life".

(O'Driscoll 2008, 431)

It was as if Saddlemyer had told him he could return to his 'personal helicon'—his source of muses and poetic gifts—at Mossbawn.

As it turned out, some of the emotions that Freud associated with uncanny experiences bedeviled Heaney at Glanmore Cottage. Hunkering down in his new womb-like space aroused Oedipal anxiety and guilt. In his sonnet sequence 'Glanmore Revisited', he says he was determined to preserve the 'low and closed ..., claustrophobic, nest-up-in-the-roof/Effect' he'd cherished at Mossbawn. When his wife orders builders to cut a hole in the roof for a skylight, he reacts with anger and dread. He suggests she is threatening to 'unroof' him once again, expose his fetal state to the outside world, and make him vulnerable. He is so fixated on preserving a 'closed', Edenic womb inside the cottage that he considers himself a trespasser 'breaking and entering' (Heaney 1988, 324–325) his own home. In the end, Heaney's wife prevails; builders cut open the roof and install a skylight. As in Heaney's other experiences of *Unheimlich*, the change proves to be transfiguring. He soon thinks of the skylight as a portal that gives him access to supernatural marvels and in-spiriting gifts.

Heaney explains in *Stepping Stones* that Glanmore Cottage was his 'completely silent place of writing' that stood 'for what Wallace Stevens said poetry stands for, the imagination pressing back against the pressures of reality' (O'Driscoll 2008, 325). Stevens in 'The Noble Rider and the Sound of Words' had defined the imagination as 'a violence from within that protects us from a violence without' (Stevens 1951, 36). Heaney's 50-page sequence 'Squarings' plays variations on this idea. Heaney began writing these 'square' poems in September 1988 while annotating a selection of Yeats's poems for Faber. Earlier that year, in a lecture titled 'W.B. Yeats and Thoor Ballylee' given at Emory University, he had reflected on Yeats's square-shaped stone tower as a fortified and fortifying place of writing. The structure, according to Heaney, was 'a sacramental site, an outward sign of an inner grace' (Heaney 1989, 24), and a symbol of imagination's rock-hard defense against the 'pressures of reality'. At the beginning of 'Squarings', Heaney expresses his eagerness to turn his own place of writing into a well-fortified, sacramental site. Worried that the 'unroofed scope' of a skylight would expose him to the 'pressures of reality', he declares: 'Roof it again. Batten down. Dig in./Drink out of tin. Know the scullery cold/A latch, a door-bar, forged tongs and a grate' (Heaney 1988, 332–333). His emphatic directives point in one direction—back to the *Heimlich* of Mossbawn.

Heaney received the initial section of 'Squarings' as a surprising gift. 'It felt given, strange and unexpected', he said. 'I didn't quite know where it came from, but I knew immediately it was there to stay' (O'Driscoll 2008SS, 320–321). Rain hitting glass in the domed roof of the

Seamus Heaney's Uncanny Encounters   47

National Library, where he read Yeats's poems, had an uncanny effect. It transported him back to familiar places: Glanmore Cottage with its glass skylight and Mossbawn with its thatch roof. The title of the first section, 'Lightenings', refers to both a spirit rising toward the light of heaven before death (as if through a skylight) and to a fetus beginning its journey toward the everyday light of the world at birth. Shakespeare uses the word to describe Paris shortly before Romeo kills him in the tomb where Juliet lies dead. Romeo says: 'How oft when men are on the point of death/Have they been merry! which their keepers call/A lightning before death. Oh, how may I/Call this lightning?' (Act 5, Scene 3, 97–100). For Heaney, the word recalls the sensation of being unroofed and unhomed by his parents' deaths, but also the contrary sensation of being reborn as a writer in his new womb-like home.

After Heaney bought Glanmore Cottage, his letters often evinced resentment toward those who invited him to leave his comfortable 'garrison' to give readings or lectures around the world. In his mind, they were threatening to unhome or unroof him yet again. In a letter written to his friend Michael Longley on October 13, 1988, he repeated what had become his morose refrain about traveling the globe to perform: 'Do I want to keep stepping on planes? Living among the acquisitive brilliant young of [George] Bush-ville. The querulous self-salving rhetorics of the million books of useless poetry. The requests for blurbs'. He told Longley:

> The urge towards an elemental purifying move [to a solitary place of writing] is mighty. But the anxiety about dropping the safety-net of a salary … gives me pause. Eight months off work for four months on [as Harvard's Boylston Professor] is a terrific arrangement, but it may have to go, for the sake of new life.
>
> (SHP-EU, October 13, 1988)

(His salary for four months of teaching at Harvard was equivalent to about $100,000 today.) All he wanted to do, it seemed, was write in the silence and solitude of his Glanmore *bawn*.

In *Unheimlich* situations, Heaney routinely searched for familiar people and places to alleviate his sense of estrangement and frustration. One of his more anxiety-producing trips occurred in 1982 when he flew in a small prop-plane from the Scottish mainland over the North Sea to the Orkney Islands. A poet who lived there, George Mackay Brown, had invited him to read at the St. Magnus Festival and to stay with the poet Elizabeth Gore-Langton. Heaney said:

> I'll never forget the silence there on the airstrip, the first time I landed. I was on a small propeller plane: when it taxied to a halt and the engines were shut off, we had to sit and wait for the ground crew; and all the while you could feel the plane shaking slightly in the wind. Then the

48   *Henry Hart*

door was opened, the steps were let down with a clunk and, as I walked
across the grass to a little arrivals hut, I heard the cry of a curlew.
(O'Driscoll 2008, 292)

The quiet, the isolation, and the curlew engendered an epiphany that transported him back to Mossbawn, Glanmore Cottage, and the religious retreats
at St. Columb's College. Orkney was 'a place of silence and solitude where
a person would find it hard to avoid self-awareness and self-examination'
(O'Driscoll 2008, 292), he observed in *Stepping Stones*. As he wrote at the end
of 'The Tollund Man', he felt both 'lost/... and at home' (Heaney 1988, 63).

Heaney's uncanny experience on Orkney turned out to be inspirational
for several reasons. During the summer in 1985, the secretary of a Dublin
branch of Amnesty International, Mary Lawlor, asked him to write a poem
for 'Prisoner of Conscience Week', but he was almost as unnerved by the
prospect of writing the poem as he'd been when he landed in the light-weight
plane at the Orkney airport. Lawlor had sent him a dossier full of accounts
of political regimes that had harassed, censored, incarcerated, and tortured
its citizens. Although he approved of Amnesty International's work, he had
no idea how to write a poem about the unfamiliar people in unfamiliar places
being abused by unfamiliar tyrants. Then he remembered his trip to Orkney,
and he also remembered asking his Harvard students to write an allegorical
poem about a country that represented a mental or emotional state. Thinking of Orkney as another silent, isolated place conducive to meditation and
writing, he quickly composed the 'Republic of Conscience'. By grounding
the unfamiliar in the familiar, he felt at home again. *Heimlich* had to replace
Unheimlich, it seemed, before he could feel secure and confident enough to
fulfill the assignment. He mailed the finished poem to Amnesty International
as a gift on August 18, 1985.

Heaney got a chance to produce a different sort of gift when the Harvard
administration asked him to write a poem for the university's 350th anniversary in 1986. Once again, he felt stymied by the request to write a poem for
an unfamiliar occasion (multi-day celebrations drawing thousands of people,
including the keynote speaker Prince Charles, were planned.) Heaney felt as
lost and uninspired as he had with the Amnesty International assignment
until he discovered that John Harvard's father had worked in the cattle trade,
just like Heaney's father, and there were Mossbawn-like cattle barns near
Harvard's first building. He also learned that when John Harvard immigrated
from England to America in 1637, Cambridge resembled the farming region around Mossbawn. Harvard students had done the same sort of things
Heaney had done as a youth: they carried water in buckets from wells, used
outhouses and hand pumps, rode horses, and lit candles and lanterns to read
at night. '"There I was", Heaney said in an interview, "travelling back to
where I started"' (O'Driscoll 2008, 283). The personal connection with the
college's origins, which gave him a sense of *Heimlich*, was the catalyst for his
'Villanelle for an Anniversary'.

As his mind vacillated between the uncanny's *Heimlich* and *Unheimlich* polarities, Heaney tried to construct a new identity around the idea of being at home even in unhomelike situations. In 1980, he told Georgina Mills in an interview:

> My way of knowing that I'm being myself is to be displaced from home, and I think I've almost created conditions of being at home and not at home, at once .... It's the way I've come to an awareness of who I am, by being displaced from where I was.
>
> (Mills 1980, 14–18)

His first essay in *Preoccupations* underscores his obsession with returning to the security of a home he'd left or lost. The uncanny 'poetic recognition scenes' he discusses in his prose usually involve figures who resemble maternal muses and Christ-like redeemers who appear in unfamiliar guises during literary rites of passage. The figures, he says:

> provide an experience of estrangement, and then resituate ... [the poet] in the usual life, bemused, as it were, as if for a moment the gift for uttering truth had been possessed, as if from a laurel tree luxuriantly in bloom the Muses broke a branch and gave it for a staff and breathed a sacred voice into the mouth.
>
> (Heaney 1980, 32–33)

For Heaney, disorienting unhomings turned into restorative homings when he returned in memory to Mossbawn. There his Catholic parents played the roles of Christ-like, or at least Christian, muses. Communing with them and the familiar region around the family farm allowed him to dispel his uncanny fears, anxieties, and confusions and 'get back in touch with his ... proper poetic gifts' (Heaney 2008, 25).

Works Cited

SHP-EU – Abbreviation for: Seamus Heaney Papers, Emory University. These papers are stored in the Stuart A. Rose Manuscript, Archives, and Rare Book Library at Emory University.

Devlin, Christopher (ed.) (1959) *The Sermons and Devotional Writings of Gerard Manley Hopkins*, Oxford: Oxford University Press.

Eliot, T.S. (1943) *Four Quartets*, New York: Harcourt, Brace & World.

Fitzpatrick, Maurice (2010) *The Boys of St Columb's*, Dublin: The Liffey Press.

Freud, Sigmund (1919) 'The 'Uncanny', in *An Infantile Neurosis and Other Works*, Vol. Volume XVII (1917–1919), *The Standard Edition of the Complete Psychological Works of Sigmund Freud*, edited by James Strachey, 1955, London: Hogarth Press, 218–252.

Frost, Robert (1972) *The Poetry of Robert Frost*, edited by Edward Lathem, London: Jonathan Cape.

Garland, Patrick (1973) 'Poets on Poetry', *The Listener*, November 8.

Glob, P. V. (1969) *The Bog People*, translated by Rupert Bruce-Mitford, London: Faber & Faber.

Haffenden, John (1981) *Viewpoints: Poets in Conversation*, London: Faber & Faber.

Heaney, Seamus (1979) 'Letter to Ted Hughes', SHP-EU, May 24, 1979.

Heaney, Seamus (1988) 'Letter to Michael Longley', SHP-EU, October 13, 1988.

Heaney, Seamus (1988b) *Opened Ground*, New York: Farrar, Straus and Giroux.

Heaney, Seamus (1989) *The Place of Writing*, Atlanta: Scholars Press.

Heaney, Seamus (1980) *Preoccupations*, London: Faber & Faber.

Heaney, Seamus (1991) *Seeing Things*, London: Faber & Faber.

Heaney, Seamus (2001) *Electric Light*, New York: Farrar, Straus and Giroux.

Heaney, Seamus (2008) '"Apt Admonishment": Wordsworth as an Example', *The Hudson Review*, vol. 61, no. 1, 19–33.

Hyde, Lewis (2007) *The Gift: Creativity and the Artist in the Modern World*, London: Vintage Books.

Madden, F. J. M. and Thomas Bradley (eds) (2004). *Seeking the Kingdom: St Columb's College, 1879–2004*, Derry: St. Columb's College.

Mills, Georgina (1980) *Strawberry Fare*, February 5, 14–18.

McCrum, Robert (2009) 'Seamus Heaney: A Life of Rhyme', July 18, 2009, https://www.theguardian.com/books/2009/jul/19/seamus-heaney-interview.

O'Brien, Eugene (2014) "Crediting the Poet: What Seamus Heaney Means to Me," *Irish Studies South*, no. 1, Article 14. https://digitalcommons.georgiasouthern.edu/iss/vol1/iss1/14/.

O'Driscoll, Dennis (2008) *Stepping Stones: Interviews with Seamus Heaney (SS)*, New York: Farrar, Straus and Giroux.

Stevens, Wallace (1951) *The Necessary Angel*, London: Vintage Books.

Wordsworth, William (1965) *Selected Poems and Prefaces*, edited by Jack Stillinger, Boston, MA: Houghton Mifflin Company.

3 Double Agent

The Redress of Seamus Heaney's Prose Poems

William Fogarty

In between Seamus Heaney's first three books of poetry and *North* is a slim chapbook titled *Stations*. Those first three books published between 1966 and 1972 present traditional and free-verse poems of farm and family life often in a combination of onomatopoeic language and local speech as well as etymological ruminations on local Northern Irish place names and their conjuring of history and culture.[1] A few refer, mostly indirectly, to the entrenched divisions and inequalities that laid the ground for the Northern Irish Troubles. The Troubles began in 1968, two years after the publication of Heaney's first book, when student-led civil-rights demonstrations protesting unequal housing and employment for, mostly, working-class Catholics in Northern Ireland's Protestant-led hierarchical political structure escalated into rioting and clashes between Catholic civilians and the mostly Protestant police forces in Belfast and Derry. Those stand-offs initiated a thirty-year paramilitary conflict and sharpened the lines of sectarianism. *North*, published in 1975, broadened Heaney's verse terrains to include more fully the dire political realities of his homeland, transforming prehistoric cadavers unearthed in bogland into corollaries of, in Heaney's terms, the 'atrocity' of 'Irish political and religious struggles' in the famous 'bog poems' and confronting more directly in the book's other poems the corrosive effects of sectarianism and political violence on everyday life and language in Northern Ireland (Heaney 1980, 57–58). This chapter examines *Stations* as a pivotal text between and alongside those surrounding texts.[2]

North is Heaney's first sustained response in verse to the Northern Irish Troubles. However, *North* is not Heaney's first extended response to the Troubles in poetry. For *Stations*, composed largely at the same time as *North*, published in the same year, and presented directly before the *North* poems in all of Heaney's selected volumes, returns to Heaney's Northern Irish childhood and expresses in several poems the strain on that childhood caused by the social conditions that eventually led to the Troubles.[3] The poems are distinctive not just because most were only published, as Andy Brown tells us, 'in a limited edition chapbook' and in various issues of *The Irish Times* (Brown 2018, 177). They are distinct as well because they are set in the

DOI: 10.4324/9781003456148-4

52   *William Fogarty*

sentences and paragraphs that constitute prose rather than in the lines that define verse. Taken together, the sequence of twenty-one vignettes charts the development of the young poet coming to awareness of himself as a conduit for sensorial impressions of his rural Northern Irish locale and as a portraitist of the adults populating that locale.[4] He also is increasingly cognizant that he, his family and his neighbors are subjects in a precariously divided society.

In other words, *Stations* is a portrait in prose poems of the artist as a child living in uncommonly pronounced and mountingly volatile political circumstances.[5] Richard Rankin Russell points out that *Stations* and *North* 'are rarely considered in conjunction with each other' even though 'in a draft of *North*, Heaney had included a section entitled 'Seed-Time', consisting of twelve prose poems—some that would be published as part of *Stations* and others that would remain uncollected—which comes after a draft of 'Singing School', the last section of the published version of *North*' (Russell 2016, 68).[6] Russell suggests that this early inclusion of prose poems in Heaney's first manuscript of mostly political verse reveals that prose occupied an estimable place in his thinking about lyric's potentialities: 'This earlier draft of *North* ... suggests how fully he himself saw the prose poems as integrated with his lyrical poetry' (Russell 2014, 193). The prose poems of *Stations*—as well as the one prose poem in the published version of *North*, 'The Unacknowledged Legislator's Dream'—are integral lyric poems that prefigure via their prose form Heaney's earliest aesthetic impulses and illuminate some of the ways Heaney reckoned artistically with his quandary about the ethics of writing poetry in response to immediate social catastrophe.

Stations stands apart from the books of poems that surround it (and stands out in Heaney's entire corpus) because its poems are in prose, a singularizing feature that constructs a kind of bridge between the lineated poems of local life and language that comprise the first three books and the similarly formalized but highly metaphorical, mythical and overtly political poems that make up *North*. The *Stations* prose poems reach back to what Heaney terms the 'pre-reflective experience' in that book's preface and 'the pre-reflective life' in his interviews with Dennis O'Driscoll almost thirty years after *Stations* was published (Heaney 1975b, 3; Heaney 2008, 180). The phrase refers to his early years as a child growing into the adult poet he would become—the prose form itself evoking that pre-poet stage by presenting language that appears unarranged.[7] Heaney has referred to the early verse poems he wrote before 'finding a voice', to use his words, as lacking a totalizing structure, and he relates those inchoate verse efforts to the last poem in *Stations* whose title is Heaney's youthhood penname, 'Incertus':

> I called myself *Incertus*, uncertain, a shy soul fretting and all that. I was in love with words themselves, but had no sense of a poem as a whole structure and no experience of how the successful achievement of a poem could be a stepping stone in your life.
>
> (Heaney 1980, 43–45)

Stations goes back to this uncertain period, but the prose poems are fully realized poems: they suggest something like juvenilia, attempts at poems before arriving at a 'sense' of a poem's 'whole structure', while they are unequivocally not juvenilia. For even though they don't look like poems on the surface, they produce through their prose the rhythmic and associative modulations of poetry. Further, the prose of *Stations* helps carry Heaney's poems into political territory that he felt compelled to explore artistically but was anxious about exploiting. In fact, the crucial position of *Stations* in his early catalog clarifies that Heaney's worries about writing political poetry reflected at least as much a formal dilemma as it did a moral one. Prose operates in the sequence as a kind of 'trial run', to borrow a title from one of the *Stations* poems—and to appeal to Heaney's own suggestion that his earliest 'verses were what we might call 'trial-pieces', little stiff inept designs in imitation of the master's fluent interlacing patterns, heavy-handed clues to the whole craft' (Heaney 1980, 45). That Heaney titled that last section 'Seed-Time' in the drafts of *North* described by Russell intimates that he saw prose as a way to revisit his developing poetic consciousness—the seeds of his poetry—well after they had been planted.

The prose of *Stations* serves to test Heaney's responses to the political forces he sensed as a child in the redolent, highly charged registers of poetry but without the lineated patterns that could risk instilling the texts with, in the face of real-world catastrophe, a contrived and even 'programmatic' aspect, a word Heaney used for the American political poetry, some of it cast in prose, that he encountered in the 1970–1971 academic year when he was a visiting instructor at UC-Berkeley and writing some of the *Stations* poems (Hart 1992, 106; Heaney 1979, 20).[8] The prose-poem form in *Stations* provided an aesthetic space for Heaney to amble in what exists between line breaks and prose paragraphs: the texts neither pattern their rhythms into lines nor follow the extended, usually logical flow of conventional prose.[9] At the same time, they amplify rhythms that govern line breaks in verse as they unfold in unbroken sentences and paragraphs. When read as both initiating Heaney's political poetry alongside the poems of *North*, the poems of *Stations* and their in-between formal prose-poem structures wind up making a formal argument despite themselves: they reveal that Heaney's poems would not so much need in later volumes to dispense with lineation in order to avoid sliding toward the potential oversimplifications or grandiose pronouncements of political writing. After all, Heaney didn't continue writing prose poems but did proceed to write political verse. They imply that his political poems would need, if they were to be in verse, something else that was initially broached in the prose poems of *Stations* to prevent them from falling into those pitfalls of political poetry, namely the profound ambivalence and, more forcefully, the outright guilt—the self-consciousness, in other words—that he felt about writing them in the first place.

54 William Fogarty

'Consciousness' is the concept that Heaney most often connects to the prose poem—again, a form he rarely wrote in and doesn't discuss much.[10] Despite the form's modest presence in Heaney's creative oeuvre, which is almost all traditional and free-verse, and the dearth of commentary about the form in both his essays about poetry and poetics and his many interviews, the few descriptions he does supply of the form's capacities for tapping material at the periphery of awareness assign it a fundamental place in poetry. In the preface to *Stations* in the original chapbook, Heaney points up this elevating aspect of the form: the early drafts of the *Stations* texts, he writes, 'had been attempts to touch what Wordsworth called 'spots of time', moments at the very edge of consciousness which had lain for years in the unconscious as active lodes of nodes' (Heaney 1975b, 3). That Heaney relates his efforts to write prose poems explicitly to Wordsworth's conception, articulated in the twelfth book of the Romantic poet's epic blank-verse poem *The Prelude*, indicates Heaney's high regard for the form's potential for both reaching into one's memory and mobilizing the resources and connections, the 'lodes of nodes', found there. For Wordsworth, as for Heaney, certain moments in life attain, as Wordsworth describes it in *The Prelude*, a 'distinct pre-eminence' because they possess a 'renovating virtue' and can be appealed to when one's spirits have fallen due to any number of obstacles, from the 'trivial' and 'ordinary' to ordeals of 'heavier or more deadly weight' (Wordsworth 1965, 345). Heaney calls his own spots of time 'stations', evoking the stations of the cross and establishing a Catholic motif to structure his own preeminent moments.[11] He also refers to the poems as 'points on a psychic *turas*, stations that I have often made unthinkingly in my head', stamping a cultural identity on the book that is definitively Catholic and Irish—'turas' is Irish for 'journey'—and characterizing the sequence's originating memories as 'unthinking', in other words, instinctive or subconscious (Heaney 1975b, 3). Such moments accrue to gloss an entire childhood: to borrow Henry Hart's summary, 'the first section covers Heaney's preschool days, the second his days at Anahorish, and the third his journey away from home to St. Columb's', the boarding school in Derry that Heaney attended (Hart 1992, 108). They cover these periods in Heaney's life in direct relation to his development during those early stages into the poet he would eventually become.

Heaney's memories of childhood endure political pressures, too, tinged as they were by the simmering sectarian atmosphere that would eventually lead to the Troubles, which were well underway by the time Heaney was writing *Stations*. The violence and repressive policies such as internment without trial that characterized the Troubles at first obstructed Heaney's work on *Stations*: 'after the introduction of internment my introspection was not confident enough to pursue its direction. The sirens in the air … jammed those other tentative if insistent signals' (Heaney 1975b, 3). And yet the insistence of such 'signals' did not relent despite their tentativeness, while moving out of Northern Ireland and into the Republic of Ireland (from the dangerous nerve-center of Belfast to rural Wicklow across the border) eventually created for Heaney enough distance and silence (and a certain covertness implied by Heaney's following reference to Ireland's eighteenth- and nineteenth-century illegal Catholic 'hedge-schools') to absorb those signal demands: 'So it was again at a remove, in the 'hedge-school' of Glanmore, in Wicklow, that the sequence was returned to, and then the sectarian dimension of that pre-reflective experience presented itself as something asking to be uttered also' (Heaney 1975b, 3).[12] The quiet of this Irish 'hedge-school' supplied the acoustics to make those utterances audible, and Heaney finally admitted them into the *Stations* poems.

Prose also allowed Heaney to continue writing *Stations*.[13] He describes the prose poems of *Stations* as representing occasions of such import that the stored memories of them had acquired their own reluctance to being transformed into verse, the prose form apparently circumnavigating those hesitations: he says about the poems in his preface, 'I wrote each of them down with the excitement of coming for the first time to a place I had always known completely' (Heaney 1975b, 3). Over thirty years after *Stations* was published, Heaney remarked that the prose form of *Stations* operated as a resource for engaging material aesthetically when that material seemed to resist versification: prose provides, he says, 'a way to pounce on material that has been in my memory for so long it has almost become aware of me and has begun to be wary of being chosen for verse' (Heaney 2008, 180). Transforming those long memories into words contained a particularly pronounced self-consciousness that would extend beyond, say, the prose of a memoir, but that could become overwhelming or inflated if the words were also arranged in lines: 'Each [of the *Stations* texts] is a making over into words that are more self-conscious than the usual prose record and yet not justified as verse' (Heaney 2008, 180). 'Justified' here goes two ways at once, denoting both the practice of legitimizing certain actions or forms of behavior and the alignment of a text's margins for printing. The prose poem could at once permit and check the self-consciousness that often guides the writing of a poem: it could express a self-consciousness more common for poetry than other forms of writing such as essays or short stories while being literally justified on the page—aligned at the margins—as prose, not verse, qualifying that self-consciousness by presenting it in prose rather than augmenting it with wrought arrangement in lines.

Although its sources lie in memory, *Stations* is not just a recollection of childhood and adolescence arranged into poetic prose. It is, as I assert earlier, a poet's memories of himself as a child who will become that poet, a *Künstlerroman* in miniature advancing through definitive 'stations', those Wordsworthian 'spots of time', that presuppose Heaney's development as a poet. After all, Heaney has described the book as 'pre-reflective', reflecting, we might say, on what has not happened yet but is going to happen. Prose poetry could suggest this 'pre-reflective' stage when he was not yet a poet but the child who would become or is in the process of becoming a poet because it nods toward that period by conveying in prose the impressions

56 *William Fogarty*

that a poet would typically cast in lines. In a lineated poem, rhythm creates the poem's shape because it prescribes where the line breaks will land. Those breaks in a traditionally metered poem are based on received abstract patterns. Free-verse's breaks are based on its own patterns that might come very close to a traditional metrical grid (like many of Heaney's poems) or not to one at all (say, Walt Whitman's long catalogues). A prose poem is, arguably, furthest from the traditional metrical grid: there are no lines. A result is that the prose poem looks least like a template for a poem because its prose shape on the page makes it appear more like a micro essay or story. It is as if instead of presenting the juvenilia Heaney may have produced, *Stations* gives us a form that only hints at it, providing texts that have not yet found, and never actually will find, arrangement in lines. It bears repeating that the essential point here is that the poems are emphatically not juvenilia; they are prose poems by a fully realized poet. They suggest a poet's pre-development while providing poems in prose that depict the poet looking back at that time.

'Nesting-ground', the fourth poem in the *Stations* sequence and the first *Stations* poem in Heaney's selected volumes, demonstrates how the prose form can transform a 'spot of time' into words that retain and manage a guiding self-consciousness. Meanwhile, the lyrical, unlineated sentence and paragraph structure of 'Nesting-ground' creates a 'pre-poetic' rendering of the raw material the poem encounters. 'Nesting-ground' is set in the third person and in three paragraphs, the overarching narrative voice relaying a story from Heaney's youth that connects it to the other stories told by the other early poems in the series that also revisit discomfiting interactions with the natural environment of Heaney's childhood farm. The poem is not, however, a straightforward tale. Rather, it is a lyrical rendering of two memories proliferating linguistically inside another memory. As Paul Hetherington and Cassandra Atherton explain, prose poems 'are never entirely driven by narrative and are always trying to point to something about their language or their subject that sits outside of any narrative gestures they make (and frequently outside of the work itself)' (Hetherington and Atherton 2020, 14). 'Nesting-ground' is delivered by a narrator remembering himself in the third person as a child observing a group of 'sandmartins' nests', but it is more about language than nature or event (Heaney 1975b, 7).[14] The narrator describes the ominous look of the nests as 'loopholes of darkness in the riverbank' in the first sentence and then pivots both to the conditional case and, omnisciently, to the youth's thinking—the 'He' of the poem—as the narrator's and character's languages merge in the manner of free indirect discourse, the narrative technique that collapses aesthetic distance between writers and their fictional materials practiced by modernist novelists such as James Joyce and Virginia Woolf. As the child in Heaney's poem looks at the holes, the poem says, 'He could imagine' putting his arm all the way in one of them. However, this memory articulated by the poem's narrator about a boy standing before the nests conjures the boy's memory and stops him from putting his arm into one of them: he can only *imagine* inserting his arm into the dark holes but doesn't actually do so because he recalls once touching 'a dead robin's claw' and 'tiny beak', an experience that felt 'cold' with a 'surprising density'. He fears that a similar surprise could await him in the dark nests. The unsettling remembrance causes him to stare at the holes rather than to explore them with his hands, and also to devise a language to express that halt.

This sort of reaching into the unknown has, for Heaney, a direct corollary in the act of composing poetry. He has referred to poetry writing as a reaching in or, to use his own term for his own poetics, a 'digging' into 'the hiding places' and 'a dig for finds,' that activity enshrined as one of Heaney's chief poetic methods in the first poem of his first book, 'Digging' (Heaney 1966, 1; 1980, 41). The phrase 'hiding places' he borrows (again) from Wordsworth's *Prelude* (Heaney 1980, 41; Wordsworth 1965, 346). He compares writing poems to 'putting your hand into the bush or robbing the nest, one of the various natural analogies for uncovering and touching the hidden thing' (Heaney 1980, 41–42). The 'Nesting-ground', then, is not just a bird's nest but a metaphor for Heaney's poetic development: a rumination on his own poetic 'nesting-ground'. The poem is a portrait of an adult poet remembering himself in the third person as the child who would become that poet as he contemplates reaching into nests. He is triggered by other, similar memories that stop him from surveying the nests physically, though not from exploring that interruption as an adult poetically. Since the poet's tools are, largely, the visual and sonic elements of language, and since the lyric poem usually circulates around a self, the poet can make a poem about this pre-reflective experience of fearful hesitation that enacts the rhythms of that experience and that rehearses the self-conscious tentativeness he felt as a child before the curiosities of the natural world without having to 'reach in' with his arm. The prose both indicates a time before the writing of verse while also producing those images, sound effects, rhythms and self-consciousnesses that make lyric poems. In other words, 'Nesting-ground' conveys the tension between the urge to unearth what lies within the nests and the reluctance that curtails that urge and changes it.

Studies of the prose-poem form typically view it as imbedded with tension and even conflict and subversion: it's been called 'the literary genre with an oxymoron for a name' (Riffaterre 1983, 117), 'a genre that does not want to be itself' (Monroe 1987, 15), 'absolute counter-discourse' (Terdiman 2018, 259). For Robert Hass, the form is by nature both archetypal and multidirectional:

> The thing developed from the invention of writing. And print gave it its principal formal character, two justified margins. The word comes from the Latin *prosus*, which means 'straightforward', and is also derived from *provertere*, which means 'to turn forward'. Pro + versus, so it is distantly related to the etymological root of 'verse.; Prose turns forward. Verse turns.

(Hass 2017, 385)

58   William Fogarty

Hass finds in the form an inevitable push and pull between reality and imagination, calling to mind Wallace Stevens's conception of poetry as 'the imagination pressing back against the pressure of reality' (Stevens 1997, 665): Hass remarks, 'there is a tension in the form between prose as the medium of realist representation and poetry as the medium of the transformation of the world through imagination' (Hass 2017, 388). The form is predisposed to being a 'medium' for facilitating an exchange between artistic and realistic realms which protracts to the discord between imagination and reality. 'Nesting-ground' imparts such discord: it turns *back*, to modify Hass's terms, as the speaker recalls youthful imaginings of what lies within hidden places and 'turns forward' as it articulates the reality of being wary of delving into those imaginings.

And yet if prose poetry differentiates imagination and reality, it also joins them. Heaney himself sees poetry as a bridge between actuality and the imagination:

> within our individual selves we can reconcile two orders of knowledge which we might call the practical and the poetic; ... each form of knowledge redresses the other and ... the frontier between them is there for the crossing.
>
> (Heaney 1995, 203)

Heaney argues that poetry counters reality by weighing it against a counter-reality 'which may be only imagined but which nevertheless has weight because it is imagined within the gravitational pull of the actual and can therefore hold its own and balance out against the historical situation' (Heaney 1995, 3–4). Prose poems can employ the rhythms of prose not only to press back against reality but also to admit reality without precluding the imaginative or imagistic capabilities of poetry. A prose poem, then, not only 'avails itself of the elements of prose ... while foregrounding the devices of poetry', as Edward Hirsch says, but also, to expand this, employs prose to shuffle those devices repeatedly back and forth from the foreground to the background (Hirsch 2014, 239). Prose is thought generally to supply exposition while poetry makes music; prose poetry can manage both: it can keep shifting from explaining to intoning, and back again, becoming a site of movement, or, to appeal again to Hass's terms, 'turning forward' and, in my addition to Hass, turning backward. To come at the form another way, Jeremy Noel-Tod claims that prose poems have a 'tendency to dwell on image over narrative' (Noel-Tod 2018, xxvi). We can add to this that the prose poem generates narrative *from* images rather than solely from exposition. The images of 'Nesting-ground' don't so much emerge from the narrative but conduct it as the poem proceeds from sandmartins' nests, to a robin's claws, to a rat's nest, to chaff and cornstalks. One suggests the other then the next, and so on, producing through associations its lyrical rhythms in prose. Hetherington and Atherton note that what often propels poets to write poems in prose is a preoccupation with the potential for prose's suggestiveness: 'Prose poets are particularly interested in how prose sentences and paragraphs may be poetically suggestive even when they may not have the kind of heightened tonality one would usually associate with the "poetic"' (Hetherington and Atherton 2020, 11). A prose poem, then, is not just a collaboration between an overarching prose structure and the elements that conventionally make a poem other than line breaks; rather, the poetry of a prose poem *is* its prose rhythms. It is produced by its arrangements of prose.

'Nesting-ground' employs its prose sentences and paragraphs to create the kind of suggestiveness and heightened tonality that Hetherington and Atherton refer to. The poem's second paragraph is a single sentence that repeats the long sentence structure of the previous one, creating verbal patterns that both link memories and accumulate words that reflect the repellent 'density' of the figures they describe. Here, the narrator turns from imagining the feel of what is inside the nests to gazing at them in order not to risk unsettling surprises. The poem also turns in this paragraph toward imagining the child hearing rather than touching: 'He heard cheeping far in but because the men had once shown him a rat's nest in the butt of a stack where chaff and powdered cornstalks adhered to the moist pink necks and backs he only listened'. Again, his apprehension of the unknown keeps him at once physically out of the nests and imaginatively intrigued by them. The prose gives a matter-of-fact impression of essayistic reportage: 'the sandmartins' nests were loopholes', 'He could imagine his arm going in to the armpit', 'but because he once felt the cold prick of a dead robin's claw and the surprising density of its tiny beak he only gazed'. Meanwhile, the arrangement of the prose also makes its own music. Repeated phrases that begin, link and end clauses create a kind of refrain: 'He could imagine' in the first paragraph is picked up by 'he heard cheeping' in the second and 'he stood sentry' in the third; 'but because he once felt' and 'but because the men had once shown him' link sonically and logically the memories in their respective paragraphs, explaining in replicated syntax the causal relationship between the memories and the boy's reluctance to examine the nests with only safely removed ears and eyes. What we have here is a portrait in an especially rhythmic prose of the young Heaney before he is a poet but who is already fielding the impressions and the cautions that will make him a poet. The poem is a lyrical prose rendering written by the mature poet of the self-consciousness that wracked him when he was a child as he stood before the natural elements of the farm that constitutes the central poetic subjects of his first books. And yet *Stations* strikes different notes than those earlier books do: 'Nesting-ground' isn't a lyrical enactment of the nests, nor does it attempt to sound 'the silence under the ground' that the poem figures the young Heaney thinking about at the end. Rather, the prose poem is an expression of the adult Heaney remembering his youthful trepidations as he contemplated his raw material—and it sounds like Heaney through and through; it has, to use Heaney's own words to describe a poet's individuated voice, 'the feel of [him] about them' in every

60   William Fogarty

way (Heaney 1980, 43). The prose form centers the images of the nests, the robin's claw and beak, the rat's nest, the chaff and cornstalks, the rats' 'moist pink necks and backs', while permitting the self's reluctances and worries, his self-consciousness, without letting those aspects of the self's ambivalence take over the poem.

Poetic tentativeness about form conveyed in 'Nesting-ground'—where the adult poet revisits in prose his youthful, pre-poetic uncertainties before the real-word natural figures that will comprise much of his early poetry in verse—is a major theme for Heaney. It emerges most forcefully in the political poems in *North*. For example, 'Viking Dublin: Trial Pieces' wonders if its own poetic lines are comparable to a prehistoric relic's 'interlacings elaborate/as the netted routes/of ancestry and trade' or if they're merely 'dithering, blathering' like Hamlet, 'smeller of rot//in the state' (Heaney 1975a, 13–16). 'Punishment' concludes with the confession, 'I am the artful voyeur', just after the poem has related a prehistoric bog cadaver to young Catholic women in 1970s Northern Ireland who are tarred and feathered when accused of indiscretions with British soldiers.[15] The voyeur is artful, but also 'dumb': the volatile situation requires him to strategize about how and when to speak, which includes staying silent (Heaney 1975a, 31). In 'Exposure', Heaney fears his move to Wicklow from Belfast at the height of the Troubles to write poetry evinces his evasions: 'How did I end up like this?', he asks, 'weighing and weighing/My responsible *tristia*', escaping 'from the massacre/Taking protective colouring/From bole and bark ...//... blowing up these sparks/ For their meager heat' (Heaney 1975a, 68). Such compunction shows up in subsequent books as well. He stages a discourse between books when the subject elegized in 'The Strand at Lough Beg' in *Field Work* (1979), Heaney's cousin who was executed by paramilitaries, returns to reproach Heaney in the eighth section of the title poem of *Station Island* for confusing 'evasion and artistic tact' (Heaney 1984, 83). The latter poem criticizes the earlier poem's ceremonial, mannered Dantesque diction that 'whitewashed' the brutality of political violence. What these examples disclose is that Heaney's worries are not just moral—they don't just involve questions of his evasions in the real world—they are formal; they are about aspects such as diction and style as they ask how political, real-world atrocity can be managed in poetry in ways that won't aestheticize and trivialize them.

Indeed, Heaney has described these dilemmas as struggles to identify aesthetic strategies for preserving 'creative freedom' as a poet when he found himself under 'social obligation' to address the Troubles (Heaney 1995, 194). Although he felt 'socially called upon ... to render images of' the Troubles and even 'to show solidarity with one or other side in the quarrel', he was adamant in maintaining a commitment above all to his art rather than to 'better community relations' (Heaney 1995, 193–194). In his verse poems, one strategy Heaney devised to handle these pressures was to make verse that dramatized the very guilt he felt about his own sometimes tentative role in that predicament and about aestheticizing political violence. He writes lines

Double Agent 61

of verse—some of his most famous, and some quoted above, that are, to use his own words in an unpublished letter to a potential translator, 'haunted by the problem ... of art in the context of deprivation/violence/suffering ... , [and] animated by a sense of guilt' (Heaney 1981). Prose poetry in *Stations* also provided Heaney with a strategy for finding ways to write aesthetically in response to the Troubles, a strategy not so much reliant on guilt as an animating force because the prose poems take recourse against overt aestheticization by modulating elements of prose instead of verse lines.[16] According to Heaney, harmonious aspects of verse such as 'the felicity of a cadence, the chain reaction of a rhyme, the pleasuring of an etymology' could counter real-world crisis in a kind of imaginative 'counter-reality' suggesting 'possibilities of political harmony' (Heaney 1995, 203). But they could also risk aestheticizing such crisis. Because poetry has this redressing ability, Heaney claims, it is 'being appealed to constantly' for political purposes (Heaney 1995, 5). He is thus adamant that poetry must not be confused with activism:

> Poetry cannot afford to lose its fundamentally self-delighting inventiveness, its joy in being a process of language as well as a representation of things in the world ... . And while this may seem something of a truism it is nevertheless worth repeating in a late-twentieth-century context of politically approved themes, post-colonial backlash and "silence-breaking" writing of all kinds.
>
> (Heaney 1995, 5)

The prose poems of *Stations* produce less mellifluous poetic elements to re-envision reality, thereby mitigating such risk. Rather than amplifying cadence and rhyme as loudly as verse does, they switch between registers of speech, interweave simple and complex sentences, inflect active-voice statements with passive-voice reflections, and shift from first to second to third person. If prose explains and poetry makes music then prose poetry does both while also relating in a productively strained way to its own form: there is, in other words, a tension between explaining and harmonizing just as there is a tension between the practical matters of the real world and the imaginative realm of poetry.

The prose-poem form of 'Nesting-ground' portrays Heaney as a child in poetic pre-development and conveys his youthful tentativeness on the farm as he confronts the real-world figures that he would reimagine in verse in his early books. It registers as well Heaney's uncertainties about such subject matter as do the other naturalistic recollections that come early in the sequence. Later poems in *Stations* sound broader political undertones from beyond the farm that permeate that domestic environment and operate similarly to 'Nesting-ground' in terms of their formal hesitations. For example, in 'Patrick and Oisín', the young speaker weighs the 'polysyllabic', 'hard' lexicon of the catechism he learns at school (the 'Patrick' or Catholic language) against the 'tenebrous', 'back-biting' adult banter about neighbors

62 *William Fogarty*

at the kitchen table (the 'Oisín' or Irish nationalist talk) (Heaney 1975b, 10). The poem shifts back and forth between the two modes, resulting not in lingual clarities but in stalled, evasive 'tongues' ('atrophied' and 'camou-flaged', the poem calls them). In 'Sweet William', the 'words' that name the flower have 'the silky lift of a banner on the wind'. And yet that banner con-notes William of Orange, too, evoking a 'heraldry' that the young speaker 'cannot assent to' because he's an Irish Catholic, that understanding taint-ing his engagement with the silky, lifting, breezy sounds of words that lure him as a poet-to-be (Heaney 1975b, 11). Such poems contain in their prose recounting and juxtapositions the conflicting signals that appear to pull the young Heaney in various directions at once: toward the enticing language of the parish and the farm and away from the allegiances and divisions such language reveals. In 'July', the adult poet recalls not just the goading annual marches of pro-British 'Orange' drummers he heard as a child, but himself in his youth trying to describe those provocations: first their sound is like 'hail' from above, then 'No', it's 'murmured from beneath' not from above, then the speaker corrects that impression, too: 'the drumming didn't murmur rather hammered' (Heaney 1975b, 15). The poem stages the early problems of writing about political calamity: the young Heaney's 'ear was winnowed annually' by the charged July marches, but 'winnowed' in such a way as to be uncertain about how to construe those political affronts in his own po-etic language. He uses the prose-poem form to write not so much about the marches but to capture the difficulty of identifying sufficient verbal strategies in which to do so. Rather than construe political reality, the prose poems convey the very anxieties about doing so, just as 'Nesting-ground' did with sand martin's nests and other figures from the natural world.

The poem after 'July' in *Stations*, 'England's Difficulty', is one of the first instances in Heaney's body of work in which he explicitly presents this anxi-ety in his poetry in terms that express his own sense of being personally di-vided about the larger political divisions he and his family must exist in. That Heaney includes both 'July' and 'England's Difficulty' in *Opened Ground* (1998), his largest single volume of selected poems, but had not included 'July' in his earlier *Selected Poems: 1966–1987* (1990) underscores at once Heaney's regard for his categorically political poems and his wavering about them. In 'England's Difficulty,' he hints at the guilt that animates the verse poems he was writing at the same time about the Troubles that eventually comprised *North*. 'England's Difficulty' is the thirteenth in the *Stations* chap-book sequence and either the second or third in those volumes of selected poems chosen for those books as, like 'Nesting-ground', one of the repre-sentative texts of the sequence. Set in Anahorish, Heaney's hometown com-memorated in the place-name poems in *Wintering Out* (1972), as Germany drops bombs on Belfast during World War II, the prose poem announces itself in definitively political terms: its title 'England's Difficulty' refers to the Blitz but also to the six counties that constitute Northern Ireland where seg-ments of the divided society could align with England and the allies or with

Double Agent 63

Ireland's controversial position of neutrality (and, at least indirectly, with Nazi Germany). The poem begins with the young speaker referring to himself as a 'double agent', not so much because he feels politically torn between sides but because he is a double agent in relation to language: 'I moved like a double agent among the big concepts', the opening sentence declares (Heaney 1975b, 16). The 'big concepts' he moves among are 'The word 'enemy'' uttered during a radio broadcast from Germany on the household radio, a precarious sense of 'opaque security' and an ironic 'autonomous ignorance' about allegiances. While the word 'enemy' is at first just 'noise' on the radio, it returns later in the poem to refer directly to Heaney and his family as Catholics in Northern Ireland: 'I lodged with "the enemies of Ulster", the scullions outside the walls', the poem's seventh and final paragraph begins, reaching back to and aggravating the poem's opening declaration. These enemies are subsumed also as part of England's difficulty.

'England's Difficulty' circulates such energies in the house in different strands of interposing language as they both conflate and clarify, depicting in its prose arrangements movement between the various connotations of the word 'enemy' and movement in general within language to regulate its potentially loaded intentions and meanings. The poem gives us in straightforward sentences an orderly mix that includes Heaney's first-person childhood recollections, newscasts on the radio such as reportage that 'When the Germans bombed Belfast it was the bitterest Orange parts were hit the worst', a catalog of the parts of the radio that distributed the news from Germany, the local-speech commentary by the adults in the house on 'this Haw Haw', the name given to William Joyce who delivered the Nazi propaganda to the UK, and Heaney's concluding identification with the 'enemies of ulster' as well as his sense of himself as, like 'this Haw Haw', a manipulator of speech. In other words, the poem effects a transformation enveloped by the announcement that Heaney is a double agent who proceeds both to separate himself from Ulster and 'the bitterest Orange parts' of Northern Ireland as an enemy and to compare himself to the 'Haw Haw' propagandist, referred to by the adults in Heaney's home as 'an artist' who 'can fairly leave it into them' with his rhetorical skill. The poem depicts the adult poet looking back at himself as a child who is learning similar linguistic skills himself, becoming 'An adept at banter' who even back then strategically 'crossed the lines with carefully enunciated passwords, manned every speech with checkpoints and reported back to nobody'. The prose-poem form itself reflects Heaney's adult adeptness as a poet: he employs prose to untangle strands of language, to move among that language, to relay the reportage transmitted from the radio, to point up the 'mechanical and distant' quality of that reportage by cataloging the parts of the radio's hardware, to characterize the awareness of the adults in his home via their local speech, and to acknowledge finally his own sense of becoming an 'artist' who will learn how to 'fairly leave it into them' in his own constructions of language. What we have here is Heaney's first inklings that writing about politics could risk propagandizing those politics and that

64   William Fogarty

a strategy not to skirt around it but to cut right through it is to write about that very risk, to turn it into the raw material for poems about the Troubles.

The use of prose poetry to convey the risks of writing political poetry would come to even fuller fruition in a prose poem not in *Stations* but that, like *Stations*, occupies a crucial position between surrounding verse poems, 'The Unacknowledged Legislator's Dream' that begins the second section of *North*. The first section of *North* is composed mostly of the bog poems. Pared down, set mostly in quatrains with two- and three-beat lines, the long, narrow shapes of those poems suggest a downward movement as if into the ground, a manifestation of Heaney's poetics of digging. They rely mostly on visceral description that connects the physical images of the bog cadavers to contemporary images of Northern Ireland and to the poet's personal, conflicted disposition toward the violence in his homeland. In the second section, the poems take on, for the most part, more expansive shapes as the lines become less compressed, usually extending to five beats and written in and about colloquial versions and usages of Northern Irish speech. Instead of narrow stanzas moving downward, the lines stretch across the page. It is as if the poet has come out of the ground in the second section and entered the wide world. Linking these two sections is 'The Unacknowledged Legislator's Dream', a prose poem, the book's only one, in which the poet expresses his anxieties about writing political poetry, mocking, for instance, his grandiose desire to be a poet-liberator.

Prose provides Heaney here with a way to confront rather than to escape his self-consciousness about the ramifications of, say, subordinating political atrocity to line breaks. It is not an uncomplicated method. 'The Unacknowledged Legislator's Dream' occurs in the disorienting realm of a dream where the poet grapples explicitly with his anxieties about balancing his dual commitments to his people and his art. He envisions himself first as a liberator with Archimedean power: 'I sink my crowbar in a chink I know under the masonry of state and statute' (Heaney 1975a, 51). But he is also a cartoonish amalgamation of Tarzan, who 'shook the world when he jumped down out of a tree', and French insurgent: 'I swing on a creeper of secrets into the Bastille'. Prose as opposed to verse lines befits a poem in which the speaker dreams of himself as a French revolutionary poet: French symbolists like Baudelaire wrote prose poems to tap the 'prickings of the unconscious' and to rebel against the rigid conventions of eighteenth-century neoclassicism (Caws 2012, 1112). But Heaney also questions the sincerity of his rebelliousness: the desire of this 'Unacknowledged Legislator' for acknowledgement by 'his wronged people' who 'cheer from their cages' preempts his desire to write poems. His obsession with being recognized as a certain kind of poet restricts him and threatens the very possibility for poetry: 'I am blindfolded with my hands above my head until I seem to be swinging from a strappado'. The need for acknowledgement restrains and incapacitates the poet.

As we have seen, the prose poem was for Heaney a form for material that he has been eager to write about but that over time has increasingly resisted versification. It provides a way for Heaney to write a poem even when he is unable to eschew the self-consciousness that could make verse seem overly affected. Prose is, then, a resource to justify self-conscious content, to legitimatize material that may come across as preachy or programmatic in poetry and quite literally to align it with the margins of the page rather than to organize it in lines. Heaney employs it between the bog poems and the poems on the ground to ruminate on a poet's capacity to write political poetry when political concerns threaten to impede poetics. The 'Unacknowledged Legislator' is actually imprisoned in the poem's 'verse-free' prose paragraphs just as he is imprisoned in his dream of veneration: 'In the cell, I wedge myself with outstretched arms in the corner and heave, I jump on the concrete flats to test them. Were those your eyes just now at the hatch?' The poem illumines something of the subtlety in Shelley's famous reference to poets as 'the unacknowledged legislators of the World' (Shelley 2002, 535). Shelley's phrase invites different readings. When the emphasis is placed on 'legislators', the adjective 'unacknowledged' means unofficial or unrecognized, and therefore unappreciated. But the phrase emphasizes, too, the condition of being 'unacknowledged'. Acknowledgement can preclude artistic inspiration, and it is only when poets do not acknowledge themselves as political authorities that they can then be legislators in his sense. Shelley believed that when poets write with an agenda and attempt to 'teach certain doctrines' or 'moral truths'—when they are, in other words, too self-righteous—poetry ceases. Doctrines and truths can be expressed at will but poetry, according to Shelley, cannot:

> Poetry is not like reasoning, a power to be exerted according to the determination of the will. A man cannot say, "I will compose poetry." The greatest poet even cannot say it: for the mind in creation is as a fading coal which some invisible influence, like an inconstant wind, awakens to transitory brightness.
>
> (Shelley 2002, 520)

Poets, then, must not be concerned with how others perceive them because writing poems for acknowledgement, either by pandering to political expectations or soliciting revolutionary glory as a political poet, may result in no poetry at all. The prose form for Heaney's dream is able to stake that claim while also remaining in the realm of poetry.

Stations is more than a side experiment, or the outcome of a brief engagement with American political poetry of the early seventies, or Heaney's attempt to weigh his efforts against the achievement of Geoffrey Hill's *Mercian Hymns* (1971), a book of incantatory prose-like lines published four years before *Stations* that Heaney refers to in the *Stations* preface as possessing such 'complete authority' that it 'headed off' his own efforts to write prose poems (Heaney 1975b, 3). If Hill's hymns headed off Heaney's stations, they did so only temporarily: Heaney eventually published the *Stations* prose

66   William Fogarty

poems as a special publication and always included at least seven of them in his selected volumes. For Heaney, the triumph of Hill's book is partly due to its 'double-focus': 'one a child's eye view ... the other the historian's and scholar's eye' (Heaney 1980, 159). Such doubleness is similar to the complex viewpoint of *Stations*: the adult looking back as a poet to the child who would become that poet. The prose poems of *Stations*, and the one prose poem in *North*, illuminate something essential about Heaney: that in his early work he didn't only transform his County Derry farm and 'images and symbols' of the Troubles into verse (Heaney 1980, 56). For in the prose poems that also comprise his early work, Heaney began centering artistic tentativeness as one of his most profound poetic subjects. The prose poems portray him reflecting on his earliest impulses and hesitations to turn his local world—its nature, people, language, culture—into poems. They cautiously encounter in prose the raw material of that locale before it would ostensibly be configured into lines of verse. They also represent some of Heaney's earliest explicit renderings of the political reverberations he heeded even on the childhood farm, decades before the Troubles began. *Stations* and 'The Unacknowledged Legislator's Dream' reveal Heaney learning that he could make poetry that does not avoid the risks of political writing but stages the very dilemmas those risks incite. Such prose poems are specimens themselves of complete authority because they face head-on the ambivalence and the self-consciousness that Heaney felt about writing poetry in response to Northern Ireland's social and political contexts and crises. Those dilemmas were always formal dilemmas that he didn't so much try to resolve but rather examined and confronted in poetic form. Prose poems supplied one of those forms to execute that lifelong project.

Notes

1   The first three books are *Death of a Naturalist* (1966), *Door into the Dark* (1969), and *Wintering Out* (1972).
2   *Stations* has been largely absent in Heaney studies, but a handful of scholars have grappled with the poems to come to terms with their place in Heaney's oeuvre. Henry Hart and Richard Rankin Russell provide extensive details about the writing and publication of the poems. Hart examines the poems in relation to the influence of American prose poetry and 'the Symbolists and Modernists' (Hart 1992, 100). Russell reads the poems as 'companion pieces' to the poems in the second part of *North*, having discovered that an early draft of *North* included some of the *Stations* prose poems (Russell 2014, 193–194). Going in a different direction, Jonathan Hufstader asserts that the *Stations* poems depict a young Heaney repudiating an ingrained 'anti-Protestant and anti-British provincial mentality which nurtured him', rejecting the very experience of hostility and violence (Hufstader 1999, 27–29). Most recently, Christopher Laverty has challenged the commonly held notion, one that Heaney himself has sometimes reinforced and sometimes contradicted, that the *Stations* prose poems were the result of a significant influence of less traditional American poetics that he was exposed to when he was a visiting instructor at Berkeley. Laverty argues that the 'claimed traces' of such an influence on *Stations* are, at best, 'allusive': Heaney's prose poems sound

Double Agent 67

a lot like his verse poems and not much like Robert Bly's work within the form (Laverty 2022, 74). Andy Brown notes that 'Much existing criticism . . . misreads *Stations* by not taking the work on its own technical terms from within the prose poetic tradition'; his close readings of the poems do exactly that (Brown 2018, 177). Brown provides a summary of writings about *Stations* by Patrick Crotty (1982), Blake Morrison (1982), Anne Stevenson (1982), Thomas Foster (1989), Elmer Andrews (1993), and Neil Corcoran (1998).

3 Seven *Stations* poems were chosen for Heaney's *Selected Poems: 1966–1987*, which was first published in 1990 and reissued in 2014. *Opened Ground*, another volume of Heaney's selected poems published in 1998, include the same seven and add two more.

4 *Stations* is out of print. However, a digitized version of the book is at the moment available on *HUMAN: Honest Ulsterman Magazine Archive Network* at this link: https://www.huarchive.co/items/viewer/190#page/n2/mode/1up. When citing from *Stations*, I refer to this version of the digitized original chapbook.

5 Heaney was somewhat reluctant to call the texts prose poems: 'I'm not sure ... that the things should be called 'prose poems': maybe it would be better to use David Jones's word 'writings' about them' (Heaney 2008, 180).

6 For the publication history of *Stations* see Hart, Russell, Brown, and Laverty. Heaney states in the preface to *Stations* that the 'pieces were begun in California in 1970/1971 although the greater part of them came to a head in May and June of last year', which would have been 1974 when Heaney was living in Wicklow in the Republic of Ireland (Heaney 1975b, 3). In his interviews with Dennis O'Driscoll, Heaney indicates that the writing of *Stations* and *North* intertwined. He appears to have started *Stations* before *North* but kept working on *Stations* after *North* was completed: 'I believe it was after I handed in the manuscript of *North* that I took them up again' and turned to those prose poems, which, he says, were 'backlit by awareness of the historical moment or the political circumstances' (Heaney 2008, 180).

7 Heaney says he began to 'dabble in verses' in 1962, when he would have been 23 years old (Heaney 1980, 41).

8 Sarah Bennett remarks that '[d]uring his year at Berkeley Heaney also experimented with prose poems, inspired by [Robert] Bly's renowned ventures in the form; these later appeared in the pamphlet *Stations*' (Bennett 2021, 54). The influence of American poetics on *Stations* is an ongoing narrative that Heaney himself has corroborated. He tells O'Driscoll that he was attracted to the 'lyric core' and 'a certain religious disposition' in Bly and Gary Snyder and that 'it was partly under the influence of Bly's prose poems that I experimented with my own—the ones that appear early on in *Stations*' (Heaney 2008, 141). He also tells James Randall that 'probably the most important influence I came under in Berkeley' was an 'awareness that poetry was a force, almost a mode of power, certainly a mode of resistance' (Heaney 1979, 20). However, Christopher Laverty argues that although many of the prose poems of *Stations* were composed during his time at Berkeley where he encountered American political poetry, the influence of American poetics on Heaney has been not only overemphasized but misunderstood: 'When considered in the broader view of Heaney's American influences, the Berkeley period is more useful for highlighting his resistance to certain forms of US poetry due to the critical-literary values he had already absorbed' (Laverty 2022, 62).

9 Jonathan Allison remarks that the state of being 'in-between' is a prominent concept for Heaney: the 'quarrel within himself between poetry and politics, between writing and political commitment was a dominant theme of his writing throughout his life' (Allison 2021, 231). Allison quotes Heaney's poem 'Terminus' from *The Haw Lantern* to substantiate the point: 'Two buckets were easier carried than

68 *William Fogarty*

one./I grew up in between' (Heaney 1987, 4–5). Allison notes that Heaney 'came to regard being culturally and even geographically 'in-between' as a formative influence, citing Heaney's description of the 'in-between' aspect of his childhood home' (Allison 2021, 231): 'I grew up between the predominantly Protestant and loyalist village of Castledawson and the generally catholic and nationalist district of Bellaghy' (Heaney 2002, 53).

10 Brown remarks that Heaney's comment in the preface of *Stations* that the prose poems represented the 'excitement of coming for the first time to a place I have always known completely' indicates his 'delight in the form that remained throughout his career' (Brown 2018, 178). However, Heaney's prose poetry output is small: only nine of the twenty-one *Stations* poems have made it into Heaney's selected poems and only three other prose poems appear in his individual collections, 'The Unacknowledged Legislator's Dream' in *North* and the three 'Found Prose' pieces in *District and Circle* (Heaney 2006, 37–39).

11 Elmer Andrews notes that *Stations* is the first Heaney sequence that adapts the Stations of the Cross for its structure (Andrews 1993, 6). Heaney will also use it for his long, major poem 'Station Island' in the book of the same name that was published in 1985.

12 Heaney moved in 1972 with his family from Belfast, where he was a lecturer at Queens University, to Glanmore Cottage in County Wicklow in the Republic of Ireland (Heaney 2008, xxiii).

13 Hart connects Heaney's move across the border from Northern Ireland to the Republic to his work in prose, citing an unpublished letter Heaney wrote to him: Hart writes, '[r]emoved from direct confrontation with the Troubles, he could experiment with a new form that, as he states in a letter, 'the rather stricter, mocking, and self-mocking atmosphere of Belfast would not have allowed" (Hart 1992, 100–101).

14 I cite the *Stations* poems from the digitized version of the book available on *HUMAN: Honest Ulsterman Magazine Archive Network* at this link: https://www. huarchive.co/items/viewer/190#page/n2/mode/1up. I indicate the page number the first time I quote from a poem then proceed without citations.

15 The bog poems were inspired by P. V. Glob's 1965 book *The Bog People* that includes photos of exhumed corpses, some probably murdered, that were preserved in Scandinavian bog land.

16 For Russell, the binary quality of the prose poem form provided Heaney with a structure to mirror the divisions of Northern Ireland:

> Heaney's turn to prose poetry as a hybrid genre evinces both a desire to register the divide in Northern Ireland between Catholics and Protestants through an inherently divided form and his further attempt to connect the two traditionally distinct genres of prose and poetry, perhaps as a formal model for cultural connection in the province.
>
> (Russell 2014, 188)

Similarly, Hart sees the form itself as a representation of doubleness that Heaney felt free to explore once out of Northern Ireland:

> The judicious, measured style of *Stations* is above all the product of a culture besieged by enemies from without and within. The prose poem, which stalks the border between genres like a double agent, depends on the sort of freedom Heaney must have felt in California and Wicklow.
>
> (Hart 1992, 100)

Works Cited

Allison, Jonathan (2021) 'Politics', in *Seamus Heaney in Context*, edited by Geraldine Higgins, Cambridge: Cambridge University Press, 231–240.

Andrews, Elmer (1993) *Seamus Heaney: A Collection of Critical Essays*, London: Macmillan, 1993.

Bennett, Sarah (2021) 'America', in *Seamus Heaney in Context*, edited by Geraldine Higgins, Cambridge: Cambridge University Press, 48–58.

Brown, Andy (2018) "I Went Disguised in It': Re-evaluating Seamus Heaney's *Stations*', in *British Prose Poetry: The Poems without Lines*, edited by Jane Monson, Cham: Palgrave Macmillan, 177–191.

Caws, M. A. (2012) 'Prose Poem', in *The Princeton Encyclopedia of Poetry and Poetics*, edited by Roland Greene and Stephen Cushman, fourth edition, Princeton, NJ: Princeton University Press, 1112–1113.

Corcoran, Neil (1998) *The Poetry of Seamus Heaney: A Critical Study*, London: Faber & Faber.

Crotty, Patrick (1982) 'All I Believe That Happened There Was Revision: *Selected Poems 1965–1975* and *New Selected Poems 1966–1987*', in *The Art of Seamus Heaney*, edited by Tony Curtis, Bridgend: Seren Books, 192–204.

Foster, Thomas C. (1989) *Seamus Heaney*, Dublin: The O'Brien Press.

Glob, P. V. (1969) *The Bog People*, Ithaca, NY: Cornell University Press.

Hart, Henry (1992) *Seamus Heaney: Poet of Contrary Progressions*, New York: Syracuse University Press.

Hass, Robert (2017) *A Little Book of Forms: An Exploration into the Formal Imagination of Poetry*, New York: Ecco.

Heaney, Seamus (1966) *Death of a Naturalist*, London: Faber and Faber.

Heaney, Seamus (1969) *Door into the Dark*, London: Faber and Faber.

Heaney, Seamus (1972) *Wintering Out*, London: Faber and Faber.

Heaney, Seamus (1975a) *North*, London: Faber and Faber.

Heaney, Seamus (1975b) *Stations*, Belfast: Ulsterman Publications, 1975, available at *HUMAN: Honest Ulsterman Magazine Archive Network*, https://www.huarchive.co/items/viewer/190#page/n2/mode/1up [Accessed 21 September 2023].

Heaney, Seamus (1979) 'An Interview with Seamus Heaney', interview by James Randall, *Ploughshares* (5.3): 7–22.

Heaney, Seamus (1980) *Preoccupations: Selected Prose 1968–1978*, New York: Farrar, Straus and Giroux.

Heaney, Seamus (1981) Letter to 'Ramon', 15 October 1981, Box 1, Folder 1, Subseries 1.3 (Outgoing Correspondence, 1968–2004), MC 960, Seamus Heaney Papers, Stuart A. Rose Manuscript, Archives, and Rare Book Library, Emory University, Atlanta, GA.

Heaney, Seamus (1985) *Station Island*, New York: Farrar, Straus and Giroux.

Heaney, Seamus (1987) *The Haw Lantern*, New York: Farrar, Straus and Giroux.

Heaney, Seamus (1995) *The Redress of Poetry*, New York: Farrar, Straus and Giroux.

Heaney, Seamus (1998) *Opened Ground: Selected Poems, 1966–1996*, New York: Farrar, Straus and Giroux.

Heaney, Seamus (2002) *Finders Keepers: Selected Prose 1971–2001*, New York: Farrar, Straus and Giroux.

70 William Fogarty

Heaney, Seamus (2006) *District and Circle*, New York: Farrar, Straus and Giroux.

Heaney, Seamus (2008) *Stepping Stones: Interviews with Seamus Heaney*, interviews by Dennis O'Driscoll, New York: Farrar, Straus and Giroux.

Heaney, Seamus (2014; 1990) *Selected Poems: 1966–1987*, New York: Farrar, Straus and Giroux.

Hetherington, Paul and Cassandra Atherton (2020) *Prose Poetry: An Introduction.* Princeton, NJ: Princeton University Press.

Hill, Geoffrey (1971) *Mercian Hymns*, London: André Deutsch.

Hirsch, Edward (2017) *The Essential Poet's Glossary*, New York: Mariner.

Hufstader, Jonathan (1999) *Tongue of Water, Teeth of Stones: Northern Irish Poetry and Social Violence*, Lexington: University Press of Kentucky.

Laverty, Christopher (2022) *Seamus Heaney and American Poetry*, Cham: Palgrave Macmillan.

Monroe, Jonathan (1987) *A Poverty of Objects: The Prose Poem and the Politics of Genre*, New York: Cornell University Press.

Morrison, Blake (1982) *Seamus Heaney*, London: Methuen.

Noel-Tod, Jeremy (2018) *The Penguin Book of the Prose Poem: From Baudelaire to Anne Carson*, New York: Penguin.

Riffaterre, Michael (1983) 'On the Prose Poem's Formal Features', in *The Prose Poem in France: Theory and Practice*, edited by Mary Ann Caws and Hermine B. Riffaterre, New York: Columbia University Press, 117–132.

Russell, Richard Rankin (2014) *Seamus Heaney's Regions*, Notre Dame: University of Notre Dame Press.

Russell, Richard Rankin (2016) *Seamus Heaney: An Introduction*, Edinburgh: Edinburgh University Press.

Shelley, Percy Bysshe (2002) *Shelley's Poetry and Prose*, edited by Donald H. Reiman and Neil Fraistat, Second edition, New York: Norton.

Stevens, Wallace (1997) 'The Noble Rider and the Sound of Words', in *Wallace Stevens: Collected Poetry and Prose*, edited by Frank Kermode and Joan Richardson, New York: Library of America, 643–665.

Stevenson, Anne (1982) '*Stations*: Seamus Heaney and the Sacred Sense of the Sensitive Self', in *The Art of Seamus Heaney*, edited by Tony Curtis, Bridgend: Seren Books, 47–51.

Terdiman, Richard (2018) *Discourse/Counter-Discourse: The Theory and Practice of Symbolic Resistance in Nineteenth-Century France*, New York, Cornell University Press.

Wordsworth, William (1965) *William Wordsworth: Selected Poems and Prefaces*, edited by Jack Stillinger, Boston, MA: Houghton Mifflin.

4 Preoccupied with Redress

Heaney Meditates on Getting his 'Feel into Words'

Ruth Macklin

I have argued elsewhere that redress 'is a deeply considered intellectual construct which facilitates the process of writing, and that Heaney's critical explorations of redress are best described as a "troubled, not wholly consistent... meditation"' (Macklin 2017, 56). By provisionally naming the construct 'redress' in the Oxford Lectures, Heaney strikes upon a term whose many definitions allow him to explore his own process under the guise of issuing an apologia. In this chapter I would like to focus on *Preoccupations* in order to illustrate one way in which redress facilitates composition early in Heaney's career. Though it is not nearly as flexible a term as redress, an old definition of 'preoccupation' as 'anticipating and meeting objections beforehand' allows the young poet to counter the recrimination that his poetry 'didn't sound very Celtic' – that it did not exhibit the requisite soundscape of Ireland, 'pre-occupation' (Heaney 1980, 36). The charge is simplistic, perhaps even naive, in light of the geographical, historical and cultural complexities that Heaney lays out in 'Mossbawn' and 'Belfast', but it is also troubling enough for him to record it.

At the time of writing *Preoccupations*, Heaney can reflect on the difficulty of getting his 'feel... into words' over the previous two decades (Heaney 1980, 41). His deep interest in the many elements of composition and his sense that at any stage subtle missteps can lead to a 'still-birth' indicate the high stakes for a poet of finding one's voice (Heaney 1980, 41). The language of labour and delivery might seem gratuitous in relation to composition, but as Heaney argues repeatedly throughout his prose work, '[n]ature forms the heart that watches and receives but until the voice of the poet has been correspondingly attuned, we cannot believe what we hear' (Heaney 1980, 69). In the case of a young Irish poet in Northern Ireland who desires to write English lyric poetry in the 1960s and 1970s, there are additional challenges. At this stage of Heaney's career, the corrective function of redress as a challenge, revision or readjustment enables him to transform an inherited cultural and linguistic conflict into a poetically generative tension.

Heaney's belief that 'in any poetic music, there will always be two contributory elements' introduces a potential sense of conflict or negotiation into

DOI: 10.4324/9781003456148-5

72 Ruth Macklin

the process of composition before a poet even puts pen to paper (Heaney 1980, 62). One element is 'illiterate', 'pre-verbal' and 'instinctual', comprising '[w]hat kinds of noise assuage him, what kinds of music pleasure or repel him, what messages the receiving stations of his senses are happy to pick up from the world around him and what ones they automatically block out' (Heaney 1980, 62). This aspect fosters and excites the vatic impulse, as these are the sounds that reach the poet 'as a fibre from a tap-root' (Heaney 1980, 36). They may at various times admonish, assuage or satisfy, but in all cases, they restore a 'sensation of rightness', to use the language of *The Redress of Poetry* (Heaney [1995] 1996, 83). While the 'illiterate' element is significant as the source of 'connection between the core of a poet's speaking voice and the core of his poetic voice, between his original accent and his discovered style' (Heaney 1980, 43), the second contributory element stems from the poet's education and is therefore 'literary' (Heaney 1980, 62). This element is responsible for establishing 'structures' which create 'certain kinds of aural expectations' in a poet's work, thereby functioning as a directive rather than a source (Heaney 1980, 62).

For a poet born into the dominant culture there is little to no conflict between these two elements, but for those who discover that they must now 'think twice' about their natural speech, these dual elements necessitate conscious decision-making during the process of composition (Heaney [1995] 1996, 63). Word by word such poets must reject, adjust or emphasise their native dialect in order to work within a given form, unhelpfully aware of future readers, and with each deliberation potentially interrupting or redirecting the flow of composition. Heaney remains alert to the decisions linguistically marginalised poets make, and the consequences of those decisions, throughout his career. While Heaney admires the ease with which John Clare worked within the conventions of the eighteenth century, he feels that the resulting poetry lacks the spark of the dialectal and vernacular poetry of his early middle years (Heaney [1995] 1996, 69–70). The poetry that Clare produces when he is 'out of step with himself', 'operating within a received idiom that he half-knew was not the right one for him' (Heaney [1995] 1996, 74) today 'moves fluently and adequately but it moves like water that flows over a mill-wheel without turning it' (Heaney [1995] 1996, 70). By contrast, Wordsworth experiences the world as moving 'like a waterwheel under the fall of his voice', and consequently, the reader experiences the same (Heaney 1980, 68).

The corrective function of redress enables Heaney to negotiate his even greater linguistic marginalisation as a poet from rural County Derry by privileging the preliterary element of his auditory imagination. Later in this chapter I will illustrate that this position, taken out of necessity in order for him to begin, is short-term and somewhat gestural. Throughout my analysis I will describe the two elements of Heaney's auditory imagination as the preliterary ('illiterate') Germanic and the Latinate of his education. Germanic because though Irish is Celtic and not Germanic, Heaney perceives an enabling

Preoccupied with Redress   73

connection between the aural qualities of Old English as it is echoed in the alliterative poetry of Gerard Manley Hopkins and his own Ulster speech:

> Looking back on it, I believe there was a connection, not obvious at the time but, on reflection, real enough, between the heavily accented consonantal noise of Hopkins's poetic voice, and the peculiar regional characteristics of a Northern Ireland accent.
>
> (Heaney 1980, 44)

And Latinate because while the child hiding in the hollow in 'Oracle' absorbs his native soundscape effortlessly and tenderly, the process of formal education in poems like 'Alphabets' and 'Freedman' takes place in the starkly juxtaposed halls of the 'Latin forum' (Heaney 1987, 1–2).

In *Preoccupations*, Heaney privileges the preliterary element of a poet's auditory imagination by aligning it with the vatic impulse, that first nudge to write that is confirming throughout a poet's lifetime. 'Call it apt admonishment', he writes decades later, 'call it contact with the hiding places, call it inspiration, … call it what you like, but be sure it is what a poet's inner faith and freedom depends upon' (Heaney 2008, 33). In *Preoccupations*, 'Feeling into Words' (1974), 'The Makings of a Music: Reflections on Wordsworth and Yeats' (1978) and 'The Fire i' the Flint: Reflections on the Poetry of Gerard Manley Hopkins' (1974), form a triad in which Heaney mentions the literary almost in passing, and then only as an instructive foil. The main focus in these lectures is the problems that arise from a poet's attempt to engage with the preliterary element, an engagement that is especially problematic when it derives from a register like the Germanic, the employment of which is largely unprecedented in the tradition of the English lyric. Heaney therefore dwells on the preliterary imaginations of Hopkins and Kavanagh, leaving aside those more easily suited to the English lyric, such as Wordsworth, Keats and even Yeats, for whom 'Gaelic is my national language, but it is not my mother tongue' (Yeats 1961, 520).

Heaney also gives the preliterary element greater weight by arguing for its role in the novice poet's ability to channel inspiration inimitably by 'finding a voice' (Heaney 1980, 47). This occurs, he states, through the poet's first receptive encounter with the 'in-fluence' of another writer: 'you hear something in another writer's sounds that flows in through your ear and enters the echo-chamber of your head and delights your whole nervous system' (Heaney 1980, 44). His analyses of Gerard Manley Hopkins and Patrick Kavanagh are especially illuminating in relation to finding a voice, because while the aural quality of both poets reaches Heaney in the physiological way he is describing, only one of them helps him to write.

In 'Feeling into Words' Heaney recalls that his first encounter with the highly alliterative poetry of Hopkins ignited his desire to write (Heaney 1980, 43–44). Like Heaney, Hopkins grew up between traditions, and as I have already mentioned, Heaney's preliterary ear is attracted to the echoes of

74   Ruth Macklin

Ulster speech he finds in the 'bumpy alliterating music, the reporting sounds and ricochetting consonants typical of Hopkins's verse' (Heaney 1980, 44). These qualities are highly crafted and therefore imitable, and Heaney attempts his own version in the early poem 'October Thought' (Heaney 1980, 44). And yet, discovering and even emulating Hopkins's poetry does not help Heaney to find his own voice. This is because of the highly intentional way in which Hopkins deals with the conflict between his two inherited traditions, and between his preliterary and literary sources:

> His masculine powers of powerful and active thought were consciously developed, as consciously as his theories of sprung rhythm and his private language of instress and inscape: behind the one was a directed effort in Welsh and classical versification, behind the other a scholastic appetite for Scotism.
>
> (Heaney 1980, 86)

Hopkins's verse exhibits a 'directed effort' to include what had been acquired through education, the appreciation for 'Welsh and classical versification' and a shared interest in the soundscape of 'Scotism' which is clearly an attraction for the young Heaney (Heaney 1980, 86). However, the masculine effort at classical versification is too pronounced for Heaney, and Hopkins's deliberate development of instress and inscape, although stemming from an interest in Old English which initially attracts Heaney to him, develops into too 'private' a 'schema' (Heaney 1980, 86).

Significantly, while Hopkins ignites his desire to write, Heaney suggests that it is the aural quality of Kavanagh's poetry that first helps him to do it. In *Preoccupations* he emphasises Kavanagh's feat of getting the Germanic source of his own auditory imagination into poetry, despite a lack of precedence. 'Much of his authority and oddity', Heaney writes, 'derive from the fact that he wrested his idiom bare-handed out of a literary nowhere' (Heaney 1980, 116). Writing about Kavanagh's influence on him in 'The Placeless Heaven: Another Look at Kavanagh', a lecture delivered five years after the publication of *Preoccupations*, Heaney asserts:

> Kavanagh's genius had achieved singlehanded what I and my grammar-schooled, arts-degreed generation were badly in need of – a poetry which linked the small farm life which produced us with the slim volume world we were now supposed to be fit for. He brought us back to what we came from.
>
> (Heaney 1988, 9)

By linking a rural upbringing with literary tradition Kavanagh gives Heaney permission to challenge the centrality of Standard English. The distinction Kavanagh makes between parochialism and provincialism in 'The Parish and the Universe' is an enabling one for Heaney. His declaration that

Preoccupied with Redress   75

'[a]ll great civilizations are based on parochialism' allows Heaney to trust the validity of his own experience and the resources of his auditory imagination that develop from that experience (Kavanagh 1967, 282). Thus, *Preoccupations* begins by relocating the *omphalos* from Delphi to Mossbawn, a landscape which provides him with ample 'secret nests' in which to hide as a boy (Heaney 1980, 17). To return to the poem 'Oracle', what appears to be passivity in the child-listener, absorbing the soundscape as if by osmosis, is really the storing of potential in light of the directive to hide and blend with the landscape. By contrast the student in 'Freedman' is hard at his task, obeying endless direction which only renders him '[s]ubjugated' (Heaney [1975] 2001, 56).

Heaney conceives of 'Digging' as the first poem in which he achieves 'technique', 'where', he states, 'I thought my *feel* had got into words' (emphasis original) (Heaney 1980, 41). The poem features the vernacular quality of Heaney's County Derry origins and is clearly worlds away from Hopkins or Heaney's early pastiche 'October Thought'. Heaney's own description of 'Digging' is closer to his assessment of Kavanagh's poem 'Inniskeen Road, July Evening' in 'The Sense of Place' where he claims that Kavanagh's words are:

> natural and spoken; they are not used as a deliberate mark of folksiness or as a separate language, in the way that Irish speech is ritualized by Synge. Inniskeen English is not used as a picturesque idiom but as the writer's own natural speech and again this points to Kavanagh's essential difference from the Revival writers. There is nothing programmed about his diction, or about his world.
>
> (Heaney 1980, 138)

'Digging' and what Heaney has to say about it is important because a poet's ability to develop technique is not guaranteed. Young Heaney may recognise technique in the work of other poets and experience the sense of rightness that is its consequence, but unlike craft, technique cannot be imitated. In 'Digging' Heaney has found that it is possible to incorporate the preliterary element of his auditory imagination and to feel that sense of rightness, but the effort must be repeated, and having found his voice there is still an anxiety about how to use it.

In the early poetry there is a feeling that Heaney needs the notion of elegance that redress – by achieving balance and decorum – can offer him. He famously describes 'Digging', for instance, as 'a big coarse-grained navvy of a poem' (Heaney 1980, 43) and relays his disquiet of using Ulster pronunciation in poetry:

> I tried to write about the sycamores
> And innovated a South Derry rhyme
> With *hushed* and *lulled* full chimes for *pushed* and *pulled*.

76   Ruth Macklin

Those hobnailed boots from beyond the mountain
Were walking, by God, all over the fine
Lawns of elocution.

> (Heaney [1975] 2001, 58–59)

The Ulster dialect rhymes that Heaney perceives to be 'hobnailed' are due to Irish. G. B. Adams notes that:

> To some extent of course Irish has affected all Ulster dialects; the sound given to short *u* (as in *drum*, *but*) in most of Ulster, and the 'clear' sound of *l*, without the raising of the back of the tongue which accompanies this sound before consonants in English and in all positions in Scottish speech, are due to this influence, which extends also to idiom.
>
> (Adams 1964, 3)

Heaney perceives his attempts to use the Germanic, the preliterary and the vatic, as a hobnailed trampling of the English lyric to which he is attracted. His concluding comment in 'The Ministry of Fear' that 'Ulster was British, but with no rights on/The English lyric' suggests that despite gathering exemplars such as Ted Hughes and R. S. Thomas, the aural quality of the Germanic register seems incompatible with the received pronunciation of Standard English (Heaney [1975] 2001, 60). I would like to turn to Heaney's early poetry to examine some ways in which redress as a corrective helps Heaney to negotiate his conflicting linguistic inheritances.

The linguistically driven poetry that predominates in Heaney's early volumes indicates that diction provides one means of enacting redress. Heaney's education brings him into conflict with the preliterary element of his imagination. He is unable to feel faithful to his own voice by excluding the Latinate, although this second element of his auditory imagination represents the literary tradition from which he feels excluded. One useful image Heaney finds for admitting both traditions and registers into his poetry is that of the water carrier from the eponymous poem by John Montague (Montague [1961] 1977, 11). Here is the image as it appears in Heaney's poem 'Terminus III', from *The Haw Lantern*:

Two buckets were easier carried than one.
I grew up in between.
My left hand placed the standard iron weight.
My right tilted a last grain in the balance.
Baronies, parishes met where I was born.
When I stood on the central stepping stone
I was the last earl on horseback in midstream
Still parleying, in earshot of his peers.

> (Heaney 1987, 5)

Like Kavanagh's view of parochialism, the image supplied by 'The Water Carrier' is 'irrigating and confirming' (Heaney 1988, 7). The poet as fulcrum maintains two traditions which exist in a relationship of balance. But to what extent is such a claim operative in Heaney's early poetry?

One way in which redress is enacted is through Heaney's treatment of etymology and pronunciation, which he uses to gain Ulster some rights to the English lyric. Although he studied Latin at school, remnants of the language were part of Heaney's preliterary imagination. He grew up hearing Latin spoken, both through the catechism and his mother parsing from memory, and later as a parent he incorporated Latin into playful everyday interactions with his family. When Heaney brings the two registers into balance by challenging the authority of Received Pronunciation and authoritative definitions, he is claiming Latin as part of his Ulster inheritance. Upon first inspection, unwieldy constructions like 'I took the embankment path/(As always, *deferring*/The bridge)', '[a] *transfer* of gables and sky', 'I *established* a dreaded/Bridgehead' (emphasis mine) (Heaney [1966] 1969, 18) convey the same awkwardness with the process of learning that Bernard O'Donoghue notes in the phrase 'my hitherto snubbed rodent', from 'An Advancement of Learning' (O'Donoghue 1994, 44). But it seems to me that Heaney is also deploying Latinate diction in particular to suggest the familiarity that comes from centuries of vernacular use. Latinate diction is not necessarily used to elevate Heaney's poetry in accordance with the English poetic tradition, as a 'hallmark of his high style' (Kerrigan 1992, 238). Its unwieldiness in these poems seems rather to suggest a deliberately archaic quality not in accordance with the traditional elegance of the English lyric. Heaney's deployment of Latinate diction suggests long use and a quaintness to the ear of the Standard English speaker which is usually reserved for dialect. By appropriating the Latinate into his vocabulary it becomes part of the local, supporting his claim to parochialism.

Heaney's appropriation of words from the Latinate register is also signalled by his use of archaic, rare or obsolete definitions. This manner of appropriation challenges the claim of superiority made by the Standard English speaker to the English language. At the same time, the poet quietly affirms his extensive learning and intimate knowledge of etymology. In *Death of a Naturalist*, for example, the narrator witnesses the 'obscene threats' of frogs spawning in a flax dam. Their obscenity is of course immediately understood in the usual sense of the word as '[o]ffensively or grossly indecent, lewd', but it is illuminated by awareness of the Latin etymon *obscenus* and its derivatives. One derivative, *caenum*, meaning 'mud, filth' echoes Heaney's description of the frogs as 'mud grenades' (Heaney [1966] 1969, 16). At the same time a second derivative, *scaevus*, meaning 'left-sided' and therefore 'inauspicious', adds a touch of menace to the Biblical element of invasion which is already implied. A second example indicates that Heaney affirms his familiarity with the Latinate by using words in which a Latin definition is itself more

78   Ruth Macklin

relevant than the English one currently in use. In 'A Lough Neagh Sequence', for instance, Heaney alludes to the technical use of 'describe' when he writes '[t]he eel describes his arcs without a sound' (Heaney 1969, 41). The Latin *describere*, meaning 'to copy off, transcribe, write down', is historically paired with 'arcs' in a geometric description of the 'arches of circles'. After years of excelling at Latin in school the origins of words are as readily available as the conjugations were for his mother.

Heaney's treatment of Germanic diction in such cases is markedly different, indicating that he is bringing these two traditions into balance through redress. It seems to me that Heaney takes care to select dialect words that will support a balance between the two registers. His early poem 'Follower' provides an instructive example. In the Oxford lecture 'John Clare's Prog', Heaney explains how in the famous opening line he removed his initial choice of 'wrought', replacing it with Standard English 'worked' so that the published line reads 'My father worked with a horse-plough' (Heaney [1966] 1969, 24) but keeping 'headrig', a regional term for 'the headland, the strip at the top of the field where the horses or tractor turn, afterwards ploughed at right angles'. It may be that using 'headrig' relates to Heaney's own experience of 'finding a voice', since he earlier recalls encountering 'headland', a word he had believed to be similarly peculiar to County Monaghan, in Kavanagh's poem 'Spraying the Potatoes' (Heaney 1988, 7). But it seems more likely to me that Heaney is willing to employ dialect only if it will sound foreign to the Standard English ear, while 'thinking twice' about words which are familiar to a Standard English reader but which might either be misunderstood or conceived of as quaint or archaic (Heaney [1995] 1996, 63). A further example is evident in Rand Brandes's analysis of the development of Heaney's working titles. Brandes states that Heaney abandoned the title 'Polder' for *Field Work* (1979) at his editor Charles Monteith's urging: 'Never call a book by a title that people aren't sure how to pronounce' (Brandes 2009, 19). Brandes suggests a problem of 'marketing and memory' which seems likely from a publisher's point of view (Brandes 2009, 25). At the same time, this example is indicative of what appears to be Heaney's concern to be viewed as parochial rather than provincial. Before deploying a dialect word, Heaney carefully considers the relationship that will arise between the two registers.

Heaney's treatment of Germanic diction also indicates an acute awareness of the historical and geographical usage of the two registers. The place-name poems in *Wintering Out*, especially, suggest connections between geography, language and history through which Heaney asserts continuity between his native Ulster vernacular and Old English. This form of redress is enacted through pronunciation. The opening lines of 'Fodder', for example, which read 'Or, as we said/*fother*', assert the local pronunciation which according to the *OED Online* is now obsolete except in such dialect usages. What Heaney is asserting through pronunciation is the immediacy of the word 'as we said' to the Old English fóðer (Heaney [1972] 1973, 13).

The poem begins with authority, offering 'fother' as a legitimate alternative, and continues 'I open/my arms for it/again' (Heaney (1972) 1973, 3).

'Fodder' reminds the reader of what Kevin McCafferty describes as 'Ireland's position as a recipient of large numbers of English-speakers in the earliest phases of the overseas spread of the language' (McCafferty 2010, 141). Heaney's interesting demarcation of the area 'north of that Berwick/Bundoran line' as one 'where the language of Shakespeare and the Bible meets the language of Dunbar and the ballads and where new poetic combinations and new departures are still going on' also claims Scots as part of his own Ulster inheritance (Heaney 1997, 220). As Heaney wrote in 'Mossbawn',

> In the names of its fields and townlands, in their mixture of Scots and Irish and English etymologies, this side of the country was redolent of the histories of its owners... They lie deep, like some script indelibly written into the nervous system.
>
> (Heaney 1980, 20)

Like Stephen Dedalus's discovery of the English origin of 'tundish', '[w]hat had seemed disabling and provincial' is transformed into something 'corroborating and fundamental and potentially universal' (Heaney 1983, 10–11). The Ulster dialect from which he has been displaced through his education, and which in the process threatened to become 'an embarrassment, a kind of Firbolg birthmark rebuked by the Milesian superiority of the standard English "funnel"' is viewed instead as a linguistic store rich with potential for poetry (Heaney 1983, 10). To return to the image of the water carrier, redress has momentarily corrected the historical imbalance between the two traditions Heaney has inherited.

Despite the correction, as the image of the water carrier also suggests, the Latinate and the Germanic remain separate, monological registers. Commenting on Heaney's 1973 interview with Patrick Garland, partially reproduced in *The Listener*, in which Heaney suggested that the English consonants and Irish vowels combine to create 'a harmony of some kind' (Heaney 1973, 629), Rob Jackaman writes: '[h]armony, then, is the ideal, a balance between English and Irish – but to put this in perspective it might be worth considering for a moment how *unlikely* harmony actually was in the context of Northern Ireland in the 1970s' (emphasis original) (Jackaman 2003, 152). This is of course an unlikelihood acknowledged by Heaney in 'The Water Carrier' through his allusion to the 1607 Flight of the Earls, Hugh O'Neill among them and the end of Gaelic Ireland.

Because each register remains a discrete monologue, the relationship between them also operates as a challenge rather than a corrective, and so I would like to examine the extent to which the Germanic is set against the Latinate. I have already suggested that Heaney's framing of the aural quality of the Latinate and the Germanic indicates that they develop in the poet's imagination from opposing sources. Here the aural quality of Hopkins's poetry

80 *Ruth Macklin*

is illuminating. In Heaney's estimation, Hopkins's poetry is highly directed, composed in support of a preconceived rhetorical argument: 'the whole figurative life of the piece is analogous and diagrammatic; what is mimetic in the words is completely guaranteed by what is theological behind them' (Heaney 1980, 90). Concord between diction and imagery is the operative means by which Hopkins achieves the directive. His poems 'are most fully achieved when siring vision is most rapturously united with a sensuous apprehension of natural life. United, and not simply in attendance upon each other' (Heaney 1980, 95). In Heaney's poetry, however, as the image of the water carrier suggests, each register speaks only to itself.

The challenge is made by the Germanic register, which Heaney endows with what Geoffrey Leech calls 'degrees of linguistic audacity' (Leech 1969, 29; 33). This audacity can be the result merely of the difference in aural quality between the Latinate and the Germanic. In 'Bone Dreams II', for instance, Heaney differentiates between the sounds of various registers in what Edna Longley points out is an instance of 'linguistic decolonisation' (Longley 1994, 69):

> I push back
> through dictions,
> Elizabethan canopies.
> Norman devices,
> the erotic mayflowers
> of Provence
> and the ivied Latins
> of churchmen
> to the scop's
> twang, the iron
> flash of consonants
> cleaving the line.
>   (Heaney [1975] 2001, 20)

Heaney brings the comparative whimsy of 'canopies', 'devices', 'erotic mayflowers' and 'ivied Latins' into sharp contrast with the abruptness of the 'scop's/twang'. Like his reference to John Clare's '[p]rog' (Heaney [1995] 1996, 63), Heaney's description of the Germanic register suggests that its very aural quality challenges the 'gorgeousness of the polysyllable', as he describes his earliest impression of the 'literary language, the civilized utterance from the classic canon of English poetry' in 'Mossbawn', inseparable to his childhood ear from the impressive but essentially foreign sounds of the catechism (Heaney 1980, 26).

Linguistic innovation is another means of displaying audacity. In the following statement, Heaney suggests that the particular 'linguistic energy' of the Germanic register is incompatible with traditional notions of how diction should operate in poetry. In setting the Germanic against the Latinate,

Heaney challenges the balance that is maintained by redress. Through the audacious use of the Germanic register, he resists what Czesław Miłosz calls 'merely graceful writing' (Miłosz 1983, 65):

> I'm a different kind of animal from Ted [Hughes], but I will always be grateful for the release that reading his work gave me. I have gone through all that education about Eliot's bringing in irony and urban subject matter and intelligence, and nothing in that connected with the scripts written in my being. Then I read Hughes, Kavanagh, R. S. Thomas, and I realized their work was dealing with my world. One of the poets I got a charge out of early on was Hopkins, and Ted's poetry had that kind of linguistic energy, arrest and power, textures and surfaces.
>
> (Haffenden 1981, 74)

Although Heaney does make frequent use of such monosyllables as 'glib' (Heaney [1975] 2001, 4) and 'bleb' (Heaney [1975] 2001, 11) a word need not be unfamiliar to readers outside Ireland in order for it to display audacity. In the following example, linguistic audacity results from innovative use of a familiar term. The audacity of the term arises from its refusal to be arch or ironic.

There are several familiar senses in which the word 'neighbourly', recurrent in *North*, might be traditionally used. The *OED Online* defines 'neighbourly' as '[f]riendly but reserved *Obs.* (With implicit contrast with a less reserved emotion, feeling, etc.)' and '[o]f a person, etc.: inclined to act as a neighbour; situated as a neighbour'. On the basis of such definitions, as well as biblical dicta such as 'Charitie worketh no ill to his neighbour', it is perhaps inevitable that 'neighbourly' should lend itself readily to irony (*Romans* 8.10). There is a healthy dose of it in Portia's summation of her Scottish suitor in *The Merchant of Venice*, whom, she says, 'hath a neighborly charity in him, for he borrowed a box of the ear of the Englishman and swore he would pay him again when he was able' (I. ii. 74–76). The term is similarly deployed in *Sense and Sensibility* with the wry irony characteristic of Jane Austen's narrators, as when Mr. John Dashwood reneges on his promise to care for his half-siblings. The narrator remarks that Dashwood 'finally resolved, that it would be absolutely unnecessary, if not highly indecorous, to do more for the widow and children of his father, than such kind of neighbourly acts as his own wife pointed out', namely, the withholding of their income (Austen 2006, 15).

The audacious force of 'neighbourly' in *North* therefore arises from the lack of irony with which Heaney uses it. It is used as an adjective for 'murder' in 'Funeral Rites II' (Heaney [1975] 2001, 7) and as a modifier for 'score-taking/killers' in 'Viking Dublin: Trial Pieces' V (Heaney [1975] 2001, 15). Heaney's use of 'neighbourly' is neither darkly ironic, as in *The Merchant of Venice*, where Portia's subsequent statement, 'I think the Frenchman became

82 *Ruth Macklin*

his surety and sealed under for another', hints at France's continual promises to aid the Scottish in battle against the English (I. ii. 76–78), nor wickedly self-delighting as in *Sense and Sensibility*. Rather, the audacity of 'neighbourly' stems from its resonance with uses of the word as a commonplace, notably as a descriptor of strained relations between Northern Ireland and the Republic during the Troubles. In August 1969, following Taoiseach Jack Lynch's call 'for a United Nations peacekeeping force to be sent to the province', Prime Minister Chichester-Clark 'responded by saying neighbourly relations with the Republic were at an end and that British troops were being called in' (BBC 2008). In light of the mock-scoretaking graffiti message ('PARAS THIRTEEN, the walls said,/BOGSIDE NIL') the unironic use of 'neighbourly' exhibits linguistic audacity through its placement as a paradoxical yet chillingly appropriate modifier (Heaney 1979, 22).

Another example of the audacity of the Germanic register is the way in which it challenges narrative flow, especially noticeable in the tightly bound poems in *North*. Constructions such as kennings, for instance, disrupt the shapeliness of these poems by injecting vividness into an otherwise smooth line. Neil Corcoran suggests that:

> The poems are not aggressive towards the reader, exactly, but neither are they accommodating. Hard-edged, all elbows with their constantly jolting line-breaks and lexicographical diction, they disrupt the smoothness of English lyric in a way appropriate to the violence of their material.
>
> (Corcoran 1998, 63)

In 'Viking Dublin: Trial Pieces', the aural quality of kennings such as 'skull-handler' waylays the graceful snaking progression and gathering momentum of the poem. In 'Bone Dreams II', the eye slides easily over the short lines until it arrives abruptly at 'the scop's/twang', which both breaks and adheres immovably to the line (Heaney [1975] 2001, 20). The suddenness with which it appears on the page enhances its unexpected break into the measured, fluid pace of the lyric. The audacious effect of this 'flash of consonants' is a resistance to the enjambment which threatens to counteract the compactness of the poem's form, and which lends the poem a smooth grace. Heaney's use of audacity in these poems 'cleaves the line', resisting the Latinate grace that might otherwise become the aural watermark of his poetry (Heaney [1975] 2001, 20).

Importantly, however, there is still a significant tension created by the fact that this challenge is to some extent gestural. Heaney does not carry out his claim to Frank Kinahan that 'that music, the melodious grace of the English iambic line, was some kind of affront, that it needed to be wrecked' (Kinahan and Heaney 1982, 412). The 'scops/twang' is a slightly pejorative description of the aural effect of the Germanic register, and the violent challenge ('push back') of its 'iron/flash of consonants/cleaving the line' becomes less straightforward upon closer examination (Heaney [1975] 2001, 20). Cleaving is the traditional method by which many craftsmen, including the Viking boat builders whose longships haunt the pages of *North*, work with raw materials. Such craftsmen identify points of weakness in the grain of a felled oak tree before patiently wedging them open in a line. Through careful repetition they split the wood into planks that, because they have not been cut or sawed, retain the strength of their original form. Like the Viking boat builder, Heaney is thoughtful and methodical, engaged in a process that is slow and constructive, rather than single-minded or destructive. By 'cleaving the line', he uses the Germanic register to reconfigure rather than to 'wreck' his linguistic raw materials. In doing so, Heaney maintains the characteristic decorum produced by redress. The 'hard-edged' compactness of the early poems, which Corcoran finds 'all elbows' and 'jolting', is largely visual and dissolves upon reading (Corcoran 1998, 63). 'Bone Dreams', like 'Viking Dublin: Trial Pieces' and another poem which I have not discussed, 'Kinship', is a lengthy single breath divided into multiple parts. As each stanza leads into the next the poem lengthens and becomes more like the English lyric, despite retaining its tight shape visually. The 'skinny quatrain', as Edna Longley calls it, becomes less a drill moving down and boring into the earth than a reluctant discursiveness (Longley 1994, 88). Longley is critical of poems that 'can dwindle to mere layout unjustified by stress or sense' (Longley 1994, 89). In her expectation of the concord and proportion which govern the iambics of the English lyric Longley misses the tension created by Heaney's resistance to it. At the same time, Heaney's likening of the poems to 'drills and augurs' (Randall and Heaney 1979, 16) conceals the increasing sway of that lyric as it enters his longhand and 'turns cursive, unscarfing' (Heaney [1975] 2001, 14).

While Heaney's early poems benefit from the creative tension that is the product of redress, over time his use of the Germanic register becomes increasingly obligatory. At first, privileging the vatic impulse allows Heaney to assert the importance of the Germanic register as one of two traditions he inherits. In 'North', this privileging is made explicit by an instruction Heaney issues himself through the Viking 'longship's swimming tongue' (Heaney [1975] 2001, 10) to 'Lie down/in the word-hoard' (Heaney [1975] 2001, 11), an instruction reminiscent of the bidding in 'Oracle', and one which places Heaney under a certain obligation to keep the Germanic register functioning at its highest currency. This induces the poet to use this register at the expense of the rest of his auditory imagination. While proclaiming his fidelity to the word-hoard at first allows Heaney to challenge the English lyric while maintaining balance, ultimately it threatens to yield poetry that is programmatic. In theory, Heaney's association of the Germanic register with the preliterary element of his auditory imagination aligns the Germanic with technique. In practice, however, his fidelity to the Germanic register necessitates a greater degree of craft – of 'cleaving the line' – than is natural to the poet, who once

84   *Ruth Macklin*

quoted Keats that 'if poetry comes not as naturally as the leaves to a tree it had better not come at all' (Keats 1971, 474).

Heaney admires craft just as he admires technique, and his view of the poetic process as one of digging requires him to be both vatic and craftsman-like. Impacted no doubt by growing up in a rural environment, Heaney has a strong sense of the creative powers of makers. He describes local blacksmith Barney Devlin as 'in his late eighties now, but still capable of striking the epic out of the usual' (O'Driscoll 2008, 91), and his carpenter neighbour Joe Ward as 'a kind of poet too' (Heaney 1971, 660). Heaney himself ascribes to the notion of discovery through industry that is initiated by the 'reconcili-ation' between the pen and the spade in 'Digging' (Parker 1993, 63). Elmer Andrews's suggestion that '[i]t is the natural, easy movement, the precise rhythmic control of his father and grandfather that he particularly wishes to embrace' (Andrews 1988, 39) touches on the skill which separates an expert craftsman like Heaney's grandfather, '[n]icking and slicing neatly' (Heaney [1966] 1969, 14), or a painter whose brushstrokes 'split', 'hone' and 'slice' (Heaney [1966] 1969, 54) from the eager and inspired schoolchildren who, through lack of skill, manage only a 'blundering embrace of the free//Word' (Heaney [1966] 1969, 56). Like technique, craft has the power to produce the unwilled and the unexpected. But while technique, as a mysterious vatic process, originates from within and acts as a catalyst, craft is the product of action. The blacksmith in Heaney's early poem 'The Forge' (Heaney 1969, 19), for instance, exhibits a masterful carelessness that Heaney admires, and which is reminiscent of Hopkins's procedure as Heaney describes it in 'The Fire i' the Flint'. In contrast to Wordsworth's process, whereby the 'gentle flame/Provokes itself', in the case of Hopkins the 'fire i' the flint/Shows not till it be struck' (Heaney 1980, 79).

The high degree of forethought in Hopkins's process leads to poetry which is too 'forged' (Heaney 1980, 87), too much the product of 'a labour of shaping' (Heaney 1980, 88). In 'Feeling into Words', despite having speci-fied Hopkins as the 'in-fluence' whose aural quality first awakened his desire to write, Heaney's focus is on the high degree of craft in Hopkins's verse (Heaney 1980, 44), and in 'The Fire i' the Flint', he perceives a programmatic use of alliteration in Hopkins's poetry that he associates with craft rather than technique:

> The words are crafted together more than they are coaxed out of one another, and they are crafted in the service of an idea that precedes the poem, is independent of it and to which the poem is perhaps ulti-mately subservient. So much for the dark embryo. We are now in the realm of flint-spark rather than marshlight. 'Heaven-Haven' is conso-nantal fire struck by idea off language. The current of its idea does not fly the bound it chafes but confines itself within delightful ornamental channels.
>
> (Heaney 1980, 84)

This degree of craftedness – Hopkins's dedication to 'the pointed masonry of Anglo-Saxon verse' (Heaney 1980, 46) – removes the child-listener that Heaney depicted in 'Oracle' from the process entirely (Heaney 1980, 46). Rather than answering the nudge of the vatic impulse in hopes of 'delivering a poem of the first intensity out of its labour' (Heaney 1980, 117), Hopkins instead alienates the poem from the natural process of composition 'in the service of an idea that precedes' it. In 'Freedman', the student labouring to develop a literary ear is alienated from himself and '[s]ubjugated' (Heaney [1975] 2001, 56), and here, the poem itself, similarly detached and separated from the natural process of composition, is rendered 'subservient'. Either Hopkins chooses not to honour the preliterary element of his auditory imagination, or his use of the Germanic register is itself prescribed.

In 'The Fire i' the Flint', Heaney suggests that this directedness is in effect even at the earliest stage of Hopkins's composition. Unlike Yeats, another maker, Hopkins requires an element of making in order for him even to begin. As Heaney views it, Hopkins's preliterary imagination has to be instructed to create a poem. The Anglo-Saxon consonantal nature of his poetry is therefore not a natural extension of his aural imagination but is selected with a view to an end. Also unlike his view of Yeats, Heaney approaches his analysis of Hopkins's poetry from the completed poem backwards towards its inception, from 'the circumference of his art rather than from the centre of himself' (Heaney 1980, 79). Hopkins's use of the Germanic register is therefore not a genuine reflection of his preliterary voice. Because of the degree of directedness in Hopkins's poetry, the Germanic ceases to be aligned with the vatic impulse in Heaney's estimation. Using language that closely echoes his description of the technique of the water diviner, Heaney writes: 'Hopkins's consonants alliterate to maintain a design whereas Keats's release a flow' (Heaney 1980, 85).

By the mid-1970s, Heaney has outgrown the need for redress as a corrective in relation to his conflicting linguistic inheritances, and he is beginning to find it constrictive rather than enabling. The kind of highly 'disciplined' (Heaney 1980, 85) writing that Heaney encounters in Hopkins precludes the accidental and stifles opportunities for the linguistically 'risky or "chancy" successes' which Bernard O'Donoghue notes Heaney admires (O'Donoghue 1994, 101). Heaney repeatedly describes Hopkins's poetry in terms of confinement and constraint. 'Heaven-Haven' is 'fretted rather than fecund' (Heaney 1980, 84). It 'confines itself within delightful ornamental channels' (Heaney 1980, 84). Hopkins's 'sound and sense always aim to complement each other in a perfectly filled-in outline' and 'his poems are closer to being verbal relief-work than to being a receding, imploding vortex of symbol' (Heaney 1980, 87). Heaney describes his own early imitations of Hopkins as '"trial-pieces", little stiff inept designs in imitation of the master's fluent interlacing patterns, heavy-handed clues to the whole craft' (Heaney 1980, 45). But having found his voice and developed as a poet, a new constraint is evident in his poetry throughout *North*, where images of spaces in which to discovery freely can also be read as increasingly restrictive moulds. For

86   *Ruth Macklin*

example, Paul Scott Stanfield notes that in 'Viking Dublin: Trial Pieces', in which Heaney dwells on the image of the trial piece, the poem:

> only imitates improvisation ... for soon enough we see that the shifts of metaphor are not governed by whim. ... The criss-crossings of the pattern are both a cage – obviously suggestive of confinement – and a trellis which enables the plant to grow upward and outward.
>
> (emphasis original) (Stanfield 1995, 103)

With few exceptions, Heaney does not admire the 'unmoored' form of American verse, and he has no precedent for the tight lines he has been writing (Heaney [1999] 2000, xxii). Like Hopkins, Heaney's early work in the Group Sheets reveals an attraction to lyricism. But while for Hopkins the lyricism of a poet like Keats abandons 'itself to an unmanly and enervating luxury', Heaney desires a more mellifluous language and a traditional poetic form (Heaney 1980, 86). As he suggests to Frank Kinahan in a 1981 interview:

> the line and the life are intimately related; and that narrow line, that tight line, came out of a time when I was very tight myself. Especially the poems in North. I remember looking at them when I was just going to send them in and saying: This is a very habit-formed book – these little narrow lines. Can I open this? And I wrote out a couple of poems in long line, and the sense of constriction went; and when the constriction went, the tension went.
>
> (Kinahan and Heaney 1982, 411–412)

Alongside the cage that Stanfield points out there is evidence of Heaney's inclination towards the well-noted 'unbuttoning' that takes place between *North* and *Field Work* (O'Driscoll 2008, 160). Outlines such as the Viking trial pieces are 'provisional', as Rob Jackaman illustrates (Jackaman 2003, 169). The poem is barely and only somewhat superficially rescued from formlessness by its own 'cage/or trellis', the constricting form of the short-line stanza (Heaney [1975] 2001, 12). There is the image of the inscribed longship, 'buoyant' and 'migrant', and the narrator's 'longhand', which 'turns cursive, unscarfing' (Heaney [1975] 2001, 14). And along with what Stanfield calls the 'Joycean nets' in Part II, the final stanza's direct quotation from Synge's *The Playboy of the Western World* operates as a somewhat superficial return to an Irish concern, an afterthought which only just rescues the form from its own lyricism (Stanfield 1995, 103).

After writing a series of highly worked, shapely poems, Heaney abandons this form, and in Part II of *North*, the two registers vanish in favour of a more prosaic diction. His next volume, *Field Work* contains a sonnet he wrote at this time:

> when the cuckoo and the corncrake 'consorted at twilight', almost two years after we had landed, I gave in. I wrote at that moment, involuntarily, in 'smooth numbers' – iambic lines that were out of key with the

more constrained stuff I was doing at the time, the poems that would appear in North.

(O'Driscoll 2008, 198)

Like the experience of getting his 'feel into words' for the first time, writing these naturally lengthened lines and employing more relaxed diction restores a sense of rightness for Heaney. Technique and craft work together and the poem flows freely and in a form that redresses what has come before. Having challenged the English lyric he can continue to enact redress and can explore it in other ways, within the form of the sonnet.

Years later, when Heaney explores Clare's work in *The Redress of Poetry* his analysis is that of a mature poet who has moved past the concerns that Clare himself is grappling with. Heaney's reading of Clare is illuminating but it is no longer the particularised, intricate analysis of composition that his explorations yield in *Preoccupations*. While he remains grateful throughout his career that the vatic impulse continues to return, and anxious that someday it might not, the potentially disabling anxiety of how to use his voice as a linguistically marginalised poet has passed. His explorations and contemplations of the corrective power of redress, as a challenge, revision, or readjustment, have helped him get his 'feel into words' during a pivotal time in his life as a poet. And while his concerns may change, the prose remains an important lifelong locus of his inquiry into redress.

Works Cited

Andrews, Elmer (1988) *The Poetry of Seamus Heaney: All the Realms of Whisper*, Basingstoke: Macmillan.

Austen, Jane (2006) 'Sense and Sensibility', in *The Cambridge Edition of the Works of Jane Austen*, edited by Edward Copeland, Cambridge: Cambridge University Press, 1–431.

BBC (2008) '1969: British Troops Sent into Northern Ireland', *On This Day 1950–2005* (August 14, 1969), available: http://news.bbc.co.uk/onthisday/hi/dates /stories/august/14/newsid_4075000/4075437.stm [Accessed 22 September 2023].

Brandes, Rand (2009) 'Seamus Heaney's Working Titles: From "Advancements of Learning" to "Midnight Anvil"', in *The Cambridge Companion to Seamus Heaney*, edited by Bernard O'Donoghue, Cambridge: Cambridge University Press, 19–36.

Corcoran, Neil (1998) *The Poetry of Seamus Heaney: A Critical Study*, London: Faber.

Haffenden, John (1981) *Viewpoints: Poets in Conversation with John Haffenden*, London: Faber.

Heaney, Seamus ([1966] 1969) *Death of a Naturalist*, London: Faber.

Heaney, Seamus (1969) *Door into the Dark*, London: Faber.

Heaney, Seamus (1971) 'A Poet's Childhood', *The Listener*, November 11, 1971: 660–661.

Heaney, Seamus ([1972] 1973) *Wintering Out*, London: Faber.

Heaney, Seamus (1973) 'Poets on Poetry: Auden and Others', *The Listener*, 8 November: 629.

Heaney, Seamus ([1975] 2001) *North*, London: Faber.

88   Ruth Macklin

Heaney, Seamus (1979) *Field Work*, London: Faber.

Heaney, Seamus (1980) *Preoccupations: Selected Prose 1968–1978*, London: Faber.

Heaney, Seamus (1983) *Among Schoolchildren: A John Malone Memorial Lecture*, Belfast: John Malone Memorial Committee.

Heaney, Seamus (1987) *The Haw Lantern*, London: Faber.

Heaney, Seamus (1988) *The Government of the Tongue: The 1986 T. S. Eliot Memorial Lectures and Other Critical Writings*, London: Faber.

Heaney, Seamus ([1995] 1996) *The Redress of Poetry: Oxford Lectures*, London: Faber.

Heaney, Seamus (1997) 'Burns's Art Speech', in *Robert Burns and Cultural Authority*, edited by Robert Crawford, Edinburgh: Edinburgh University Press, 216–233.

Heaney, Seamus ([1999] 2000) *Beowulf*, London: Faber.

Heaney, Seamus (2008) '"Apt Admonishment": Wordsworth as an Example', *The Hudson Review*, 61 (1): 19–33.

Jackaman, Rob (2003) *Broken English/Breaking English: A Study of Contemporary Poetries in English*, London: Associated University Presses.

Kavanagh, Patrick (1967) *Collected Pruse*, London: MacGibbon and Kee.

Keats, John (1971) 'Letter to John Taylor February 27, 1818', in *Critical Theory Since Plato*, edited by Hazard Adams, New York: Harcourt Brace Jovanovich, 474.

Kerrigan, John (1992) 'Ulster Ovids', in *The Chosen Ground: Essays on the Contemporary Poetry of Northern Ireland*, edited by Neil Corcoran, Bridgend: Seren Books, 235–269.

Kinahan, Frank and Seamus Heaney (1982) 'An Interview with Seamus Heaney', *Critical Inquiry*, 8 (3): 405–414.

Leech, Geoffrey N (1969) *A Linguistic Guide to English Poetry*, New York: Longman.

Longley, Edna (1994) '*North*: "Inner Emigré" or "Artful Voyeur"?', in *The Art of Seamus Heaney*, edited by Tony Curtis, Chester Springs: Dufour Editions, 63–95.

Macklin, Ruth (2017) 'Seamus Heaney and the "Place of Writing": Technique as Evidence of Redress as a Construct', *Irish Studies Review*, 25 (1): 56–70.

McCafferty, Kevin (2010) '"[H]ushed and *Lulled* Full Chimes for *Pushed* and *Pulled*"', in *Varieties of English in Writing: The Written Word as Linguistic Evidence*, edited by Raymond Hickey, Philadelphia, PA: John Benjamins, 139–162.

Miłosz, Czesław (1983) *The Witness of Poetry*, Cambridge, MA: Harvard University Press.

Montague ([1961] 1977) *Poisoned Lands*, London: MacGibbon and Kee. Reprint, Dublin: Dolmen Press. Citations refer to the Dolmen edition.

O'Donoghue, Bernard (1994) *Seamus Heaney and the Language of Poetry*, London: Harvester Wheatsheaf.

O'Driscoll, Dennis (2008) *Stepping Stones: Interviews with Seamus Heaney*, London: Faber.

Parker, Michael (1993) *Seamus Heaney: The Making of the Poet*, Iowa City: University of Iowa Press.

Randall, James and Seamus Heaney (1979) 'An Interview with Seamus Heaney', *Ploughshares*, 5 (3): 7–22.

Shakespeare, William. 2002. *The Merchant of Venice*, in *The Complete Pelican Shakespeare*, edited by Stephen Orgel and A. R. Braunmuller, New York: Penguin, 285–323.

Stanfield, Paul Scott (1995) 'Facing *North* Again: Polyphony, Contention', in *Critical Essays on Seamus Heaney*, edited by Robert F. Garratt, New York: G. K. Hall, 97–109.

Yeats, W. B. (1961) *Essays and Introductions*, London: Macmillan.

5 'The Makings of a Music'
Musicality and Seamus Heaney's Prose

Ian Hickey

Seamus Heaney's prose has mainly been relegated to the function of providing a meta-commentary to the poetry, acting as a sort of supplementary feature to it. There have only been two full length studies of the prose to date – Michael Cavanagh's *Professing Poetry: Seamus Heaney's Poetics* and Eugene O'Brien's *Seamus Heaney as Aesthetic Thinker*. This in itself is interesting, as Heaney has written extensively in prose form. Prose writing is something that he constantly turned to throughout his writing life, and we find these works collected in *Preoccupations: Selected Prose 1968–1978, Place and Displacement: Recent Poetry of Northern Ireland, The Government of the Tongue: The 1986 T.S. Eliot Lectures and Other Writings, The Place of Writing, The Redress of Poetry: Oxford Lectures* and *Finders Keepers: Selected Prose 1971–2001*. To publish this amount of writing over a lifetime would be an achievement in itself, but to do so while being one of the most celebrated and lauded poets of the twentieth century, and indeed the twenty-first century, is testament to Heaney's dedication to writing. That he would also spend such a great amount of time writing prose, delivering lectures and writing critical work on other writer's is suggestive of an intensity to understand the craft, and himself, in a means outside the creative act of poetry. Prose allows Heaney to air his thoughts in more detail, to trace his insights into his poetic exemplars, and to get a sense of the world around him. Common to all of his prose work across the texts mentioned above is a reverent and fervent attention to poetic music. The musicality of words, their connection to feeling and the metrical span of those words across the page become emblematic of Heaney's approach – he consciously tunes the ear to the metrical patterns and the musicality of words, and his thinking on this is reflected in his prose.

Perhaps one of the most often quoted lines of Heaney's poetry is from 'Song' in *Field Work*: 'that moment when the bird sings very close/To the music of what happens' (Heaney 1979, 53). Indeed, *Seamus Heaney and The Music of What Happens* was the title of a recent BBC documentary charting Heaney's life, and these lines are also present in the Foreword to his first collection of prose *Preoccupations: Selected Prose 1969–1978*. Writing of the prose collected in this book, he outlines the following:

DOI: 10.4324/9781003456148-6

90   *Ian Hickey*

The longer pieces were written to be delivered from the podium so now and again that lecturing note creeps in. And if there is sometimes a strait-laced quality about the writing, that too is all part of 'the makings of a music', the slightly constricted utterance of somebody who underwent his academic rite of passage when practical criticism held great sway in the academy. Nevertheless, I am grateful for that discipline: as Finn McCool said in his time, the best music in the world is the music of what happens. We go on, of course, to blunder after the music of what might happen, a quest which requires confidants and mentors, and this book is a response to some who came to my assistance. A number of the essays are obviously a matter of 'breaking bread with the dead', an activity which W. H. Auden judged essential to the life of poetry. Others are just as clearly engagements with the achievements of the living; and others still are inspections of myself.

(Heaney 1980, 13–14)

From this short piece we can gather some intuition as to Heaney's sensibility when it comes to writing. He is aware of the register of the prose, swaying between dry academic criticism and at other times, a more personalised approach. Both approaches are successful in the collection but the musicality of Heaney's poetry is also gleaned from his 'confidants and mentors', both living and dead, acquaintances in life and through reading, sometimes both. The equation with Finn McCool that life mirrors music is important, as the different rhythms, patterns, experiences, approaches and interpretations of each of our lives vibrate to different beats, literally and metaphorically. That Heaney would associate music and experiences together in this fashion is in synecdoche to the act of writing poetry itself – where life and poetic metre (or lack of) can rhyme together in a harmonious relationship of implied meaning. The prosody of poetry is important to him and Angela Leighton has noted of the lines quoted from 'Song' above that they have 'often seemed the keynote of Heaney's work: not music which sounds for its own sake, lifting words into tunes, but rather a poetic song, which comes close up to the reality of the world, to the gritty or gravelly reality of fact' (Leighton 2015, 20). Heaney's poetry has tended to grasp at, and successfully capture, the events of his life, and our lives more generally as readers. It has swayed successfully to the music of what happens and the poetic music evoked by words.

However, the focus here is not primarily aimed at the events of Heaney's life chiming with that expressed in his poetry. My attention is aimed at musicality in terms of word choice, poetic form and tune. Heaney's attention to the musicality of poetry might owe something to T.S. Eliot's prose work, specifically 'The Music of Poetry'. Eliot writes of the necessity to create a unique metrical style, one that is learned from other poets but which is separate from imitation. He argues that the ear is tuned by the study of individual poems,

'The Makings of a Music' 91

and not the systems of poetry. During the first stages of beginning to write it is the ear that must be trained, not the selection of themes or words. In 'The Music of Poetry', Eliot makes this point clearly:

> Even in approaching the poetry of our own language, we may find the classification of metres, of lines with different numbers of syllables and stresses in different places, useful at a preliminary stage, as a simplified map of a complicated territory: but it is only the study, not of poetry but of poems, that can train our ear. It is not from rules, or by cold-blooded imitation of style, that we learn to write: we learn by imitation indeed, but by a deeper imitation than is achieved by analysis of style.
>
> (Eliot 1975, 107)

Eliot is writing here about English verse, and the English canon more specifically, but it does have some purchase on how Heaney may have begun to think about the musicality of poetry. He had read Eliot in detail while attending Queen's University, Belfast as a student and digested much of his poetry and prose there. We can draw many similarities between Heaney's thinking and Eliot's in terms of their approach to the musicality of poetry, but also in terms of the notion of tuning the ear. Of course, this poetic music is not garnered at the expense of meaning as Eliot rushes to remind us – 'the music of poetry is not something which exists apart from the meaning. Otherwise, we could have poetry of great musical beauty which made no sense, and I have never come across such poetry' (Eliot 1975, 110) – but it is something to which both pay sincere and detailed attention. If Eliot notes that the ear must be trained by reading poems, Heaney trained and strained his to Eliot's *The Waste Land*. In 'Learning from Eliot' in *Finders Keepers*, Heaney notes that at 'Queen's University I packed myself with commentaries and in particular advanced upon *The Waste Land* with what help I could muster in the library. I even read chunks of Jessie L. Weston's *From Ritual to Romance*. I began to hear the music and to attune myself, but chiefly I obeyed the directives of the commentaries and got prepared to show myself informed. Yet perhaps the most lasting influence from this time was Eliot's prose' (Heaney 2002, 33). In the following sections I will argue that Heaney's ear was tuned by his childhood experiences, his schooling and his attention to other poet's work. However, at this early stage I would like to point out that the illuminating moment that signalled the fine tuning of his poetic music was laid when he read Eliot's prose – it acts, much like the poetry of Hughes and Kavanagh in terms of image and content, as a passport towards creating a musicality.

Eliot's prose becomes a particular source of inspiration, a blueprint for the young Heaney, at university as he began collating the rhythms and cadences of his life and laying them down in verse form. Indeed, he writes in 'Learning from Eliot' that the 'auditory imagination', as Eliot terms it, has as much importance as the image and theme – there is a symbiotic relationship at play:

92   *Ian Hickey*

There I read and re-read 'Tradition and the Individual Talent', essays on 'The Metaphysical Poets', on Milton on Tennyson's *In Memoriam.* On the music of poetry. On why *Hamlet* doesn't make it as a play, as an objective correlative. But most important of all, perhaps, was a definition of the faculty which he called "the auditory imagination". This was "the feeling for syllable and rhythm, penetrating far below the conscious level of thought and feeling, invigorating every word; sinking to the most primitive and forgotten, returning to the origin and bringing something back... [fusing] the most ancient and civilized mentalities".

(Heaney 2002, 34)

It should come as no surprise that Heaney's poetic imagination revolves around this significant point of the auditory imagination and that his prose writing about the nature of his own writing, and that of other writers, generally involves an eye, and ear, tuned to the rhythms, cadences and music of their work. Eliot's lines on the auditory imagination could easily be transplanted into Heaney's prose and were obviously deeply influential on his writing style:

it is at least more nearly possible to distinguish the pleasure which arises from the noise, from the pleasure due to other elements, than with the verse of Shakespeare, in which the auditory imagination and the imagination of the other senses are more nearly fused, and fused together with the thought.

(Eliot 1975, 262)

Once we begin to read Heaney's thinking on poetry through this lens, it is near impossible not to see traces of it across his prose collections, and other uncollected articles and writings.

It would be disingenuous, and indeed incorrect, to assume that reading Eliot's prose was solely the catalyst for such a mode of thinking. However, Heaney's acknowledgment of Eliot's prose in terms of musicality is important. There are many others who led Heaney along this path such as Yeats, Lowell, Wordsworth and Hopkins, to mention but a few, but Eliot's thinking seems to stand out in its similarity to Heaney's own poetic interests. For example, the language and word choice of Heaney's prose mirrors that of Eliot's with his attention to the musicality of poetry in terms of poetic form. Consider for a moment Heaney's comments on Edwin Muir's poetry from 'Edwin Muir' in *Finders Keepers*:

Muir's music is a combination of primal song chant and the differentiated, alienated precisions of the modern world. There is a haulage job being done by the metre; the rhymes are like a system of pulleys over which the argument drags forward a positive meaning. And allied to this metrical vitality is a brisk diction which keeps the poem from indulging in longueurs or relishing its own effects.

(Heaney 2002, 249)

'The Makings of a Music'   93

The specific focus on metre and rhyme is suggestive of the musicality of the poetry and the soundings of the form that 'drags forward a positive meaning'. This sort of approach is shot through much of his prose work and extends as far back to his thinking as a young poet, even as far back as childhood. Two other prime exemplars in terms of their prose writing are Yeats and Hopkins. In *Autobiographies* Yeats writes about going to see the first showing of Henrik Ibsen's *A Doll's House* and being somewhat underwhelmed by the language Ibsen employed, as well as its tonal resonance. The lack of music in the language is what he finds problematic, not the content but the delivery of the content: 'I resented being invited to admire dialogue so close to modern educated speech that music and style were impossible' (Yeats 1995, 279). Hopkins' prose also mirrors this approach to language, and specifically that used in the creative endeavour. Hopkins, in a letter dated 15 February 1879, writes the following:

No doubt poetry errs on the side of oddness. I hope in time to have a more balanced and Miltonic style. But as air, melody, is what strikes me most of all in music and design in painting, so design, pattern or what I am in the habit of calling 'inscape' is what I above all aim at in poetry. Now it is the virtue of design, pattern or inscape to be distinctive and it is the virtue of distinctiveness to become queer. This vice I cannot have escaped.

(Hopkins 1980, 77)

That Eliot, Yeats and Hopkins, three major influences on Heaney, would use such language in their prose obviously had a deep impression on him. So often, as we will see throughout this chapter, Heaney consistently engages with the musical qualities of words, the cadence and rhythm of words and poetic metre in his prose.

Casting ourselves back to Heaney's first collection of prose, *Preoccupations: Selected Prose 1968–1978*, we can see this sort of thinking shot through the first essay, indeed the very first paragraph, 'Mossbawn'. The first memory from childhood that he brings to our attention is the sound of the water pump at the back of his house. He associates this sound with a word:

I would begin with the Greek word *omphalos*, meaning the naval, and hence the stone that marked the centre of the world, and repeat it, *omphalos, omphalos, omphalos*, until its blunt and falling music becomes the music of somebody pumping water at the pump outside our back door.

(Heaney 1980, 17)

For Heaney, the rhythmic vibrations of the word 'omphalos' connect with the ear to make a music that has a very real purchase on the lived experience. It is this interconnectedness between word and sound, between theme and musicality, word selection and rhythm, that is at the very centre of his

94   *Ian Hickey*

thinking. Music moves beyond what we could consider music performed with a musical instrument to create vibrations that resonate with the ear. Instead, Heaney sees words as having a musicality, something that connects with the metrical patterning of lines and stanzas and that allows for a certain beat to be created throughout a poem. Drawing on Harry White's thinking in *Music and the Irish Literary Imagination*, Eugene O'Brien notes that 'music allows for [the] unconscious, associative, and suggestive aspect of language to be enabled' (O'Brien 2016, 10). What we find in his prose writing is a poet very much in tune with, and thinking about, the act of writing. Ever open to opportunities and new avenues, Heaney recorded some his poems to the sound of music, or had musical interpretations of them delivered. In a wonderfully personal account, Meg Tyler details her attendance at, and introduction of, 'a performance of "Anything Can Happen", the result of a recent collaboration (2012) between the Arab-American composer, Mohammed Fairouz, and—why was I surprised—Seamus Heaney' (Tyler 2017, 160):

> The first time I heard the music accompanying the poems was the night of the performance. I wasn't sure how it would all work. The idea of poems set to music unnerved me. Poetry was a sanctuary, a place of quiet, where the music I heard was in my head or sometimes came to me through a poets voice. At the beginning of the show, I stood up before the audience and gave a short spiel about the poems, then I sat back and let the occasion unfurl. By evenings end, I was made to think anew of the way one art form can help illuminate another, how the blending of two creates a third form. What the collaboration achieved was in a nutshell one of the things I most admire about Heaney. He brought together languages and the sensibilities attached to them—English and Arabic—into a co-habitable space. The work teaches us how these two different cultural shapes and forces can find consonance amid the dissonance.
>
> (Tyler 2017, 160)

It is not exactly this sort of musicality that I have in mind in this chapter, though it does emphasise the rhythms and patterns of poetry that are conducive to musical performance.

The focus here will not be to use the poetry as a guiding force to offer examples, but rather to connect the common strands across his prose writing where he discusses notions of musicality. Little attention has been paid to how Heaney tunes his ear to the words being put on the page, to his negotiation of word and sound as he details in his prose writing. Returning to his essays on Hopkins, Yeats and Wordsworth, Heaney consistently turns towards the musicality of their poetry. He generally moves beyond the implied meaning, or interpreted meaning, and focuses on the musicality of their work. The same image is used across his prose writing when discussing musicality too – that of the tuning fork. In 'The Makings of a Music: Reflections on Wordsworth

'The Makings of a Music' 95

and Yeats', he comments on a section of Wordsworth's *Prelude* that the image of a river in the poem means that 'the passage flows, shifts through times and scenes, mixes, drifts and comes to rest with the child composed into a stilled consciousness, a living tuning fork planted between wood and hill, bronzed in sunset' (Heaney 1980, 70). In this sense, the musicality of the poem mimics the undulating flow of the river whereby both form and content interconnect.

In 'The Fire I' the Flint: Reflections on the Poetry of Gerard Manley Hopkins', the image of the tuning fork appears again in the context of his discussion of Shakespeare's *Timon of Athens*, where in the use of the word 'slipp'd' Heaney notes that it 'acts like a tuning fork for the music and movement of the whole piece' (Heaney 1980, 80). Again, in *Stepping Stones*, Heaney's book of interviews with Dennis O'Driscoll, that phrase is referenced when he notes that he

> sat down and deliberately took the hammer to my own scrap and tried to beat sense and shape out of the loss of friends like Sean Armstrong and Louis O'Neill. That was the one time when Yeats was an actual tuning fork for a poem I was writing. "Casualty" commemorates the eel fisherman Louis O'Neill – whom I've mentioned – and I was counting out the metre to keep in step with "The freckled man who goes/To a grey place on a hill/In grey Connemara clothes".
>
> (O'Driscoll 2009, 194)

Unsurprisingly, this trope crops up again in *Stepping Stones* when Heaney is talking about the poem 'The Pitchfork'. The section where he discusses the physical activity of lifting hay with the fork, that the action creates a music, is reminiscent of his opening lines in *Preoccupations* – the connections between the act and the sound, the word and the rhythm, the form and content are constantly undulating on the page and the poet's mind:

> I loved handling the fork and the rake, their lightness and rightness in the hand, their perfect suitedness to the jobs they had to do. It meant that the work of turning a swathe, for example, was its own reward; angling the shaft and the tines so that the hay turned over like a woven fabric – that was an intrinsically artistic challenge. Tasty work, as they say. Using the pitchfork was like playing an instrument. So much so that when you clipped and trimmed the head of a ruck, the strike of the fork on the hay made it a kind of tuning fork.
>
> (O'Driscoll 2009, 336)

Beyond the clear resonances in the lines quoted above that Heaney has an ear tuned to the linguistic resonances and cadences that make up the language, the clear precision and execution of selecting words that offer such a pattern is demonstrative of the quality of his work. Of course, anybody who reads the poetry will immediately recognise this, but the fact that he is so consciously

96   Ian Hickey

aware and deliberate in his prose makes that execution all the sweeter when we encounter the musicality of his work. That he would consistently turn towards the same image of the tuning fork some thirty years after the publication of *Preoccupations* is important to consider. It implies that his thinking on the importance of musicality remains a central part of how he thinks about writing. It also emphasises the notion that the foundations of how he thinks about poetry laid down in 'Mossbawn' remain the same. Even if the eye and ear develop throughout his writing life, the bedrock of his approach does not change – it is the music and rhythm of the work that endures.

The image of the tuning fork is a good metaphor to carry the discussion here, and the attention to poetic music in Wordsworth and Yeats draws Heaney to think about the ways in which the poetry that both writer's read in their youth 'laid down certain structures in their ear' (Heaney 1980, 62). In his lecture on Yeats and Wordsworth, delivered as the first Kenneth Allott Memorial Lecture in Liverpool University in 1978, and collected in *Preoccupations*, he closes with the revealing lines that 'poetry depends for its continuing efficacy upon the play of sound not only in the ear of the reader but also in the ear of the writer' (Heaney 1980, 78). It is this precise preoccupation with the musical qualities of words that interests him – their lasting sway aurally in the creator and receiver. It should come as no surprise that Heaney would turn towards such musical and metrically astute poets such as Wordsworth and Hopkins, for example, or be interested in Yeats's recitation of his lines. What interested Heaney about Yeats's performance of his poetry was that the stresses and emphasis garnered in the performance easily adapted to the mouth but may have seemed stressed on the page. Elizabeth Butler Cullingford, writing of Yeats, makes the point that his method of composition 'involved what Schuchard calls "eerie poetic murmuring", began with a sound scheme' (Butler Cullingford 1996, 168). The oral and aural qualities of poetry would have had an impact on Heaney, so much so that we can trace the almost incantatory cadences and rhythms of his work back to his childhood. If, as I have noted earlier in this paragraph, Heaney acknowledges the structures of Wordsworth's and Yeats's ear were tuned by the poets that they read, I would argue that Heaney's ear was first tuned to the nursery rhymes and songs that he was exposed to during his childhood.

If the themes and images of much of the poetry were inherited in childhood – in areas surrounding Mossbawn, Bellaghy, Magherafelt – so too is the auditory imagination. In an article entitled 'Encounters with Poetry', written for the Poetry Book Society, Heaney makes the point that the ear is tuned to poetry, very much like searching for the right frequency. He states that this tuning occurred at school, in the lecture hall and through hearing other poets read their work. These are important milestones in the development of a poetic sensibility, but he makes the telling point that before that

> there was a period when verse of an unofficial sort was absorbed entirely un-selfconsciously, when the ear attuned itself unthinkingly to what James Joyce called "the rite words in the rote order", to the speech

'The Makings of a Music' 97

of Northern Ireland rigged and jigged and rhymed for effect, the kind of flotsam and jetsam that blows in one ear and out the other in every childhood, but that finally ends up lodged between the ears of the adult.

(Heaney n.d.)

He gives specific examples of these rhymes such as the following: 'The praties are boiling/And that's a fine joke/For the herrings they're coming/In Doherty's boat' and 'Too late, too late, shall be the cry,/The Bellaghy bus goes sailing by' (Heaney n.d.). While these are childish rhymes, they do get under the skin of the lilt and metre that is a central feature of writing poetry. They offer localised images, the Bellaghy bus for example, and create a flowing, metrical pattern of rhyme and rhythm that reflects local speech. These examples are not just remembered in that article, but also take up a significant place in *Preoccupations* in 'Mossbawn'. The section from 'Mossbawn' that deals with this is called 'Rhymes' and in it Heaney remembers the localised rhymes of his childhood – these in many ways become a poetry in motion as each rhyme had a response. Terming these as nursery rhymes here seems sensical, but in Heaney's imagination and perception they are poetry (Heaney 1980, 26). An example of these rhymes follows below:

Up the long ladder and down the short rope
To hell with King Billy and God bless the Pope.
To which the answer was:
Up with King William and down with the Pope
Splitter splatter holy water
Scatter the Paypishes every one
If that won't do
We'll cut them in two
And give them a touch of the-
Red, white and blue.
To which the answer was:
Red, white and blue
Should be torn up in two
And sent to the devil
At half-past two.
Green, white and yellow
Is a decent fellow.

(Heaney 1980, 25)

There is a childishness to these rhymes. There is also a sectarian element to them that Heaney acknowledges children would 'fling at one another' (Heaney 1980, 25). However, to my mind the most important of these rhymes to the Heaney canon comes in the form of a rhyme that involves digging for potatoes using a spade which obviously has connections with the first poem in his first collection, 'Digging', and which would become a central metaphor throughout his poetic life up until the final collection *Human Chain*: 'Are

98   *Ian Hickey*

your praties dry/And are they fit for digging?/Put in your spade and try,/Says Dirty-Faced McGuigan' (Heaney 1980, 24). It is important to acknowledge the imagery and the rhyme scheme here, elementary at best but a strong, forging pattern for the later Heaney's poetic imagination when he began writing poetry seriously. While these rhymes may not be overly respectful and may even be distasteful in some quarters, they are specifically childish in their nature with Heaney noting himself that 'they constitute a kind of poetry, not very respectable perhaps, but very much alive on the lips of that group of schoolboys' (Heaney 1980, 24). They are a kind of poetry that tuned Heaney's ear to the imagery and cadence of what would influence his poetry as he moved into adulthood – he mentions that many of these rhymes were recited during the ages of eight or nine. They are part of the spoken word nature of poetry, elevating it from the page and worshipping the oral and aural qualities of the words. They are, to return to Heaney's lines in 'Encounters with Poetry', 'a proof, given at the very first level of the poetic operation, of just how effective the rite words in the rote order can be' (Heaney n.d.). This sort of thinking was laid down in Heaney's imaginative work from a young age and tuned his ear to the rhythms of poetry before he encountered it in the classroom, in the lecture hall, shared it with friends, and read other poets' work. Given that these rhymes were remembered in adulthood is also significant as it shows the lasting impact that they had on his imagination. The foundation notes of the ear were tuned during these years of childhood and resonate with Heaney as a poet in adulthood.

The connection in childhood to the linguistic patterning of poetic music extends further than this. We might also consider Heaney's exposure to music and song at home in terms of his mother singing and listening to traditional Irish music. Writing of lyric poetry and music in Heaney's work, Simon B. Kress makes the point that

> the word *music* and its siblings – *song, chorus, rhythm, note,* etc. – appear throughout Heaney's poetry and criticism. Attending to the role music plays in Heaney's poetics is crucial to understanding his work. Music intersects with the central elements of Heaney's work – place, politics, the public voice, the body, the folk, Ireland – marking both its aspirations and its limits.
>
> (Kress 2021, 157)

This suggestion is apt in the context of Heaney's friendship with musicians like David Hammond and Seán O'Riada, for example. As well as that, poems like 'At the Wellhead' and 'The Given Note' display his interest in music and his celebration of it. To return to Heaney's childhood again, it is pertinent to my argument here that the ear was tuned to an interest in musicality during these years, an ear that matured as he grew older. While *Stepping Stones* is a book of interviews with the poet, it is worth noting that the book was created not in the traditional sense of conducting an interview through talking, but

'The Makings of a Music' 99

through writing. In the illuminating *The Letters of Seamus Heaney*, edited by Christopher Reid, we get a flavour of the back and forth process of *Stepping Stones* in letters sent to Dennis O'Driscoll. In one dated as 23 February 2004, Heaney writes that 'I didn't get back to the interview until to-day. Did another few pages on the Nobel subject and hope to-morrow to dip into the "politics" section' (Heaney 2023, 609). In another letter dated 26 March 2002 to O'Driscoll, Heaney explains that there was a decision to dedicate three months to each collection and that he doesn't

> want to get behind with our three month to a book programme, but on the other hand don't want you to be overloading yourself with that formidable task. The amount of thought and note-taking and ordering and re-ordering that went into the questions so far has been immense.
> (Heaney 2023, 571)

The interview was conducted through email which adds a sense of a prose-like nature to the responses. It also means that Heaney's pen and mind hones the narrative and avoids any momentary slips of the tongue. We are exposed to a controlled, certified and selective collection of memories in *Stepping Stones* – much like prose itself, and quite the opposite of speech which cannot be deleted once spoken.

Focusing on music then becomes a central feature of many of the discussions that take place in terms of the various collections of poetry, but also Heaney's early years. He makes the point in the book to O'Driscoll that he remembers his mother singing nationalist ballads like Boolavogue and Who Fears to Speak of 98 among many 'old school songs, things like 'Loch Lomand', and others she remembered from barn dances in her younger days' (O'Driscoll 2009, 135). Close to home was a blind neighbour Rosie Keenan who lived a few fields over from the Heaney's. She was a contemporary of his mother's that he would often hear playing music as he passed her house, or who would visit the Heaneys to play her violin or sing. There is something poetic about the act of playing an instrument while being blind, the natural flow and trust in the hand, the tune being guided by the ear rather than the eye. Maybe this is what resonates with Heaney the poet, and what intrigued Heaney the child – it is much akin to writing in this regard. She would visit the Heaney's and play 'Irish dance tunes mostly, jigs and reels. Thomas Moore songs. So her visit would turn into a little home concert. She made that musical dimension a living thing for us' (O'Driscoll 2009, 367). That the Heaneys, and indeed Heaney himself, had such an interest in music is interesting considering the house itself was not musical. When the family moved from Mossbawn to Bellaghy, a second-hand piano became a part of the furniture and was rolled out if people came for a party (O'Driscoll 2009, 367). Heaney had no major skills on the piano because he was attending St. Columb's College as a boarder at the time. Instead he was more of a witness to music, listening rather than partaking in the performance.

100   *Ian Hickey*

That being said, these frames of reference and the inheritances of these musical traditions and exposures during his younger years obviously had a major impact on his sensibility. He notes that his interest in music and concert going 'lapsed' (O'Driscoll 2009, 368) when the focus changed to poetry. This is the very crux of Heaney's creative, musical impulse. It transcends the musical instrument and makes the pen an instrument where words themselves take on a musical quality. We might look towards his admiration for John McGahern's writing as an example of this. The lapsed approach to music and concert going broadens out to the cadence of words and what Heaney recognises in writing as being musical. His connection to McGahern was not simply because both grew up in rural backgrounds, McGahern in Leitrim, nor the themes or subject of his novels and short stories. It was the register of the notes that McGahern's words struck on the page that caught Heaney's ear. He makes the point to O'Driscoll that

> I felt closer to McGahern not because of the rural background and subject matter but because of his register, his distinctive rhythm. The undertone is important, the melancholy of his music. Cadence was as important to his sentences as content, maybe more important.
>
> (O'Driscoll 2009, 251)

I would argue that the same is true of Heaney's poetry – though I would put the musicality on an equal par with that of the content, both pulling and pushing the ear and imagination in tandem. Heaney's poetic form is calculated and well-thought out and springs from his exposure to music throughout his life – whether poetic, songlike or instrumental.

If Heaney felt closer to McGahern's music than he did to the narrative of the novels themselves, then we can begin to see clearly how he thought about writing. Writing, the physical words printed on the page, lifts off the page and extends to the ear. In his Nobel Lecture 'Crediting Poetry', it is all the more significant that Heaney speaks about listening to the radio as a child, tuning it in to find the right frequency to hear multiple dialects, languages and intonations as the dial swept across the frequencies:

> I grew familiar with the names of foreign stations, with Leipzig and Oslo and Stuttgart and Warsaw and, of course, with Stockholm. I also got used to hearing short bursts of foreign languages as the dial hand swept round from BBC to Radio Eireann, from the intonations of London to those of Dublin, and even though I did not understand what was being said in those first encounters with the gutturals and sibilants of European speech, I had already begun a journey into the wideness of the world beyond. This in turn became a journey into the wideness of language.
>
> (Heaney 1995, 11)

'The Makings of a Music' 101

His recollection of the 'gutturals' and 'sibilants' of the different speech patterns is paradigmatic of poetry – one that emphasises a metrical pattern of words in, oftentimes, a very small space to carry both a feeling and theme. In other words, the words tune themselves to the theme and not the other way around. The musicality of the words must match, even go beyond, the very theme that they are addressing. In his Oxford lecture delivered on Dylan Thomas in November 1991, collected as 'Dylan the Durable?: On Dylan Thomas', in *The Redress of Poetry*, Heaney writes of the oral qualities of poetry and Thomas' incantatory performances of poetry. He connects Thomas with a sort of Orphic prowess, singing his poems to the crowd. Of course this connection to Orpheus by Heaney is important as there is something of Orpheus in Heaney too. What Heaney writes about Thomas and Orpheus in the closing pages of that piece is also true of himself, especially when we think of Orpheus' appearance in 'Route 110', the central sequence to *Human Chain*. Ranging the discussion between Thomas, Virgil, Rilke and Plato, Heaney expertly draws us towards the complexity of Orpheus as an image of poetic creation. Writing of Virgil and Rilke's thinking on Orpheus he notes:

> [T]heir treatments emphasize the truth-to-life-and-death in the story and they abstract meanings from the drama of Eurydice that are variously sombre or symbolic. Thus, from one perspective, Orpheus's trip to the land of the dead and his initially successful bid to have Eurydice released from the underworld can represent the ability of art—poetry, music, language—to triumph over death; yet from another perspective, Orpheus's fatal backward look must equally represent "the failure of art before the ultimate reality of death"—or, to put it in Charles Segal's more drastic formulation, the loss of Eurydice expresses "the intransigence of reality before the plasticity of language".
>
> (Heaney 1996, 144)

This is the complexity of art and both angles are true of the creative endeavour. Art triumphs over death and a prime example of this is the fact that we are still reading, examining and enjoying the body of work that Heaney has left behind. The other argument also holds sway because the 'plasticity of language' allows us to bend and shape reality to suit our own artistic or personal needs. Indeed, Orpheus is still recognised today but transported into different contexts and arenas. That being said, what I am interested in here is Heaney's association of art with 'poetry, music, language'. This is the main endeavour of his work. It is the very definition of his poetic practice – the combination of poetry, which is made up of music and language, to create a finished piece of writing. We must think beyond music performed with an instrument and begin to think of it simply as a rhythm, sound, cadence or vibration caused by the words said aloud, or in our head. Without all three (poetry, music, language), then the poem or piece of prose does not deliver.

102 Ian Hickey

Orpheus also appears as an example in 'Orpheus in Ireland: On Brian Merriman's *The Midnight Court*' whereby the recurring image of the tuning fork appears again in Heaney's criticism. It is not only the narrative of Merriman's poem that particularly attracts Heaney, but it is also the metrical pattern and poetic form that he pays attention to: 'the true motive force is the couplet which gives the poem its metrical form and its distinctive music' (Heaney 1996, 52). After quoting from a section of the poem in Irish, he notes of the lines that they are not entirely original, nor do they establish anything particularly innovative. His attraction to them is that they 'establish a melody. They strike a tuning fork and immediately a whole orchestra of possibility comes awake in the poet's ear and in the language itself' (Heaney 1996, 52). Again, it is difficult not to acknowledge the precise and consistent attention that he pays towards poetic form, metre and musicality in poetry, or the recurrence of that image of the tuning fork some seventeen years after the publication of *Preoccupations*. It is as if the search for a line lies in the search for a particular prosody, a particular tune that burrows into the mind through the ear. In a letter dated 28 November 2009, Heaney writes to Thomas McCarthy on the latter's *The Last Geraldine Officer*. Beyond his admiration for the collection, Heaney's focus hones in on the tune of McCarthy's words, their specific musicality:

> the pillars of meditative stanzaic narrative/reminiscence at the start and finish have a beautiful cello tone to them, but a cello that can play woodnotes and wartones, as it were, can tune eros and Eire, and can stand like unbroken columns, with their rhyme and rumination.
>
> (Heaney 2023, 739)

For Heaney, the shape of a poem adds a physical structure but the metrical music of what happens in those lines adds flavour. What we find in Heaney's prose writing is a conscious endeavour to understand and articulate the practicality and technicalities of producing a musical poetry, one that is in touch with the sonic rhythms of speech, dialect, place and other poetry.

We find a particularly good example of this in 'The Jayne Lecture: Title Deeds: Translating a Classic', later reworked into an edited version named 'Thebes via Toombridge: Retitling *Antigone*', where Heaney writes of the hunger strikes in the Maze prison and the death of one of those strikers, Francis Hughes. He outlines that it was his endeavour to write a version of *Antigone* that would have some purchase on the contemporary moment because the play had become somewhat stifled by 'commentary and analysis' (Heaney 2004b, 426). In order to reinvigorate the play and breathe new life into it he does not just take the play out of its context and rework it into a Northern Irish one. Although that is one of the major features of Heaney's writing in terms of culture, identity and history as it allows us to understand ourselves in a clearer way from a more European vantage point, it is not the sole tool that adds new life to this already much translated piece of classical literature. By naming his version of *Antigone The Burial at Thebes* Heaney universalises the notion of death and suffering, while at the same time arguing that life is what is important, as well as our human connection to each other. By placing the word 'burial' in the title of the play Heaney notes that:

> it is a word that has not yet been entirely divorced from primal reality, because it recalls to us our final destiny as members of the species, it also reminds us, however subliminally, of the solemnity of death, the sacredness of life and the need to allow in every case the essential dignity of the human creature. Wherever you come from, whatever flag is draped on the coffins of your dead, the word "burial" carries with it something of your *dúchas*.
>
> (Heaney 2004b, 426)

Beyond the obvious connotation that this has to Northern Irish politics, and its connection with the death of over 3,500 people during the thirty-year period of the conflict known as 'The Troubles', what we find Heaney addressing in the article before making this point is music. It is not just the act of bringing a new context and audience to Antigone that Heaney is focused on, or that he believes will be the strength of the play, it is the musical quality of the words themselves:

> In poetry, we only believe what we hear. *Antigone* is poetic drama, but commentary and analysis had dulled it. I wanted to do a translation that would be true to the original in so far as it would be as much musical score as dramatic script, one that actors could speak as plainly or intensely as the occasion demanded, but one that still kept faith with the ritual formality of the original. I have written elsewhere about the way the metre of *Caoineadh Airt Uí Laoghaire* provided a tuning fork that got me started on the first speeches between Antigone and Ismene.
>
> (Heaney 2005, 14)

Some of Heaney's most exciting prose comes when he is talking about his own work. We might notice that he again uses the image of the tuning fork when talking about word selection and poetic music. Beyond the implied thematic implications of the play he is drawing us towards the importance of the musicality of the words. His preoccupation seems to be how the words actually make us feel when we hear them, whether spoken aloud, performed on stage or in our heads while reading. That it was the metre of *Caoineadh Airt Uí Laoghaire* that set Heaney off on the first speeches is important. It was the sound of words and their metrical beat that influenced him to get those first speeches going, and not just the content. A false note in a song can be easy to distinguish and the same can be said of poetry. What the eye can miss, the ear can see. In this sense, the placement of words, the selection of words above others, becomes a driving force for the writing of good poetry in Heaney's poetic practice.

104   *Ian Hickey*

Returning to the Jayne lecture offers us an insight into the coherent and conscious vibrations of language that Heaney was engaging with when he was writing *The Burial at Thebes*. When he first recognised the tone that the translation would take, that of *Caoineadh Art Uí Laoghaire*, the prosody came as if out of the blue – 'Then suddenly, as if from nowhere, I heard the note. Theme and tune coalesced. What came into my mind, or more precisely, into my ear, were the opening lines of a famous eighteenth-century Irish poem, called in the original *Caoineadh Airt Ui Laoghaire*':

> Mo ghrá go daingean thu!
> Lá dá bhfaca thu
> Ag ceann tí an mhargaidh,
> Thug mo shúil aire duit,
> Thug mo chroí taitneamh duit,
> Deélaíos om charaid leat
> I bhfad ó bhaile leat.
> (Heaney 2004b, 423)

The ear connects with the theme for Heaney and this is something that is resonant throughout his writing. Some examples of this are the constrained, tight lines of the bog poems in *North* where these narrow lines and stanzas act like drills, digging downwards into history, culture and identity, among other issues. Likewise, the *terza rima* form becomes a significant feature of *Station Island* and many later collections such as the 'Squarings' sequence in *Seeing Things* and is used throughout *Human Chain*. The lines of the later poetry are also longer than many of those poems that we find in *North*, for example, and so the expansiveness of Heaney's thematic vision is reflected in poetic form. That *terza rima* form, or Heaney's variation of it, is significant because Richard Rankin Russell draws us towards the notion that it is the 'form for last things' (Russell 2016, 363), and therefore, the structure, form and music of the poem become connected with the thematic impulses. While scholars may draw us towards this notion, Heaney was outlining these ideas in his prose work from as early as *Preoccupations* and beforehand when the pieces had been published in newspapers and journals, or delivered as lectures. What I am getting at here is the very considered approach that Heaney takes and which he makes us distinctly aware of in his prose work.

To continue our focus on his writing on *The Burial at Thebes* reinforces this point and shows us the specifics of his attention to his craft (Heaney 2004b, 424–426). Of course, there is always something eerily unconscious about the formation of literature. Feeding the unconscious over a lifetime of reading perfectly placed him to conjure up the right metre, almost serendipitously: 'the listening posts of the unconscious had been attending all along and had come up with exactly the right register' (Heaney 2004b, 423). This is the very crux of creativity, the momentary flash of illumination that springs from the unconscious. But, as Heaney draws us towards in his prose writing

'The Makings of a Music' 105

that flash needs steady honing and crafting. Something that inspires his steadied, crafted approach is Yeats's own drafts of poems that were constantly drafted and redrafted. The inspiration was met with pen to mould the idea, and much the same can be said of Heaney too. For example, Heaney notes of the metrical pattern of *The Burial at Thebes* that

> the three-beat line established a tune that I could carry, and that the sisters could carry. And with a first tune established, it was easy enough to play variations. The speeches of the chorus, for example, almost spoke themselves in an alliterating four-beat line, one that echoed very closely the metre of Anglo-Saxon poetry.
>
> (Heaney 2004b, 425)

He also goes on to note that 'the traditional iambic pentameter, with its conventional tee-tum, tee-tum, tee-tum, seemed right for Creon, who must in every sense hold the line, so I tuned his speeches to a fairly regular blank verse form' (Heaney 2004b, 425). Again, writing of the specifics of poetic form and musicality he comments that 'Antigone rises to her final heroic utterances, I moved from trimeter toward pentameter and tried to make the pitch of the lines rise with her' (Heaney 2004b, 426). It should come as no surprise to us that this level of attention to metre is present in the poetry, but what is interesting is that Heaney consistently likens it to music – words and phrases like 'pitch', 'tee-tum, tee-tum', 'three-beat line' and 'four-beat line' all convey the attentive musical qualities of the work here. That this is consciously at work, and that Heaney uses the language of music to articulate his points is all the more emblematic of his poetic approach. The imbrication of text and sound, word and vibration, becomes central to Heaney's poetic music.

This close attention to form is not coincidental when we consider the environment that Heaney grew up in, the schooling he received at St. Columb's and Queen's University, Belfast, and his poetic influences. Throughout his prose he is reverting back to his childhood and the past at different stages. Those formative years are when many of the major themes, interests and tunes of Heaney's work became embedded in the psyche. The farming background, the rural images, the multiple identities that he encountered in the local area such as the two religious traditions of Catholic and Protestant, but also elements of pre-Christian Ireland and Viking remnants along the river Bann encourage the adult Heaney to create a poetry reflective it. In 'Belfast' from *Preoccupations* he writes about the education system informing the voices that influenced his creative endeavours. Those voices, as he terms them in that essay, are those of an Irish and English heritage – there is a dual influence at work here that acts in synecdoche of the very parameters of his identity, but also the poetry that he writes:

> [O]ne half of one's sensibility is in a cast of mind that comes from belonging to a place, an ancestry, a history, a culture, whatever one wants

106   *Ian Hickey*

to call it. But consciousness and quarrels with the self are the result of what Lawrence called 'the voices of my education'. Those voices pull in two directions, back through the political and cultural traumas of Ireland, and out towards the urgencies and experience of the world beyond it. At school I studied the Gaelic literature of Ireland as well as the literature of England.

(Heaney 1980, 35)

This very specific, broad education and exposure to different literatures encourages Heaney to engage with the multiple, varied and often opposing voices of literature. Indeed, he would be influenced by such writers as Hopkins, Yeats, Shakespeare, Kavanagh, Eliot, Wordsworth, Keats, Stevie Smith and Ledwidge. What we can see here is a complex variation of voices, tones and themes that all of these poets embody from Elizabethan, Romantic and twentieth century writing. Of course, Heaney was widely influenced by poetry from Eastern Europe, classical literature and America, such as Mandelstam, Brodsky, Lowell, Roethke, Virgil and Dante, but the impact of his schooling to enable him to engage with literature from across the political and religious divide from a young age is imperative to his poetic development. Even his exposure to Virgil's *Aeneid* in school by Father McGlinchey is something that remains with him. This education, like all education, first began at home and Heaney points out his godmother, his aunt Sarah, known as Sally, as being a major influence on him. It is all the more interesting that it was English literature that she exposed him to at a young age, the likes of Thomas Hardy and Rudyard Kipling:

I was close to her, and when I showed some academic promise she kept me in view. It was in her house I got a feel for books – she had a bookcase with sets of Hardy and Kipling that she'd bought as a young teacher, and it was always strange to see my own initials on the inside flyleaf of all of them: "S. Heaney, 1925".

(O'Driscoll 2009, 26)

This sort of reading and approach set a trajectory for Heaney in later years to make a music that chimes with the stresses and strains of his literary encounters during his youth.

As has been mentioned earlier in this chapter, perhaps the greatest and most influential of these encounters is with the work of W.B. Yeats, with whom Heaney has been much likened and even compared with. His attention to the musicality of Yeats's work lies in the achievement of syntax, melody and poetic form. Of course, the content of the poetry is also deeply influential but when Heaney writes about Yeats there is always a draw towards the older poet's musicality. For example, in 'The Place of Writing: W.B. Yeats and Thoor Ballylee' from *The Place of Writing*, Heaney makes the point that the political and cultural climate of the early twentieth century forces him

'The Makings of a Music'   107

to create a music that reflects and refracts that environment. While Yeats may have been writing himself into future history, and indeed the political actions of the period with poems like 'Easter 1916' and 'September 1913', or through the establishment of the Abbey Theatre in order to uplift and implore a spirited nationalism, Heaney doesn't seem to think in that same way. Instead, Heaney makes that point that the first purpose of poetry should be to 'satisfy a need in the poet' (Heaney 1989, 25). This need is not one that articulates a point, nor is it one that compels others to act, as the case may be in Yeats's writing. It is poetic form and musicality that will bring about a sense of peace and satisfaction amidst the chaos of the surrounding world:

> The achievement of a sufficient form and the release of a self-given music have a justifying effect within his life. And if the horizons inside which that life is being lived are menacing, the need for the steadying gift of finished art becomes all the more urgent.
>
> (Heaney 1989, 25)

What Heaney is writing about Yeats here is equally applicable to his own approach, his own way of viewing art. It is the finished product, the labour of creation and the musicality that the words create that is the imperative behind the poetry. It is not just the selection of the right words to convey meaning, but the selection of the right words in the right order that spring a musicality to the piece. This is something that Heaney admires about Yeats's writing and which sends us back to his comments in 'Belfast' about the different voices of his education becoming beacons to follow. He was tasked with writing the Introduction to *W.B. Yeats: Selected Poems* for Faber and Faber and in this piece we not only get an idea of Yeats's poetry in a broad sense but also an understanding of Heaney's mindset. He comments that 'reading Yeats, we are under the sway of a voice that offers both expansiveness and containment' (Heaney 2004a, xvi), something which is also true of Heaney's own work in the contained poems of the earlier work and the more expansive, numinous, lighter poems from *Seeing Things* onwards. However, beyond the importance of the voice here, which we could argue that Heaney sides with in his own poetic career, is his focus on the melody of poetry – the musicality that it offers: 'to string the sentence out with reinforced syntactical effect over a sequence of rhymes and line-endings. The poem is a written melody as much as it is the formulation of aims and hopes' (Heaney 2004a, xvi). Through Heaney's writing on Yeats we might begin to see the very crux of his own approach to poetry. In Heaney analysing Yeats's work, we find something of him being transplanted into that criticism that is reflective of his own artistic impulses – specifically the necessity of musicality in poetry.

Both Heaney and Yeats won the Nobel Prize for literature, Heaney in 1995 and Yeats in 1923. It is apt that the end of this chapter connects two of Ireland's greatest poets together, not in terms of what their poetry means, expresses or achieves, but because both paid such close attention to the art

108 *Ian Hickey*

of poetry. Both poets articulate a response to the creative practice that places the musicality of the words, the rhythms of words as a major factor in the achievement of good poetry. This musicality is something that followed Heaney throughout his life and that he constantly engaged with. The seeds of his interest in poetic music were planted in childhood, sprouted in adolescence and rooted in adulthood. Heaney focuses on 'what kinds of noise assuage him, what kinds of music pleasure or repel him, what messages the receiving stations of his senses are happy to pick up from the world around him and what ones they automatically block out – all this unconscious activity, at the pre-verbal level, is entirely relevant to the intonations and appeasements offered by a poet's music' (Heaney 1980, 62). That he places Mossbawn as the central location of sound and image at the beginning of his first prose collection is not surprising given the importance that his first world has as a divining rod of inspiration. The childhood sounds of water being pumped resonate with Heaney over his lifetime, and extend far beyond this. Those sounds connect with the skills and knowledge of poetry, and an ear tuned over a lifetime of reading and listening to literature, to place musicality as one of the central features of Heaney's creative endeavours.

Works Cited

Butler Cullingford, Elizabeth (1996) *Gender and History in Yeats's Love Poetry*, New York: Syracuse University Press.

Eliot, T. S. (1975) *Selected Prose of T.S. Eliot*, edited by Frank Kermode, New York: Farrar, Straus and Giroux.

Heaney, Seamus (1980) *Preoccupations: Selected Prose 1968–1978*, London: Faber and Faber.

Heaney, Seamus (1989) *The Place of Writing*, Georgia: Scholars Press.

Heaney, Seamus (1995) *Crediting Poetry*, Meath: The Gallery Press.

Heaney, Seamus (1996) *The Redress of Poetry*, second edition, London: Faber and Faber.

Heaney, Seamus (2002) *Finders Keepers: Selected Prose 1971–2001*, London: Faber and Faber.

Heaney, Seamus (2004a) 'Introduction', in *W.B. Yeats: Poems selected by Seamus Heaney*, London: Faber and Faber, xi–xxv.

Heaney, Seamus (2004b) 'The Jayne Lecture: Title Deeds: Translating a Classic', in *Proceedings of the American Philosophical Society*, Volume 148, Number 4, 411–426.

Heaney, Seamus (2005) 'Thebes via Toomebridge: Retitling Antigone', *The Irish Book Review*, Volume 1, Number 1, 13–14.

Heaney, Seamus (2023) *The Letters of Seamus Heaney*, edited by Christopher Reid, London: Faber and Faber.

Heaney, Seamus (n.d.) 'Encounters with Poetry', *Poetry Book Society*. http://www.poetrybooks.co.uk/poetry_portal/seamus_heaney_encounters_with_poetry [Accessed October 13, 2023].

Hopkins, Gerard Manley (1980) *Gerard Manley Hopkins: Selected Prose*, edited by Gerald Roberts, Oxford: Oxford University Press.

Kress, Simon B. (2021) 'Music' in *Seamus Heaney in Context*, edited by Geraldine Higgins, Cambridge: Cambridge University Press.

Leighton, Angela (2014/2015) 'Heaney and the Music', *The Irish Review*, Winter–Spring 2014/2015, Number 49/50, 19–32.

O'Brien, Eugene (2016) *Seamus Heaney as Aesthetic Thinker: A Study of the Prose*, New York: Syracuse University Press.

O'Driscoll, Dennis (2009) *Stepping Stones: Interviews with Seamus Heaney*, London: Faber and Faber.

Rankin Russell, Richard (2014) *Seamus Heaney's Regions*, Indiana: University of Notre Dame Press.

Tyler Meg (2017) 'What We Leave Behind: Poetry, Music, and Seamus Heaney', *Five Points*, Volume 18, Number. 1, Spring 2017, 159–167.

Yeats, William Butler (1995) *Autobiographies: Memories and Reflections*, London: Bracken.

6 The Limits of Redress

Heaney's Aesthetics of Grace Confronts Larkin's Struggle with Gravity

Magdalena Kay

Heaney's affirmation of the power of poetry to redress an unsatisfying reality is one of his lasting critical legacies. It has been comprehensively examined in the nearly three decades since the poet's Oxford lectures were published as *The Redress of Poetry* in 1995, but this titular notion's reliance upon the thinking of Simone Weil is not commonly traced, even while Weil's dichotomy of gravity and grace has taken on an independent celebrity of its own. We receive Heaney's notion of redress by means of Weil, and her shadow presence affects it. Given the importance of this notion to contemporary thinking about poetry, it is worth re-examining Weil's metaphor in order to better judge the adequacy of redress itself to serve as a conceptual tool for understanding the work of the contemporary lyric, and in particular, lyric that does not appear redressive.

Heaney uses this tool in order to leverage its evaluative ability. If literary texts are evaluated in reference to an ideal capacity for redress, then it becomes crucial to elaborate the relation of aesthetic form to redressive potential. This is where the Weilian roots of redress may weaken the concept's reach: as we will see, its application to a poet such as Philip Larkin reveals the peril of using Weil's metaphor as an evaluative tool. Its insufficiency is due to its very metaphorical status. The power of metaphor resides in its capacity to carry meaning from one realm into another, in which the unusual nature of the figure has the capacity to make visible further reaches of meaning. A metaphor that is carried to a further territory may illuminate yet more strangely and selectively, as the original figure will still bear the marks of its first and second homes.

Weil's dichotomy of gravity and grace was not originally a literary metaphor. It comes from notebooks posthumously compiled into an eponymous volume, and the fragmentary nature of Weil's philosophical thoughts is still evident therein. In snippets of text, she thinks through the primary analogy of the natural laws with gravity, to which grace is the only exception. These two forces 'rule the universe' (Weil 2004a, 1–2). The agonistic charge of this dichotomy, then, is central to it. The text allies the force of gravity with baseness and, oddly, superficiality (Weil 2004a, 2), and the tacit ascription of meaningfulness to grace may be notable for Heaney's eventual extension of Weil's concepts. She consistently roots her metaphor in the Christian context

DOI: 10.4324/9781003456148-7

The Limits of Redress 111

that, to her, invests it with significance and illustrative value: thus, gravity and grace come together most prominently in Christ's crucifixion, while grace inevitably, to Weil, must come from God. Humans cannot bring about their 'deliverance' themselves: 'the source of man's moral energy is outside him' (Weil 2004a, 3).

Weil exposes the antisocial impulse toward gravity inside herself, candidly exposing her need for extrahuman intervention, and viewing supplication as a 'turn to something other than myself' (Weil 2004a, 3). Her anti-humanism does not quite fit with Heaney's thinking, which consistently affirms a faith in human capacity even as it concedes what Weil would call the force of gravity within ethical life. His poetry and prose do not manifest a need for radical escape, but feature continued entreaties to plumb the human capacity for good. It is questionable whether he would agree either with Weil's dictum that grace creates the good or with her insistence that the human imagination refrain from filling 'the void', if it be discerned—rather, it can and must be filled with God's grace. Filling a perceived lack is not humanity's job. This idea, too, fits uncomfortably with Heaney's conception both of creativity and of divine presence, which rests upon affective and imagistic foundations rather than theological ones. His defense of a childhood vision of the 'universe shimmering with light' (Heaney in Brown 2002, 84) or 'ashimmer with God' (Heaney in Farndale 2001, n.p.) seeks to justify faith by means of the vision of beneficence that it provides a young poet, and its power to awaken a reciprocally stimulated creativity. Human imagination is integral to this vision (Brown 2002, 84). Although Weil does not dispute the need for metaphors to understand the divine, Heaney's exuberant acceptance of images to fill in our idea of the cosmos appears contrary to her style of thinking. Weil consistently calls for humans to wait, to leave the void open, to trust in a good that is immaterial and comes from beyond; Heaney consistently wishes to trust human imagination. If the good does indeed have an immaterial source, to Heaney, it may and must be imagined in material terms. Weil encourages a fundamentally different orientation.

Her concept of gravity is particularly useful, however, for Heaney to indicate a pressure upon the poet that can be most pronounced in times of political stress. Thus, when Eastern European poets such as Czesław Miłosz and Osip Mandelstam refuse to espouse the terms of the repressive Communist regimes of their countries, especially when they embrace the full power of the imagination, they exemplify the urge to counteract 'gravity' by means of vision (Heaney 1995, 4). This seemingly unarguable assertion, however, contradicts Weil's religious perspective. For Heaney, gravity is here a metaphor for political pressure, and the embrace of a visionary poetics may counteract it through the force of human will. Heaney repeatedly emphasizes imaginative agency. He aestheticizes Weil's terms and, in the process, invests them with a more humanist vision than she had espoused.

If we redefine grace as a force that may be summoned by human capacity, do we lose its Weilian meaning altogether? Heaney does not believe so.

112   *Magdalena Kay*

He quotes from Weil when he formulates his poetics of redress: "'Obedience to the force of gravity. The greatest sin"... Indeed her whole book [*Gravity and Grace*] is informed by the idea of counterweighting, of balancing out the forces, of redress—tilting the scales of reality toward some transcendent equilibrium' (Heaney 1995, 3). This is true when it comes to Weil's defense of the poor, but less convincing once we speak about imaginative work, which is not perfectly congruent with the fight for social justice. Heaney does not emphasize the deliberateness of the imagination's work in this passage. Rather, he focuses on the potentially aberrant nature of an imagined 'counter-reality': it 'may be only imagined but ... nevertheless has weight because it is imagined within the gravitational pull of the actual and can therefore hold its own and balance out against the historical situation' (Heaney 1995, 3–4). This view is indeed congruent with Weil's defense of the weak and her concept of 'equilibrium'. Heaney defends the poet's impulse to balance a call for practical engagement with fidelity to the aesthetic, which may even gain value as it loses practical effectiveness (Heaney 1995, 4). Perhaps, indeed, there is a sort of nobility to impracticality. Action may and perhaps must be balanced by vision and imagination.

A generally conceived principle of equilibrium, however, is less implicitly prescriptive than a principle of socio-historical redress. Heaney's initial description of poetry's capacity in 'The Redress of Poetry' is capacious: it furnishes a means of imagining our experience of 'the labyrinth' of life, allowing consciousness to 'recognize its predicaments' (Heaney 1995, 2). In this understanding, poetry may create equilibrium by offering its own vision of human predicaments, which may or may not suggest solutions. Although Heaney often suggests that inspiration may seem to come from outside the poet, this vision of creativity is centered on the human capacity to reimagine what is given. As Auden writes roughly fifty years earlier, poetry is a way of happening rather than a means toward making something happen. Importantly, this way may be informed by factors outside the individual will but is not really a matter of grace coming from above. Heaney's aesthetic judgments are informed by a view of poetry as an example of human agency—he quotes Wallace Stevens on the imagination's exertion of counter-pressure against reality. Poetry may enter the world of vision, transcendence, spirit—all concepts that Heaney vigorously defends throughout his life—but it is not formed by a passive waiting for grace.

This gap between Heaney and Weil lies beneath his fuller exposition of redress. Already in *The Government of the Tongue*, Heaney defends poetry that follows 'the laws of its own need' rather than 'external ... impositions' (Heaney 1989, 93). Could grace be seen as a beneficent 'imposition?' Heaney's argument intentionally empowers the poet to follow aesthetic rather than political authority. Inspiration need not be given by an external source of grace; rather, Heaney consistently espouses the notion that the artwork contains the principles for its making within itself.[1] The most contentious feature of Heaney's redress arises from a tacit assumption that these principles may

The Limits of Redress   113

and should be consonant with the work of grace. Although Weil importantly situates humans *metaxu*,[2] in between the transcendent and the mundane, she does not allow for the salvific quality of art that Heaney seems to allow for (if not to place absolute trust in). She emphasizes the negative nature of the law of necessity far more than Heaney, who instead focuses upon a human necessity allied with conscious intervention in historical events. This is an ethical form of the concept, then, and this form is quite different from the blind natural laws to which Weil refers. Heaney fashions his own terms differently. Thus, the influential dichotomy of gravity and grace changes as Heaney works it through an imagined opposition of Yeats and Larkin.

This opposition predates his Oxford lectures. It is usefully complicated in *Preoccupations*, his first prose collection, by fond recollections of popular rhymes heard during his childhood, which enrich the young Heaney's aural imagination and emotional life. 'Literary' language did not always reflect young people's experience, Heaney muses (Heaney 1980, 26; 44). His imagination is later educated by a more highfalutin reading list as well as more formal poetry recitations, but these different types of linguistic pleasure can, Heaney implies, happily come together. Indeed, one of his own hallmarks is precisely the union of diverse registers of language and experience.

This also happens to be a feature of Larkin's poetic oeuvre, which can startle with its leaps between the utterly demotic and the 'out of reach', which is nonetheless summoned on a regular basis.[3] Curiously, however, this is not a feature that Heaney notes in 'Englands of the Mind', an essay in which he elegantly sets apart Larkin, Geoffrey Hill and Ted Hughes as three quintessentially English voices. In this triad, Larkin stands as the voice of modern disenchantment, civil conversation and refusal—specifically, 'a refusal to melt through long perspectives, an obstinate insistence that the poet is ... a real man in a real place' who has 'deliberately curtailed his gift for evocation, for resonance, for symbolist *frissons*' (Heaney 1980, 164). True, Larkin turned from Yeats to Hardy as his preferred literary forefather (Heaney 1980, 164), even while recent scholars have reconsidered this putatively unambiguous change. There is much to say about Larkin's reputation for realism and its seemingly obvious opposition to 'symbolist *frissons*', and this is not the place to wage such a campaign. Heaney's essay is notable for its situation of Larkin in an English literary landscape and its insistence that he be seen as a poet of restriction. Heaney allows himself to recruit Keats for this purpose: 'it is by refusing to pull out the full stops, or by almost refusing, that Larkin gains his own brand of negative capability' (Heaney 1980, 165). While Keats was speaking of uncertainty, however, Heaney attributes the stronger, more negative emotion of rejection to Larkin, hinting at a sort of perversity in his eschewal of symbolist vision.

Standing against all three is the towering legacy of Yeats. Larkin's refusal is set (here tacitly) against Yeats's energetic exhilaration in his own artistic faith, based on the sense that artistic process itself has 'some kind of absolute validity' (Heaney 1980, 99). Yet its validity is underlain by an opposition

114 *Magdalena Kay*

of art and life that appears at odds with the kind of artistic recognition so convincingly described by Heaney elsewhere in *Preoccupations* (Heaney 1980, 26–27; 44). Even if 'some kind' bespeaks an irrationality which may be compared to Larkin's—just as Yeats may not be able to explain 'absolute validity', so may Larkin not be able to explain his almost-refusal to embrace the full artistry of art—it is accepted by Heaney psychologically: 'Personally, I find much to admire in the intransigence of the stance' (Heaney 1980, 100). If Yeats is a poet who 'took on the world on his own terms' (Heaney 1980, 100), Larkin seems to have allowed the world to set its terms too meekly, not permitting himself the sort of 'intransigence' that convinces readers of his own terms' validity. These early essays form the basis of Heaney's understanding of redress as a poetic and psychological (not simply political) concept in the late 1980s and 1990s.

When Heaney writes that art 'has a religious, a binding force, for the artist' later in *Preoccupations* (Heaney 1980, 217), however, he summons both Yeatsian conviction and an aesthetic faith to which Larkin is no stranger. There is now an established critical view of Larkin as young aesthete who cleaves to a faith in art: as a young man, he wishes to communicate with 'the kind of artist who is perpetually *kneeling* in his heart' and worries that in his character 'there is an antipathy between "art" and "life"' (Larkin 1992, 106; 116). Indeed, this opposition survives its placement in ironic scare quotes. Larkin cannot ironize his way out of an aestheticism that causes him to choose a lifestyle that, to other poets, may appear a rather extreme manifestation of artistic faith:

> Time and time again I feel that before I write anything else at all I must drag myself out of the water, shake myself dry and sit down on a lonely rock to contemplate glittering loneliness. Marriage, of course (since you mentioned marriage), is impossible if one wants to do this.
>
> (Larkin 1992, 116)

In these words to an artist friend, Larkin expresses a Weilian resistance to an immersive and gravity-laden 'life' which must be periodically exited, as far as one is able, to create the conditions for attunement with 'glittering' grace, areligious but perhaps not entirely secular. The young Larkin subscribes to a religion of art that may seem impossibly idealistic to the poet as middle-aged curmudgeon but which is never wholly renounced.

As Larkin moves away from extreme aestheticism, he mentions the 'fascinating effects ... got by playing off the rhythm and language of speech against the rhythm and language of poetry' (Larkin 2010, 45), moving closer to Heaney's delight in vernacular rhymes and making such 'effects' his trademark. Yet Heaney regrets the way Larkin develops his voice: 'It would seem that he has deliberately curtailed his gift for evocation, for resonance, ... [and that he] rebukes romantic aspiration and afflatus with a scrupulous meanness' (Heaney 1980, 164). Several of these terms must be put under pressure

The Limits of Redress   115

in order to clarify Heaney's later poetics of redress. The notion of deliberate curtailment and mean-tempered 'rebuke' is central to his understanding of a poetic project that seems guided by negativity rather than positive commitment. Larkin's scruples appear to be the product of an aesthetic nihilism that seeks to negate rather than to affirm. This view jars against the aestheticist Larkin and runs the risk of substituting persona for poet[4]; Edna Longley suggests viewing Larkin as a *fin de siècle* Romantic disguised as a mid-century suburbanite (Longley 2000, 178–179).

Indeed, in spite of its title, *The Less Deceived* contains several poems that testify to an ongoing interest in what Heaney calls romantic aspiration—the Laurentian swell of 'Wedding-Wind', the nostalgic tenderness of 'At Grass', the evocative vistas of 'Absences' or 'Poetry of Departures', and even the not-quite-secular perspective of 'Church Going', which fades into the 'long perspective' that Heaney more readily associates with Hughes and Hill rather than with Larkin—while others address the very point of view that Heaney finds problematic. The Petrarchan sonnet 'Spring', suffused with romantic afflatus for most of its octave, presents the poet as an 'indigestible sterility' in the sunlit greenery. The season's 'gratuitous' loveliness is not denied or even rebuked; it is juxtaposed with a speaker who has long outgrown his seedtime. Its sestet brings them into meaningful relation: 'those she has least use for see her best,/Their paths grown craven and circuitous,/Their visions mountain-clear, their needs immodest' (Burnett 2012, 40). The echo of Milton's nineteenth sonnet suggests that the speaker's middle-aged mind and body be seen in terms of disability, as cravenness and clarity come together at this time of life to diminish if not entirely extinguish the light of poetic vision. If Milton's speaker is denied the light of physical vision, thus seeing a dark world spreading around him, so its deliberate confluence of literal and figurative meaning is echoed in Larkin's sonnet. To Larkin, the undeceived sharpness of a middle-aged perspective may constitute a disability of the imagination. Reading in the most literal-minded way, Larkin may be seen as 'sterile' in his childlessness and solitary lifestyle,[5] even if he can hardly be reproached for imaginative sterility in such a lush poem. Just as Milton's sonnet does, 'Spring' questions the nature of vision and creativity while confronting the enormous need of its adult speaker. Can a poet write from outside the happy stream of human life and truly see it best? Can he continue to write lyrically once deprived of full-throated ease? These questions are at the heart of Heaney's own ethics of redress and yet Heaney assigns a greater degree of conviction to Larkin's putative disenchantment than many of the poems warrant.

Rather, Larkin's poems long for a romantic reality to which they cannot fully assent; their speaker often feels forced to confront a gravity-laden actuality. Larkin holds to a dichotomy of truth and beauty. Although its origins and purpose are obviously different from those motivating Weil, his description of composing a poem of truth bears some similarity to her descriptions of gravity: 'something was grinding its knuckles in my neck and I thought: God, I've got to say this somehow' (Larkin 2001, 49). He consistently disclaims

116 *Magdalena Kay*

his own choice of subject matter, insisting on its givenness. His histrionic statement that deprivation is for him what daffodils were for Wordsworth (Larkin 1983, 47) is defensive.

This sort of confrontation bears direct comparison to Heaney's redress. Heaney's Yeats-as-representative is defiant and intractable. Likewise, his Osip Mandelstam stands as a poetic exemplar who believes in absolute responsibility to poetry, who heroically prioritizes the lyric impulse at the cost of his life (Heaney 1989, xix). In *The Government of the Tongue*, focused upon the political pressure brought to bear upon artistic expression in Eastern Europe as in Northern Ireland, Mandelstam is brought into contrast with the Polish Zbigniew Herbert, who writes a poem expressing (though not prescribing) a minimal aesthetics of maximal ethical response.[6] Heaney wonders whether poetry should 'put the governors on its joy and moralize its song' (Heaney 1989, 99) but the answer is clear: poetry should serve as a prototype of freedom, and not be beholden to the force of gravity. Mandelstam heroically chose to write 'without the interference of his own self-censorship' since 'obedience to poetic impulse was obedience to conscience' (Heaney 1989, xix). In this context, then, the internal force of self-censorship becomes roughly parallel to the external force of gravity, with important ramifications for poetic judgment. The congruence of 'conscience' with 'poetic impulse' locates value in an impulse that must present itself as untrammeled, which creates a poem that is 'an experience of release' (Heaney 1989, xxii) rather than bondage. It is important to note, though, that terms such as 'freedom', 'release' and 'conscience' carried a specific meaning in Communist bloc countries that did not automatically carry over to Heaney's Irish and North American context, where 'freedom' could mean something far more abstract than it did in Mandelstam's Russia. Indeed, the freedom to compose a poem dedicated to exposing the forces of gravity was a freedom cherished by writers under Communist regimes. Context is key to this debate over aesthetics and ethics.

Heaney wishes a poem to allow 'a premonition of harmonies desired' if not achieved (Heaney 1989, 94), and its 'promissory' relationship to an order beyond itself (Heaney 1989, 100) implies that desire and freedom must be understood in relation to promise. A poet such as Larkin does not seek an aesthetics of promise, however, and the freedom that he reportedly feels when choosing Hardy as a model is a freedom to speak from a ground-level perspective (Larkin 1983, 175). Larkin's vision is not founded on belief in the imagination's freedom. Nor is it founded on the civilizational conflict that Heaney refers to in his renewed defense of Weil, Mandelstam and Miłosz in *The Redress of Poetry* (1995), written after the fall of Communism. Writing in disobedience to gravity, these writers espouse 'vision' seen as 'a glimpsed alternative, a revelation of potential that is denied or constantly threatened by circumstances' (Heaney 1995, 4; 5). These circumstances are elucidated by Miłosz and quoted by Heaney as an awareness of 'the void, the absurd, the anti-meaning' which is part of the contemporary 'intellectual atmosphere' (Heaney 1995, 153).

The Limits of Redress 117

There is an implicit theology in such statements. There is also an implicit opposition, eventually made explicit by both writers, between embrace of vision and awareness of the void, which is underlain by the conviction that there is, indeed, 'something more' to life than merely secular existence (see Heaney in Foster 2020, 194). In order to experience horror at 'the void', one must have a pre-existing vision of fullness. Yet Miłosz defends his childhood Catholicism more authoritatively than Heaney, who frequently expresses doubt and claims to have lost much of his faith. His twenty-first-century poems may diminish 'great theological ideas' formerly held by the younger Heaney (see Auge in O'Brien 2016, 44–45), yet the poetics of redress depend upon a spiritual notion of grace that cannot be decoupled from Catholicism. This dimension emerges most strongly when Heaney moves from defining redress in socio-political and literary terms and moves into critique of Larkin's work, which incites him to recalibrate redress not as liberation but as affirmation, while Miłosz is welcomed as an especially zealous guide. Thus, as Miłosz asserts that poetry must maintain a 'centuries-old hostility to reason, science and a science-inspired philosophy' (Heaney 1995, 153), so the metaphor of continuous antagonism is marshaled to dramatize the peril of shirking poetry's proper work.

Now, Miłosz himself is no stranger to doubt. Nor is he always as old-fashioned as he makes himself out to be in essays presenting himself as an old-world curiosity in contemporary California. In his polemic against Larkin, however, he denounces the poet for collaborating with Darwin and joining in a 'whole strain of modern literature' that has conceded victory to 'the void' (quoted in Heaney 1995, 153; n.b. Miłosz's essay was originally published in 1979). Heaney is right to see such judgments as a challenge. Their terms appear surprisingly premodern, holding to a traditionalist view of the spiritual. While Heaney may admit that Larkin 'had it in him' to write his own *Paradiso* (Heaney 1989, 22) and presents him in 'The Journey Back'[7] as an ordinary man 'who had seen poetry' as if it were a spiritual vision, Miłosz recognizes Larkin's literary talent but will not allow him such potential, asserting that he had it in him to write against writing itself. This judgment conditions Heaney's response to Larkin in 'Joy or Night: Last Things in the Poetry of W. B. Yeats and Philip Larkin', an essay which revises the idea of redress first broached in 'The Redress of Poetry' (originally published in 1990, whereas 'Joy or Night' was first delivered as a lecture in 1993).

In this essay Heaney follows Miłosz's opposition to Larkin's 'Aubade', a dark poem published somewhat cynically by the *Times Literary Supplement* in their 1977 Christmas-week edition. Instead of concession, however, Heaney sees failure: the poem 'abolishes the soul's traditional pretension to immortality and denies the Deity's immemorial attribute of infinite personal concern' in this poem, while death is given authority over humankind rather than vice versa (Heaney 1995, 156–158). This appears to be an argument over the relative Christianity of the poem rather than its literary value. Heaney uses Miłosz's notion of an 'adversary' (Heaney 1995, 158) in order to extend

118   *Magdalena Kay*

his militaristic conceit. This insistence upon a power struggle between a dark enemy and a valiant poet-hero is rather antagonistic for Heaney, who typically seeks diplomatic solutions. Thus, he adds an almost-caveat to Miłosz's negative judgment: when a poem 'provokes consciousness into new postures' by purely formal means, Heaney asserts, then it is already 'on the side of life'. Indeed, the very 'essence' of poetry is on this side, but well-formed poems may still renege on what Yeats calls the spiritual intellect's great work (Heaney 1995, 158).

This is where redress becomes far more than Weilian receptivity to grace. In defense of a neo-Yeatsian aesthetics, Heaney clarifies the poetic work that is necessary:

> in order that human beings bring about the most radiant conditions for themselves to inhabit, it is essential that the vision of reality which poetry offers should be transformative, more than just a print-out of the given circumstances of its time and place.
>
> (Heaney 1995, 159)

There is a nebulous area, then, in which poetry may still possess its essential nature but not conduce to the betterment of life. It is hard to see how any good poem could be 'just a print-out' of basic circumstances, and 'Aubade' certainly does not fit this definition (n.b. both Miłosz and Heaney make clear their appreciation of Larkin's poetic skill), so conceivably Heaney is allowing for a capacious definition of transformation. 'The Redress of Poetry' states that as long as 'the coordinates of the imagined thing correspond to those of the world that we live in and endure, poetry is fulfilling its counterweighting function' (Heaney 1995, 10)—later, this is rephrased as poetry's capacity to 'allow us to contemplate the complex burden of our own experience' (Heaney 1995, 10). Given that 'counterweighting' is here parallel to redress, these carefully worded statements point to the redressive potential of poems that encourage contemplation of a real condition. Perhaps a poem that matches the coordinates of a dismal condition of life effectively counterweighs it by encouraging empathetic response in the reader and 'transforming' dismal conditions into well-expressed feeling, a movement appreciated by Heaney as by Pope.

Yet this may be a more generous interpretation than 'Redress' allows for. Larkin's very 'coordinates' are suspect to Heaney. Poetic achievement is not, then, enough to put a poem 'on the side of life', and neither is encouragement of contemplation—for it is inarguable that most of Larkin's poems urge us to contemplate 'the burden of our own experience' and present conditions that are recognizable to contemporary readers, even if they are not often 'radiant'. Small wonder that so many readers have been surprised by the judgments levied by 'Joy or Night'. The notion of redress becomes caught between mimesis and transformation, between contemplation and resolution.

The Limits of Redress 119

'Aubade' presents a world in which the fear of death, seen as 'total emptiness for ever', is not allayed by the consolation of religious belief: 'nothing
more terrible, nothing more true'. Its denial of God's presence and abolish-
ment of the soul's pretension of immortality becomes most poignant in the
third stanza, when the speaker reckons with the terrible truth of coming
emptiness:

> This is a special way of being afraid
> No trick dispels. Religion used to try,
> That vast, moth-eaten musical brocade
> Created to pretend we never die,
> And specious stuff that says *No rational being*
> *Can fear a thing it will not feel*, not seeing
> That this is what we fear—no sight, no sound…
> (Larkin 2012, 115)

The subsequent stanza will introduce some potentially unsettling dark humor
in the epigrammatic couplet 'Being brave/Lets no one off the grave' (Larkin
2012, 116). Perhaps it is intended as a prod at the very Yeats that Heaney
so admires—the Yeats who wishes to cast a cold eye at his future death, to
make his soul and to conquer fear and uncertainty—or not, as it summons a
sly Augustan tone frequently assumed by Larkin. Such tonal shifts make clear
that 'Aubade' cannot be read as a simple expository statement even while
we cannot ignore its assertions. This is, as Heaney writes, a post-Christian
poem (Heaney 1995, 156). It is also a poem that appears longer than its fifty
lines as it moves between registers of speech, images and scenarios, with a
few stark lines containing hardly any imagery whatsoever as they evoke the
emptiness of death (Larkin 2012, 115, ll. 16–21).

Heaney counterposes 'Aubade' with Yeats's 'Cold Heaven', hardly a com-
forting poem itself. Formally, the comparison is of unlike quantities: Yeats's
almost-sonnet stops short of offering a concluding couplet, cutting itself off
after four rhymed quatrains with a wrenching question about last judgment,
positing 'the injustice of the skies'. It captures a singular though complex
moment of emotional intensity, when its final question about what happens
to 'the ghost' after death is unanswerable; Larkin's poem uses its additional
thirty-eight lines to think a similar question through, its speaker caught in a
state that is painful yet habitual. He is accustomed to the questions and problems raised within the poem and offers answers but not solutions. Yeats's poem
remains in its agonized moment, while Larkin's reaches beyond it to the numb
routines of everyday life, which are poised to submerge the speaker until his
next broken night. A poem of anaesthetized experience runs the risk of leaving
its readers in this very state rather than casting them into cathartic intensity.

'Aubade' makes clear that its bleak conclusions result from a process
of confronting now-dashed hopes. There is a diachronic backdrop of long

120   *Magdalena Kay*

duration, as the gradual decline of religious belief renders the notion of providence ludicrous to the speaker, and the rise of what Miłosz calls science-based philosophy is yet more dispiriting: while 'religion' allows for fear of death, 'specious' pseudo-scientific wisdom will not even recognize the emotional state that wracks him. Far from conceding to science-based reasoning, the poem expresses real anger at the notion that powerful emotion could be rationalized away. The irrational is as real as the rational: this is a truth known both to Larkin and Yeats.

There is, however, a difference of basic belief between them: while Yeats does not question the existence of the soul in 'The Cold Heaven', Larkin denies it and centers on 'the mind', as its thoughts, fears, 'tricks' and capacity to numb itself with work and drink are the poem's main concern. Although Heaney concedes that there is no personal God in Yeats's poem, it still 'conveys a strong impression of direct encounter' as the soul is wracked by a sense of 'answerability ... to a something out there' (Heaney 1995, 148–149). Its question of judgment and consequences suggests at least partial acceptance of the Christian belief in 'quickening' after death. Yet Yeats's spirituality cannot be too closely allied with Heaney's. Tim Kendall worries that the pieces in *Redress* show Heaney's critical tendency to admire reflections of himself with the effect that 'he will find only what he is looking for' (Kendall in Curtis 2001, 234). James Booth sees a similar tendency at work in the laudatory 'The Journey Back', in which the 'nine-to-five man who had seen poetry' is created to reflect Heaney's own artistic inclinations, thus associating Larkin with 'a very un-Larkinesque poetic ideology' (Booth 1997, 371). This is severe, yet Heaney's readings of Larkin and also Hardy—Kendall calls out his overly optimistic interpretation of 'The Darkling Thrush' as a misreading—elicit critical consternation.

Although Heaney writes compellingly of the poetic imperative to match rather than simplify reality (Heaney 1995, 8), it seems as if its bleaker aspects should not be matched but corrected toward a 'transcendent equilibrium' (Heaney 1995, 3). What if equilibrium, however, is located in mundanity rather than transcendence? Heaney praises George Herbert's 'The Pulley' for showing 'the way consciousness can be alive to two different and contradictory dimensions of reality and find a way of negotiating between them' (Heaney 1995, xiii); this could likewise serve as an excellent description of Larkin's poetic work. Negotiations, however, are not always successful. Heaney may be similar to Weil in his rock-bottom belief that grace exists, yet it cannot be forced into existence. Larkin's poetic speaker searches himself for a possible solution to his terror at 'soundless dark'. He might even agree with Heaney's statement that 'The infinite spaces may be silent, but the human response is to say that this is not good enough, that there has to be more to it than neuter absence' (O'Driscoll 2008, 471). Larkin's response is to extoll a religion of art in his youth and to consistently gaze out at a 'beyond' in his mature work. However, his conclusion is also to reject the possibility of religious faith for himself. 'Power of some sort or other will go on', he writes

The Limits of Redress 121

in 'Church Going', yet he is not a believer. Does that disqualify him from providing the poetic redress that Heaney seeks?

Peter McDonald levies a severe judgment when he writes that Heaney's *The Redress of Poetry* celebrates poetry's power of redress but does not analyze it (McDonald 2002, 85). If Heaney's pieces are celebrations more than lectures, as McDonald opines, it feels like a 'breach of etiquette' to question what we are celebrating (McDonald 1996, 85). He does, however, take issue with Heaney's 'discourse of pleasantry and complaisance' when used for analysis of Samuel Beckett's work, where such discourse is 'inevitably ill at ease' (McDonald 1996, 88–89; 94). The same should be said of Larkin's work. This circles back to Kendall's warning of finding only what one looks for: if achieved harmony and achieved transcendence are what we readers desire, then Larkin's 'Aubade' is a poor place to start. Yet this point must also be complicated: if a Herbertian movement between contraries defines one form of redress, in which a free imagination moves between poles of thought or feeling and thus serves as a model of inclusive consciousness, then such movement need not be tethered to an inevitable conclusion. If the poet honestly replicates the intricate conditions of lived life, as Heaney also desires, then radiant conclusions will not always be possible. Larkin confronts a world that does not allow him to feel the deep acceptance that is the unspoken desideratum of 'Aubade'.

McDonald importantly engages the affective dimension of criticism by proposing a felt 'breach of etiquette' caused by over-zealous interrogation of otherwise laudable notions (McDonald 2002, 88). Given the generosity of Heaney's critical perspective and the well-known geniality which shines through so much of his writing, it may seem mean-spirited to submit a particular concept to stern analysis. Heaney does not paint himself as an academic, after all, and as McDonald notes, he uses his authority as a poet in order to dissent from many of the dogmas of contemporary literary theory (McDonald 2002, 88–89). Yet precisely because the concept of redress has such tremendous potential to justify the work of poetry, its imperfect adequacy—if not total inadequacy—must be clarified, for it would also be unjust to distort Heaney's idea in order to defend its adequacy. This concept lends itself better to certain types of literary work than others. Larkin's guiding dichotomy of beauty and truth cannot be perfectly matched with Weilian gravity and grace, and his aim as a poet is to negotiate and clarify rather than to defend, to resolve, or to brighten.

If both poets have an area in which they overlap, it is differently defined, situated and even perceived. When the speaker of 'Aubade' assures himself that the curtain edges will grow light at daybreak, this potential brightening provides no consolation. It brings no glimmer of transcendence. When daytime comes the sky is 'white as clay', signifying nothing. The brightest light comes from 'the dread/Of dying', which flashes so strongly upon the speaker's inward eye that his mind (here 'the mind', indicating the general horror of vacuity which Miłosz and Heaney address) 'blanks' at the glare of

122   Magdalena Kay

it. The detail is crucial. If Heaney wishes to take a stand against nothingness in the face of death (see O'Driscoll 2008, 472), Larkin's speaker simply cannot. This is not an image of conscious capitulation but of disempowerment. It would indeed be a breach of etiquette to accuse this speaker of consciously refusing to hold his lyre up to the underworld: Larkin's speaker is more vulnerable, more helpless, than he is commonly seen, perhaps due to the brief verbal swagger of the work-and-drink pairing in the poem's first line. Redressive imagination is not an option: he is transfixed by a reality fully recognized to be creatively invalidating.[8]

For this reason, the charge of nihilism often levied against the poem should be referred back to a personal context that warrants deeper attention: 'Aubade' was started in April 1974, after he had helped to move his elderly mother into a nursing home, and was finished shortly after her death on 17 November 1977. Larkin worried over his widowed mother's care, wrote frequent letters and then picture postcards after she experienced significant cognitive decline and expressed guilt that he could not make her life happier. Unlike Heaney's mother, Larkin's did not continue to live with her family; this detail is important for differentiating 'Aubade', with its solitary and alienated speaker, from 'Clearances', with its emotionally fortifying images of extended family life. Larkin's readers are just coming to terms with the depth of the poet's filial feeling,[9] which has long been remarked by Heaney's readers. 'Clearances' and 'Aubade' demonstrate how these deaths are reckoned with cognitively and creatively as well as emotionally. As a 'space ... had been emptied/Into us to keep' in Heaney's seventh sonnet (Heaney 1987, 31), so the poet's creative task comes clear: as son, elegist and poet, the speaker must change in response to Margaret Heaney's death. Yet the poet's mind furnishes a corollary—a 'decked chestnut tree' that is his coeval—and comes to a luminous near-conclusion: the tree has become 'a bright nowhere', a soul that is now 'beyond silence listened for' (Heaney 1987, 32). There is no direct encounter with a deity nor any certain promise of continued life, but the possibility of posthumous encounter is imagined (Heaney 1987, 26) in the sort of detail that Larkin purposefully eschews in 'Aubade' ('total emptiness', 'sure extinction', 'Not to be anywhere'). 'Clearances' ends brightly while 'Aubade' ends in the blank whiteness of day ('like clay' still unformed and featureless) and inaugurates Heaney's so-called transcendent phase, implying, perhaps, the need to furnish images to fill a potential vacancy. Larkin's 'Aubade', in contrast, comes after long silence and is followed by more silence. It is not an elegy, and Eva Larkin is never named or alluded to in any way. 'Aubade' does not mourn the poet's mother; it mourns the poet himself. He is the one who is confronted with death's inexorable encroachment upon his life; he is the one held and horrified by the flash of realization. He is not able to redress Eva's death or even to 'keep' her within him; instead, he has, in the event of the poem, become her, if only in the instant that he is compelled to confront a condition that is no longer at arm's length.[10] The poem occupies neither the settled ground of elegy or of self-elegy.

The Limits of Redress   123

This positioning may explain why 'Aubade' appears so raw and, as David Wheatley calls it, 'unpalatable' to Heaney. Wheatley finds his critique behavioral as well as aesthetic: Larkin is 'unseemly' to Heaney, flouting the codes of 'literary good behaviour' and showing a different type of poet from the type Heaney celebrates in *Redress* (Wheatley in O'Donoghue 2009, 132). Yet others, such as Michael Cavanagh, puzzle over the possibility that Heaney's own terms may be used to praise 'Aubade' for not 'governing its tongue' (Cavanagh 1998, 67) and allowing itself honesty of speech as well as intricate formal shaping. He notes that Heaney's 'entry into an enlarged transcendentalism' in *Seeing Things* (1991) appropriates the language and motifs of Catholicism in one direction only: its focus on 'light and upwardness' is not complemented by the 'Roman Catholic gravity, that is, excessive awareness of sin' and of evil (Cavanagh 2009, 146). Poetry, however, is separate from critical prose, particularly when its dicta are applied to poets quite different from the author. The terms Heaney uses to define and defend redress simply do not match Larkin's context. Context, here, must be taken to mean both poetic achievement, aesthetics and worldview.

The relative persuasiveness of Heaney's re-appropriation of these Catholic motifs has not gone uncriticized. John Dennison connects Heaney's 'pseudo-religious' separation of poetry from history in the late 1980s, which allows poetry to take on a redemptive function, with the 'concerted recovery' of a metaphysical language that uses Catholic concepts of the soul, eternal life, or a transcendent realm, in overly metaphorical ways—he mordantly calls it 'a post-secular humanist re-appropriation of convenient truths' (Dennison 2015, 133–136; 153).[11] There are clear forebears for such work, such as Matthew Arnold and Wallace Stevens, yet Heaney wishes to stop short of issuing a cultural manifesto. Indeed, he consistently disclaims the fulness of his own religious belief, balancing upon a borderline between what we may call gentle disenchantment and consciously continued enchantment.[12] Even while he recognizes the ordinariness of skepticism in the late twentieth century and makes clear that he is neither dogmatist nor apologist for the Roman Catholic Church, Heaney struggles to credit the achievement of a poem that cannot be described in Christian-derived metaphysical language. Importantly, there are many poems by Larkin that can be so described, and Heaney makes distinctions between poems that can be placed 'on the side of life' and those that cannot.

Here, however, he is working against himself, both his general defense of achieved form and his earlier judgment. 'In the Main of Light', published in a 1982 festschrift for Larkin, responds gratefully to the moments of illumination in Larkin's work. Larkin's light is attached to a 'dream world' within the poet (Heaney 1989, 21) that Heaney responds to with joyful recognition. The 'blinding windscreens' of 'The Whitsun Weddings' and the 'suncomprehending glass' and 'deep blue air' of 'High Windows' are 'surprises' that are nonetheless 'extraordinary'; Heaney senses 'the brightness of belief in liberation and amelioration' (Heaney 1989, 20; 21). Significantly, Larkin's

124 *Magdalena Kay*

blue air that shows nothing is full of 'infinitely neutral splendor' (Heaney 1989, 21) in 'The Main of Light', but eerily becomes a 'glassy brilliance' lit by 'a God-curst sun', both 'frigid and negative', in 'Joy or Night'. Larkin's 'sun-struck distances' become signs of 'an infinity as void and neuter as those "blinding windscreens" which flash randomly and pointlessly in "The Whitsun Weddings"' (Heaney 1995, 152). Is this new, more negative judgment aesthetic or ontological? Or, perhaps, theological? Heaney writes, 'when Larkin lifts his eyes from nature, what appears is a great absence' (Heaney 1995, 152). In the decade since the earlier essay, then, he has gone from seeing 'splendor' to seeing 'absence' in the very same image, while 'neutral' has become 'neuter'. Some conduit has closed down between the two poets. If Larkin could have been seen as a receiver of grace in 'The Main of Light', this possibility is annulled in 'Joy or Night'. Larkin's moments of brightness are no longer happy surprises but are described as 'frigid', 'glassy', random, pointless, 'neuter'. The language of infertility bespeaks Heaney's sense that these images are not generative, perhaps even opposed to generation ('frigid'), inhuman ('glassy') and divested of forward-looking purpose (pointless). This language of generation accompanies an implicitly religious outlook. If Larkin sees 'a great absence' when he looks to the sky, that is only problematic to those who insist upon belief. Perhaps Heaney has started to view statements failing to ratify divine presence as inherently negative, uninspired and uninspiring. It is hard to see how the ending of 'High Windows' could be seen as 'neuter', however; generations of readers have read it differently, as instantiating a sort of sublimity that is palpable and even awesome even while it is non-religious.

This reading calls up a distinct terminological problem in assessments of non-religious work. In defense of Larkin, Raphael Ingelbien posits that Heaney betrays the 'unease of a spiritual imagination toward a non-believer's nihilism' (Ingelbien 2000, 481) and refers to Larkin's extraordinary effects as a 'negative' or 'nihilistic sublime' (Ingelbien 2000, 480; 482). Charges of nihilism or negativity, however, imply a failure to recognize presence or an effacement of presence; 'nihilistic' is founded upon *nihil*, nothing, and commonly implies rejection. Yet sublimity bespeaks meaningfulness even while it repels ready understanding. Again, following the term's etymology, if we are raised up beyond the threshold of normal perception or comprehension by the sublime, then charges of negativity, rejection and nihilism seem unsuitable.

If questioning Heaney's celebratory tone seems a breach of etiquette, then labeling Larkin a nihilist seems equally so. Is it possible to express disbelief in eternal life and avoid such a moniker? Cavanagh points to the 'foreclosure of possibility' in Larkin's 'Aubade' (Cavanagh 1998, 72) as a reason for Heaney's dislike, yet this judgment also constricts the realm within which poetry can dwell: is it not possible to write meaningful poetry that holds firm to its non-religious position? Must poetry remain perpetually open to religious belief? Larkin's lifelong aestheticism comes close to religious faith but the

The Limits of Redress   125

poet himself refuses to conflate the two in his adulthood (even while he does in his youth). Heaney, on the other hand, so frequently uses Christian vocabulary in his literary criticism—poetry is vision, revelation, assuagement, enshrinement, transfiguration, redemption—that it appears nearly natural to efface the line between poetry and worship. This leads to what Stephen James calls 'a quasi-mystical ideal of redress that passes understanding' (James 2017, 147–148). There is a ready vocabulary for the secular literary critic, but Heaney uses the concept of redress to clarify his need to move beyond the secular when reading, creating, or writing about poetry.[13]

This leaves Heaney's readers wondering whether poetic form itself can be credited with the power Heaney wishes it to have, but which has no necessary correlation with spiritual content. Larkin, here, is an ideal test case. 'The Redress of Poetry' affirms poetry's position 'on the side of life' whenever its form 'provokes consciousness into new postures' (Heaney 1995, 158) and whenever 'language does more than enough, as it does in all achieved poetry'. If George Herbert's work exemplifies redress at moments when 'the spirit is called extravagantly beyond the course that the usual life plots for it, when outcry or rhapsody is wrung from it as it flies in upon some unexpected image of its own solitude and distinctness' (Heaney 1995, 16), the very same could be said of 'Aubade', with the possible caveat that the latter leaves us inside 'the usual life'. Wheatley asks in puzzlement whether Heaney's valuation of form means that all art is on the side of life, and if not, what an art opposed to life would look like (Wheatley in O'Donoghue 2009, 131–132). Dennison is harsher still, opining that Heaney reneges on his own commitment to 'the achieved poem' (Dennison 2015, 167).

Yet Heaney's defense of poetic form has the potential to be the most inclusive aspect of his poetics of redress. If poets are to be capable of effecting their own means of finding grace rather than serving as passive receptacles for it, then this aspect is essential. If grace is to be a workable aesthetic concept rather than a strictly theological one, then the idea of an activist, meaning-making poetic form is necessary. Just as Heaney expands Yeats's remark that 'The Cold Heaven' was originally a poem about his mood in wintertime (Heaney 1995, 147), asserting that it goes far beyond mood and atmosphere in its achievement, so a poem like 'Aubade' goes far beyond its bleak atmospherics in its complexity of form and thinking. Perhaps mood itself, however, does have the potential for depth and complexity and should not be dismissed as a superficial effect: Larkin's poems struggle with their own moods, as an aching longing for what we may call a secular grace continuously pains the speaker. It is a source of pain, not often leading to achieved vision or heroic triumph, and this longing itself must be opposed to the clay-white sky showing nothing in 'Aubade'. The intensity of Larkin's idealism guarantees that he will not find this sort of grace easily; his sense that truth is often opposed to beauty keeps him from generating grace-filled moments by reneging on his commitment to honesty. The vulnerability of his poetic persona precludes him from taking on the heroic posture that Yeats wishes to assume—such a

126   *Magdalena Kay*

posture is not true to his own poetic spirit. His gift is to plumb the depths of vulnerability rather than to establish a new form of heroism that vanquishes the potentially disabling conditions of the contemporary moment to which he gives voice. This cannot be equated with surrender to the force of gravity. Weil's evocative dichotomy strains to accommodate a poet such as Larkin. His grace, if we can even stretch the term this far, will be non-religious and will run the risk of being dismissed or deemed insufficient; hence, his ability to provide redress may also be questioned. Larkin's devotion to form and obstinate aestheticism can be allied with what Heaney terms, *pace* Yeats, the spiritual intellect's great work, but only if the idea of spirit can be decoupled from religious belief. Heaney's notion of redress has proven controversial and complex because it carries such potential power, and that very potential urges us to refine and redefine its terms in the interest of empowering the contemporary lyric.

Notes

1 Weil furthermore insists upon the 'unintelligible nature of man's relation to God (Weil 2004b, 57). This emphasis upon not-knowing establishes a dynamic within Weil's theology that is quite different from the dynamic between gravity-laden reality and transcendence in Heaney's aesthetics. Although Heaney is sympathetic to the concept of mystery and wise passivity, his effort to define the means by which poetry summons transcendence is, in many ways, contrary to Weil's effort to defend the need for grace.

2 The concept of humans dwelling in between two realms is glossed by Rozelle-Stone and Davis as "intermediaries," and connected to the mediation of contraries. The human soul can indeed be drawn 'up' toward God while in this state. Beauty itself can be seen as '*metaxu*', attracting human souls toward the divine (see Rozelle-Stone and Davis), yet Weil does not empower art as thoroughly as does Heaney.

3 Andrew Motion sees this in literary terms as a dramatic conflict within the poems between plain speech and 'something nearly Yeatsian, Symbolist, or even Eliotic' (Motion 1993, 445).

4 Barbara Everett was one of the first scholars to argue for understanding Larkin as an aesthete made in the fin-de-siècle mold. Edna Longley has expanded upon Everett's arguments, while Andrew Waterman has argued for the importance of the 'beyond' in Larkin's work. These critics, and others, have established a rather different view of Larkin from Heaney's disenchanted view. It has also become increasingly commonplace to view Larkin's own skeptical (sometimes cynical) comments in interview with a grain of salt, even when it comes to seemingly straightforward matters of literary influence (for example, the decision to jettison Yeats in favor of Hardy).

5 James Booth notes that the working title of the poem was originally 'Spring and bachelors' (Booth 2014, 145).

6 It may be worth recalling that Mandelstam was not punished for writing poems of unmoralized joy, but for writing a critical ode to Stalin that made his political views clear.

7 'The Journey Back' was originally commissioned by George Hartley for a memorial tribute to Philip Larkin, published as *Philip Larkin 1922–1985: A Tribute* (London: Marvell, 1988). It was subsequently republished in Seeing Things, in which context the characterization of Larkin as 'a nine-to-five man who had

The Limits of Redress   127

seen poetry' would have set up a parallel between his visionary experience and Heaney's own—both poets see things. 'Joy or Night' reproaches Larkin for not using this visionary capacity for the purpose of redress.

8 Helen Vendler backs away from negotiating the debate over Larkin's relative placement on, or away from, the side of life: 'But there can be no rational argument on this plane', she exclaims, as 'each poet founds his creed on deep and convincing emotional experience'. Yet claiming that '[it] is for those who share Larkin's convictions to defend him' suggests it possible for unlike-minded critics to back away from the difficult yet necessary task of evaluating the artistry of a poet who evokes conditions they may not enjoy contemplating. See Vendler (2014).

9 *Letters Home*, containing letters from Philip to Eva Larkin, was published in 2018.

10 Larkin's identification with Eva is no secret to readers of his letters. As he writes to Eva, referring to his sister, 'Fancy [Kitty] saying we were utterly unlike each other! Only as one red is utterly unlike another red, I should have thought' (Larkin 2018, 411).

11 Dennison demonstrates the importance of Matthew Arnold as a precursor for Heaney's redressive effort. Arnold's vision of the redemptive function of the arts in a post-Christian milieu lies behind Heaney, just as Dennison believes Arnold's vision of 'adequacy' lies behind Heaney's redress (n.b. Arnold's 'adequacy' has also been critiqued in ways analogical to critiques of Heaney's redress) (see Dennison 2015, 180–181).

12 Kieran Quinlan gives a pithy and compelling account of this process in his essay entitled 'Catholicism' in Higgins (2021, 211–220).

13 Michael Symmons Roberts points to a general terminological problem for contemporary poets: those who wish to explore the area of experience that used to be called religious find themselves stuck with a vocabulary derived from a mostly Christian context. Although Roberts points to the loss of a shared symbolic language (Roberts 2013, 696), perhaps the opposite is also true: the language available for speaking of sublimity, depth, intensity and even beauty is often unsecular. See Roberts in Robinson (2013, 696–697).

Works Cited

Beisch, June (1986) 'An Interview with Seamus Heaney', *The Literary Review* 29.2: 161–169.

Booth, James (1997) 'The Turf Cutter and the Nine-to-Five Man: Heaney, Larkin, and "The Spiritual Intellect's Great Work"'. *Twentieth Century Literature* 43.4: 369–393.

Booth, James (2014) *Philip Larkin: Life, Art and Love*, London: Bloomsbury.

Brown, John (2002) *In the Chair: Interviews with Poets from the North of Ireland*, Cliffs of Moher, County Clare, Ireland: Salmon Publishing.

Cavanagh, Michael (1998) 'Fighting off Larkin: Seamus Heaney and "Aubade"', *Canadian Journal of Irish Studies* 24.2: 63–75.

Cavanagh, Michael (2009) *Professing Poetry: Seamus Heaney's Poetics*, Washington, DC: Catholic University of America Press.

Curtis, Tony, editor (2001) *The Art of Seamus Heaney*, 4th edition, Bridgend: Poetry Wales Press.

Dennison, John (2015) *Seamus Heaney and the Adequacy of Poetry*, Oxford: Oxford University Press.

128   *Magdalena Kay*

Farndale, Nigel (2001) Interview with Seamus Heaney, *Telegraph*, 5 April 2001, Telegraph.co.uk.

Foster, Roy (2020) *On Seamus Heaney*, Princeton, NJ: Princeton University Press.

Hartley, George, editor (1988) *Philip Larkin 1922–1985: A Tribute*, London: Marvell.

Heaney, Seamus (1980) *Preoccupations: Selected Prose 1968–1978*, New York: Farrar, Straus, & Giroux.

Heaney, Seamus (1987) *The Haw Lantern*, London: Faber and Faber.

Heaney, Seamus (1989) *The Government of the Tongue: Selected Prose 1978–87*, New York: Farrar, Straus & Giroux.

Heaney, Seamus (1991) *Seeing Things*, London: Faber and Faber.

Heaney, Seamus (1995) *The Redress of Poetry: Oxford Lectures*, London: Faber and Faber.

Higgins, Geraldine, editor (2021), *Seamus Heaney in Context*, Cambridge: Cambridge University Press.

Ingelbien, Raphael (2000) 'Seamus Heaney and the Importance of Larkin', *Journal of Modern Literature* 24.1: 471–482.

James, Stephen (2017) *Shades of Authority: The Poetry of Lowell, Hill and Heaney*, Liverpool: Liverpool University Press.

Larkin, Philip (1983) *Required Writing: Miscellaneous Pieces 1955–1982*, London: Faber.

Larkin, Philip (1992) *Selected Letters of Philip Larkin, 1940–1985*, edited by Anthony Thwaite, London: Faber.

Larkin, Philip (2001) *Further Requirements: Interviews, Broadcasts, Statements and Book Reviews 1952–1985*, edited by Anthony Thwaite, London: Faber.

Larkin, Philip (2010) *Letters to Monica*, edited by Anthony Thwaite, London: Faber.

Larkin, Philip (2012) *Complete Poems*, edited by Archie Burnett, New York: Farrar, Straus & Giroux.

Larkin, Philip (2018) *Letters Home 1936–1977*, edited by James Booth, London: Faber.

McDonald, Peter (2002) *Serious Poetry: Form and Authority, from Yeats to Hill*, Oxford: Oxford University Press, 2002.

Motion, Andrew (1993) *Philip Larkin: A Writer's Life*, New York: Farrar, Straus & Giroux, 1993.

O'Brien, Eugene, editor (2016) *'The Soul Exceeds Its Circumstances': The Later Poetry of Seamus Heaney*, Notre Dame, IN: University of Notre Dame Press.

O'Donoghue, Bernard, editor (2009) *The Cambridge Companion to Seamus Heaney*, Cambridge: Cambridge University Press.

O'Driscoll, Dennis (2008) *Stepping Stones: Interviews with Seamus Heaney*, New York: Farrar, Straus & Giroux.

Rozelle-Stone, A. Rebecca and Benjamin P. Davis (2022) 'Simone Weil', in *The Stanford Encyclopedia of Philosophy*, Summer 2022 Edition, edited by Edward N. Zalta. https://plato.stanford.edu/archives/sum2022/entries/simone-weil/ [Accessed 19 Sept. 2023].

Robinson, Peter, editor (2013) *The Oxford Handbook of Contemporary British and Irish Poetry*, Oxford: Oxford University Press.

Vendler, Helen (2014) 'Why Aren't They Screaming?', *London Review of Books* 36.21, 6 Nov. 2014. https://www.lrb.co.uk/the-paper/v36/n21/helen-vendler/why-aren-t-they-screaming [Accessed 22 Nov. 2022].

Weil, Simone (2004a) *Gravity and Grace*, trans. Emma Crawford and Mario von der Ruhr, London; New York: Routledge Classics.

Weil, Simone (2004b) *The Notebooks of Simone Weil*, trans. Arthur Wills, Oxford; New York: Routledge & Kegan Paul.

7 Different Animals

Heaney's Public and Poetic Ted Hughes

Caoimhe Higgins

Seamus Heaney was initially exposed to the poetry of Ted Hughes while studying as an undergraduate at Queen's University in Belfast. He 'encountered the work of Ted Hughes' in Al Alvarez's *The New Poetry* and recounted reading Hughes's second collection of poetry at the local library (Heaney 1989, 7). However, it was the latter experience of Hughes's work that seems to have had the most impact:

> I remember the day I opened Ted Hughes's *Lupercal* in the Belfast Public Library ... suddenly, the matter of contemporary poetry was the material of my own life ... I got this thrill out of trusting my own background, and I started [writing] a year later.
>
> (Randall 1979, 14)

In the poetry of *Lupercal,* with its visceral images of slaughtered animals in 'A View of a Pig' and cratered farms in 'Crow Hill', Heaney found images reminiscent, if not identical, to those from his upbringing in Derry. Hughes had inadvertently captured Heaney's childhood and, in doing so, provided him with the confidence and confirmation necessary to pursue a career in poetry. He further influenced Heaney's work through his peers as while teaching in Belfast during the 1960s, Heaney received tuition from Philip Hobsbaum, who was both a peer of Hughes and 'a fervent believer in his work' (Morrison 1982, 18). With early impressions such as these and influences that manifested in both peers and poetry, it is no surprise that upon meeting Hughes in person for the first time, Heaney recalled 'trembling with excitement and shyness' (McCrum 2009).

In the decades that followed their first real-life encounter, Hughes and Heaney formed a friendship that would span the next three decades. From a poetic perspective, they worked together to edit and publish two anthologies of poetry, *The Rattle Bag* in 1982 and *The School Bag* in 1997 and from a personal perspective, they supported and mentored each other through correspondence that they exchanged from the mid-seventies until the late nineties.

Hughes's support and mentoring of Heaney can be traced through extracts taken from the *Letters of Ted Hughes*, where Hughes can be seen 'appraising

DOI: 10.4324/9781003456148-8

Different Animals 131

and encouraging the younger poet's progress from the volume *Wintering Out* onwards' (Hughes 2009, 489). Subsequently, for every milestone in Heaney's life, literary or otherwise, there is a letter from Hughes to mark it. In 1984, following the publication of Heaney's *Station Island,* Hughes wrote, 'well, what a book! The passages where you tackle the greatest fright seem to me the most masterful successes. And I get the feeling your real kingdom is in there – that's your way in and forward' (Hughes 2009, 488). In 1989, when Heaney became the Chair of Poetry at Oxford University, Hughes wrote, 'the thought of what you might be able to do, as the voice of Irishness, at Oxford, gives me a real shock of excitement' (Hughes 2009, 565). And finally, in 1995, when Heaney was awarded the Nobel Prize for Literature, Hughes wrote, 'congratulations in a poor tame word, for what seems so naturally right, and mysteriously meant' (Hughes 2009, 683).

Heaney's support and mentoring of Hughes is just as evident in the letters that they exchanged, and particularly in those leading up to their final year of correspondence. In a letter to Heaney dated New Year's Day 1998, Hughes wrote, 'your letter overwhelmed me. I dearly wanted to know what you would feel about all of those pieces, and about the niceties and not-so-niceties of publishing them – your opinion above everybody's' (Hughes 2009, 703). Hughes was referring to his collection, *Birthday Letters*, which he had sent to Heaney four months before publication. His ask for Heaney's opinion on what was to become a controversial collection of poetry is striking as later in the same letter Hughes admits to having a 'very sudden determination to ignore every kind of reaction' to the poems and 'every possible impropriety of revealing them' (Hughes 2009, 703).

Following Hughes's death in the winter of 1998, Heaney remained supportive of his friend publicly and posthumously. At Hughes's funeral service in 1998, Heaney revealed that 'no death had been as devastating to poetry as Hughes's death, and that no death outside his family had hurt him as much' (Hart 2012, 76). At Hughes's memorial service in 1999, Heaney remembered how his friend's coffin 'rode towards the door on a clear channel of light and air' and expressed how his death was 'a heartbreak for all those who knew and loved him' (Heaney 1999). And finally, in 2011, Heaney honoured Hughes at Westminster Abbey in London by reading two poems at his plaque unveiling ceremony to celebrate his friend's esteemed new place in Poet's Corner (Westminster Abbey, 2011).

After Heaney's death in 2013, the pair's friendship was again hidden from public view until 2020, when Pembroke College at the University of Cambridge acquired what *The Guardian* described as a 'treasure trove of unseen Ted Hughes and Seamus Heaney writing' (Flood 2020). The collection of writings included published and unpublished poems by Heaney and '25 letters from Hughes, written over 30 years' (Flood 2020). The find was indicative of the poets' friendship and relationship with Barrie Cooke, who, together, Dr Mark Wormald described as the 'rough, wild equivalent of the Bloomsbury group' (Flood 2020).

132   *Caoimhe Higgins*

From their letters to their literary influence, the details of this friendship are undoubtedly welcome additions to both respective biographies, giving glimpses into a bond that seems to have been built on support and sound-boarding. Raphael Ingelbien aptly compares this bond to an image from Heaney's poem 'Casting and Gathering' from which he quotes 'when one man casts, the other gathers/And then vice versa, without changing sides' (Heaney 1991, 13). This quote, according to Ingelbien, depicts a 'bond between two imaginations that often fished in the same poetic waters' and seems to be a succinct summary of Ted Hughes and Seamus Heaney (Ingelbien 1999, 627).

Some critics were not, however, as forgiving as Ingelbien. Granted for some, writers like Ted Hughes 'were natural mentors for [Heaney] to adopt', due to the 'strong sense of place' within their poems (Parker 1993, 42), but for others, his early poems were 'at best apprentice work and at worst clumsy and derivative' (Morrison 1989, 18). Literary critic Blake Morrison went as far as to argue that Heaney's reliance on Hughes's poetry and perspectives made him guilty of 'sounding like a hobnailed version of Hughes' (Morrison 1989, 18).

The combination of these personal details and somewhat contested public opinions cast an interesting light on Heaney's prose, and particularly to Hughes's appearance in said prose. His name appears in many of Heaney's essays in a variety of different guises, with the extent of Heaney's analysis and portrayal of his friend varying throughout the collections. For example, in *Finders Keepers*, Hughes appears in an essay 'On Ted Hughes's 'Littleblood'' as Heaney performs a short analysis of the poem in question, by paying particularly close attention to its title. In *The Government of the Tongue*, Hughes appears in a chapter titled 'The Indefatigable Hoof-taps: Sylvia Plath' and is called upon as witness to the poetic processes of confessional poet, Sylvia Plath. And finally, in *The Government of the Tongue*, Hughes appears as a skilled poet and prime example of T.S Eliot's idea of the auditory imagination, in a chapter titled 'Englands of the Mind'.

This chapter will focus on two of the aforementioned essays from Heaney's prose; 'The Indefatigable Hoof-taps: Sylvia Plath' from *The Government of the Tongue* and 'Englands of the Mind' from *Preoccupations*. In the former, Hughes is referred to as a public figure who edits poetry, while in the latter, he is referred to as a skilled poet who writes poetry. This chapter will deconstruct Heaney's portrayal of the public and poetic Ted Hughes, paying particular attention to how Heaney succeeds in managing personal biography with poetic output. This biographical management will be examined both from the perspective of Heaney's friendship with Hughes and his knowledge of the celebrity that surrounded Hughes.

The Poet in Preoccupations

Preoccupations is a collection of prose that examines the work of many poets, including John Hewitt, Gerard Manley Hopkins, Patrick Kavanagh and Robert Lowell. Each of these poets is provided with the analytical scope of

Different Animals 133

an entire essay, where Heaney has space to thoroughly examine their works, alongside the biographical and historical contexts surrounding them. For example, Lowell's chapter examines his poetry in the face of what Heaney described as 'a conflict between his love of literature and his sense of his times' (Heaney 1980, 221), Kavanagh's chapter examines his poetry while acknowledging 'matters of audience and tradition' (Heaney 1980, 115) and Hopkins' chapter seeks to 'approach him from the circumference of his art rather than from the centre of himself' (Heaney 1980, 79).

In the light of these poets who are given entire chapters, it is a wonder why Heaney did not afford Hughes the same critical space. Instead, he groups him into a chapter with two other poets, Geoffrey Hill and Philip Larkin. Heaney's decision to do so seems somewhat unfounded when, in Hewitt's chapter, he remarks that 'Auden, Dylan Thomas, Larkin and Hughes have all left their traces on the decades they dominated' (Heaney 1980, 207). If Hughes did, in fact, dominate his decade, why did this not warrant further study? Furthermore, as a poet whose early influence, according to Edna Longley, 'owes a debt to the Ted Hughes of *Wodwo*', it seems strange that he would not provide his peer with a full essay analysis (Longley, 1997, 53). One could argue that while his Hughesian influence would be reason enough to give Hughes a full chapter, their closeness might have been reason enough to deny Hughes a full chapter. Longley argues that for Heaney's poetry, 'his comments on its importance to Ted Hughes interprets his own motives' (Longley 1997, 56), so perhaps an analysis of Hughes would have been an analysis of the early Heaney.

Grouped with Larkin and Hill, Hughes is the first to be examined in 'Englands of the Mind', as Heaney sets out to assess T.S. Eliot's idea of the auditory imagination. Defined by Eliot as the 'feeling for syllable and rhythm, penetrating far below the conscious levels of thought and feeling', the auditory imagination involves 'sinking to the most primitive and forgotten' parts of oneself by 'returning to the origin and bringing something back' (Eliot 1933, 119). It seems to be poetry that invokes the music of memory for a space which, over time, has become 'consciously precious' (Heaney 1980, 151). In the case of Heaney's poetic pawns, Hughes, Hill and Larkin, all three are motivated to write by a 'defensive love of their territory' as they return to the England of their minds to cast a net for their poems, in order to bring something back (Heaney 1980, 150).

Poets of the auditory imagination are, according to Eliot, not just concerned with 'the rhythmic and syllabic textures of verse', but rather with 'that strange "music" that arises from and is heard beyond these crossed acoustics' (Eliot 1933, 119). Heaney interprets this idea as 'a desire to preserve indigenous traditions' and mainly 'to keep open the imagination's supply to the past' (Heaney 1980, 151). It seems similar to an idea that Heaney entertains in an earlier chapter titled 'Feelings into Words', where, when speaking about his poem 'Digging', he admits, 'what generated the poem about memory was something lying beneath the very floor of memory' which was a childhood impression of an old warning about the bog in Mossbawn (Heaney 1980, 56). It

134   *Caoimhe Higgins*

is the idea that the auditory imagination is a retelling of 'orphaned memories', triggered by the drowned echoes of previous times and places. If, according to Heaney, 'poems come out of some previousness' from an energy that he likens to 'psychic fossil fuel', his chapter on the auditory imagination is one most aligned with his own poetic perspectives (Manufacturing Intellect 2016).

Before Heaney can characterise the England of Hughes's mind in *Preoccupations*, he first focuses on the titles of Hughes's collections, describing them as 'casts made into the outback of our animal recognition' (Heaney 1980, 153). He begins by tacking the suggestions associated with Hughes's second collection of poetry, *Lupercal*, as he shakes the word until all its connotations and contexts are left spread on the page. The first suggestion that arises is something Heaney likens to 'wolfish stinks' which upon closer inspection, leads him to suggestions of 'Shakespeare's *Julius Caesar*'. The connotations then reach their conclusion as they cast Heaney back to a sacrificial festival held in Ancient Rome, 'about the bounds of the Palatine city'. It is Hughes's focus on origin, according to Heaney, that saved 'English poetry in the fifties from a too suburban aversion of the attention from the elemental' (Heaney 1980, 153).

His complementary context of Hughes's titles resumes as Heaney moves on to *Wodwo*, which he describes as an art which 'is one of clear outline and inner richness' as Hughes seeks out 'shapes, mysteries and rituals' to unintentionally create his auditory imagination (Heaney 1980, 153). Heaney then describes the England of Hughes's mind as such:

> a primeval landscape where stones cry out and horizons endure, where the elements inhabit the mind with a religious force, where the pebble dreams 'it is the foetus of god', 'where the staring angels go through', 'where all the stars bow down', where, with appropriately pre-Socratic force, water lies 'at the bottom of all things/utterly worn out utterly clear'.
>
> (Heaney 1980, 152)

Within this landscape, Heaney focuses on Hughes's use of vowels and consonants to construct the auditory imagination. Notably, Heaney refrains from using technical or linguistic jargon to explain Hughes's use of vowels and consonants which he argues provide 'vigour' to the writing (Heaney 1980, 154). Instead, immersed in the violently descriptive world of Hughes's England, he explains the syntax and suggestions of the poet's vowels and consonants through imagery. Introducing Hughes's consonants to the reader, Heaney depicts the following scene: 'his consonants are the Norsemen, the Normans, the Roundheads in the world of his vocables, hacking and hedging and hammering down the abundance and luxury and possible lasciviousness of the vowels' (Heaney 1980, 154).

Heaney proceeds by providing an example of these Norman-like consonants with a quote from arguably one of Hughes's most famous poems, 'The

Different Animals 135

Thought Fox', capitalising on the Norsemen as he encounters them in the line: 'I iMagine this MiDnighT MoMenT's foresT' (Heaney 1980, 154). He describes these opening lines as a hush, but one that is achieved violently from a syntactical perspective 'by the quelling, battening-down action of the m's and d's and t's' (Heaney 1980, 154). It is unlikely that such a perspective was gathered from Heaney's own reading of the poem, as he once admitted to having heard Hughes read 'The Thought Fox' several times (Heaney 2012). It is therefore likely that the 'battening-down' pronunciation of these lines was a practice learned from Hughes, rather than suggested by his verse. This argument is only furthered by the fact that this is not Heaney's only mention of hearing Hughes read his own poetry. In 'On Ted Hughes's 'Littleblood' from *Finders Keepers*, Heaney again notes how hearing Hughes's read the poem in person influenced his auditory imagining of the lines; 'Ted always read it with particular delicacy and intensity, articulating the *t* of 'eating' and the *d* and hard *c* of 'medical' so finely and distinctly' (Heaney 2003, 408).

Following his example of these Norman-like consonants, Heaney turns his attention to the vowels of the poem and refers to them as music. Refraining from providing an image for the vowels, as he did for the Roundhead consonants, Heaney imagines Hughes as 'a poet-warden' and 'vowel-keeper' and commends him on his 'breaking action' between vowels in the line 'an eye,/A widening deepening greenness,/Brilliantly, concentratedly' (Hughes 2019, 7). The vowels provide, naturally, longer sounds than the general staccato nature of consonants, which Heaney notes is how Hughes polices the pronunciation of his poems. His assessment of 'The Thought Fox' is then closed out with a final quote from the last stanza, within which Heaney draws attention to 'the monosyllabic consonantal bolts' (Heaney 1980, 154):

Till, with a sudden sharp hot stink of fox
It enters the dark hole of the head.
The window is starless still the clock ticks,
The page is printed.
(Hughes 2019, 7)

These lines bring Heaney to the conclusion that the auditory imagination in Hughes's poem is created by the dictated consonantal hush of the 'midnight moment forest', combined with the arrangement of 'vowel music' in the line 'something else is alive' (Hughes 2019, 7).

Having finished with 'The Thought Fox', Heaney's examination of this vowel music continues with the poem 'Fern', as the little lives of Hughes's vowels and consonants are brought into question once again, with Heaney remarking that the subject of this poem 'might be expected to woo the tender pious vowels from a poet rather than the disciplining consonants' (Heaney 1980, 154). He is, however, mistaken as while the quote 'here is the fern's frond, unfurling gesture', is dominated by the gentle notes of e's, u's and o's, it is not long before 'the frosty grip of those f's thaws out' (Heaney 1980,

136   Caoimhe Higgins

155). The reader is then left in the command of hard d's, g's and r's, as Heaney quotes, 'among them, the fern/Dances gravely, like the plume/Of a warrior returning' (Heaney 1980, 155).

Heaney's commitment to the characterisation of these vowels and consonants as living, animate things is an echo of the style of the poet that he is assessing. Hughes's poetry is an emblem of personifying nature and things to make them as animate as the actions of animals and humans. For example, in 'Incompatibilities', from his collection *The Hawk in the Rain*, he personifies desire as 'a vicious separator in spite', and in 'The Thought Fox', he gives the clock a human dose of loneliness (Hughes 2019, 19). Heaney's mimicking of this material provides prose that not only examines poetry but also mirrors it. This results in both an encompassing argument and a successful explanation of the bounds of the auditory imagination. Heaney continues to reflect on Hughes's poetics as he brings forward a poem called 'Warrior of the North':

> Bringing their frozen swords, their salt-bleached eyes, their salt bleached hair,
> The snow's stupefied anvils in rows,
> Bringing their envy,
> The slow ships fevered Southward, snails over the steep sheen of the water-globe.
>
> (Heaney 1980, 155)

The characterisation of consonants as Norsemen at the beginning of his argument has manifested into images of genuine Norsemen in this poem, which Heaney references to show 'the Hughes voice as I see it', and seems to be an attempt to establish a poet whose voice was 'born of an original vigour, fighting back over the same ground' (Heaney 1980, 155). Heaney's assessment of Hughes and his lesson on letters subsequently turns to dialect, and to a direct quotation from Hughes, about how he came to possess what Heaney labels 'gutturals from behind the sloped arms of consonants' (Heaney 1980, 155):

> I grew up in West Yorkshire. They have a very distinctive dialect there. Whatever speech you grow into, presumably your dialect stays alive in a sort of inner freedom... it's your childhood self there inside the dialect and that is possibly your real self or the core of it... Without it, I doubt if I would ever have written verse. And in the case of the West Yorkshire dialect, of course, it connects you directly and in your most intimate self to Middle English poetry.
>
> (Hughes 1971, cited in Heaney 1980, 10)

Hughes's passage, taken from the *London Magazine* in 1971, seems awfully close to Heaney's own literary and life history and strongly suggests that the reader should go back to the first chapter of *Preoccupations*. In a chapter titled 'Mossbawn', Heaney argues that 'an old superstition ratifies this hankering

Different Animals   137

for the underground side of things' and ponders the idea that childhood foundations are rigid and unmoving (Heaney 1980, 21). Specifically, he focuses on the idea that 'orphaned memories' of first learning how to read, write and speak are never truly paved over by life experience or university degrees. They are, to use Heaney's reference to Mossbawn, an *omphalos* 'meaning the navel, and hence the stone that marked the centre of the world' (Heaney 1980, 17). Returning to Hughes, Heaney paraphrases his *London Magazine* quote to say, 'in other words, [Hughes] finds that the original grain of his speech is a chip off the old block and that his work need not be a new planting but a new bud on an old bough' (Heaney 1980, 156). Although he is speaking of Hughes, it is hard not to hear these lines as Heaney speaking of himself.

This idea of Heaney speaking for himself through the guise of Hughes and his poetry is furthered by another long extract from the *London Magazine* in 1971, and particularly in the last line:

> Crowe Ransom was the one who gave me a model I felt I could use. He helped me get my words into focus... but this whole business of influences is mysterious... and after all the campaigns to make it new you're stuck with the fact that some of the Scots Border ballads still cut a deeper groove than anything written in the last forty years. Influences just seems to make it more and more unlikely that a poet will write what he alone could write.
>
> (Hughes 1971, cited in Heaney 1980, 10)

Seamus Heaney previously admitted how, upon reading Hughes's second collection of poems, *Lupercal*, when studying as an undergraduate in Belfast, 'the matter of contemporary poetry' suddenly became 'the material of [his] own life' (Randall 1979,14). He also admitted that Hughes's poems were foundational to his early career and described them as 'a powerful magic for [him] when [he] was beginning to write' (Heaney 2012). Therefore, his explanation of Hughes's influences in poetry is an interesting topic. It almost reads as a justification for the Hughesian influences on his own poetry. Heaney writes 'what Hughes alone could write depended for its release on the discovery of a way to unjam the energies of the dialect, to get a stomping ground for that inner freedom, to get that childhood self a disguise to roam at large in' (Heaney 1980, 156). The quotation seems to echo Heaney's experience at the Belfast public library in the 1960s.

Heaney ends his analysis of Hughes, before the study of Hill is to follow, by leaving the reader with a brief description of what has become known as Hughesian language. He provides one more Hughes poem for good measure which is prefaced with a descriptive outline of Hughes's body of work as such:

> This combination of ritual intensity, prose readiness, direct feeling and casual speech can be discovered... in the best poems of Lupercal, because in *Hawk in the Rain* and indeed in much of *Wodwo* and *Crow*,

138 *Caoimhe Higgins*

we are often in the presence of that titanic extravagance Hughes mentions, speech not so much mobilising and standing up to act as flexing and straining until it verges on the grotesque.

(Heaney 1980, 157)

Heaney's final reference to Hughes's is from the poem 'Pibroch', taken from *Wodwo*, the collection to which Longley previously argued Heaney 'owes a debt to' for his earlier poems (Longley, 1997, 53). Heaney calls the poem 'uniquely Hughesian in its very title', while reiterating Eliot's idea of the auditory imagination as in this final poem, Hughes can be seen 'fetching energy and ancestry from what is beyond the Pale and beneath the surface' (Heaney 1980, 157). Hughes has returned to 'the world 'beyond' words' to find something 'real and significant, but which continues to resist the conceptual frameworks of the word-bound imagination' (Eliot 1933, 119). The poem that Heaney then quotes in full is not examined, but rather left as an afterthought and conclusion to his assessment of Hughes, in a chapter that contains two other poets waiting to be assessed. His choice of poem is quoted 'because it links the childhood core with the adult opus' and is an example of a childhood dialect and experience that 'persists, survives, sustains, endures and informs' Hughes's imagination (Heaney 1980, 159).

As an examination of the poetic Hughes, Heaney provides a good analysis. He gives the reader an introduction to Hughes's 'primeval landscape where stones cry out and horizons endure' (Heaney 1980, 151) by analysing his use of vowels and consonants. He is particularly successful in this analysis as he mirrors Hughes's poetics by personifying these elements of syntax. He shows Hughes's dedication to Eliot's auditory imagination both in terms of the poems themselves and their guiding titles. However, perhaps the only negative aspect of the analysis is its closing section, specifically where 'Pibroch' is concerned, which could have been better utilised with a close reading of some, if not all, of its vowel and consonant relations.

The Public Figure in the Government of the Tongue

Seamus Heaney's *The Government of the Tongue* predominantly covers the T.S. Eliot Memorial Lectures that he gave at the University of Kent in 1986. The collection includes many other academic and critical pieces that Heaney delivered between 1982 and 1986, including several articles written for the *London Review of Books* and the *Yale Review*. As a collection of essays, *The Government of the Tongue* critically accounts for a substantial portion of the last century's poetic output and includes explicit analyses of Anton Chekov, Patrick Kavanagh, Osip Mandelstam, W.H. Auden, Robert Lowell and Sylvia Plath. Heaney pools his research from various historical, societal and poetic perspectives for these assessments, while occasionally leaning on the assumptions and definitions of poetic peers to assist him in his analysis, some of which include the likes of Ezra Pound, Dylan Thomas, and

W.B. Yeats. Notably, one peer mentioned in *The Government of the Tongue* is Ted Hughes, whose name appears in two of the collection's twelve chapters. Hughes' first mention is hardly of note; 'I got my hands on ... Alvarez's anthology, *The New Poetry*, where I encountered the work of Ted Hughes' (Heaney 1989, 7). His name does not appear again until the closing chapter, where one could argue he was expected to be found, in an essay titled 'The Indefatigable Hoof-taps: Sylvia Plath'.

Overall, Heaney's assessment of Plath aligns with his previous assessments of Kavanagh, Auden and others within the collection, as it is an essay-analysis that combines both poetry and biography. The latter is, however, kept within the strict limitations of the poetry influenced by it as Heaney echoes a quote from Hughes's poem 'Flounders' which states 'we only did what poetry told us to do' (Hughes 1999, 66). In his examination of Plath, Heaney uses both her poetry and writing processes to investigate 'the poet's need to get beyond ego in order to become the voice of more than autobiography' (Heaney 1989, 148). He cites a range of methods that previous poets have used to overcome this issue of biography, including what Robert Frost referred to as 'original cadencing', what Yeats referred to as 'somebody who is spoken through', and what T.S. Eliot referred to as 'the auditory imagination' (Heaney 1989, 148).

According to Heaney, Eliot and Frost were 'exercised by the idea that poetry housed older and deeper levels of energy than those supplied by explicit meaning and immediate rhythmic stimulus' (Heaney 1989, 148). However, despite introducing definitions from Frost and Yeats, Heaney does not use their poetry to illustrate the point. Instead, he houses their hypothesis within the grounds of Sylvia Plath's predominantly posthumous poetic career, of which Ted Hughes was an editor. In the case of Plath's poetry, Heaney argues that she was 'a poet governed by the auditory imagination to the point where her valediction to life consisted of a divesting of herself into words and echoes' (Heaney 1989, 149). Moreover, he argues that the government of this auditory imagination, in Plath's case, was not in full session until the arrival of the poems that would eventually make up her posthumous collection, *Ariel*. It is interesting to note Heaney's iteration of the auditory imagination in relation to the poetry of Sylvia Plath, as it the same framework that was used in *Preoccupations* to examine the poems of Ted Hughes. The repetition of Eliot's idea is, however, the only similarity between Heaney's assessment of the public Hughes and the private Hughes.

As previously outlined, Eliot's auditory imagination refers to the idea that poetry's craft, cadencing and content are drawn from a well that runs far deeper than the poets who exercise it realise. For a poet, the topic of a poem may be triggered by a moment or traced by memory, but the poetic encasement of literary features allows 'a tide out of language to carry individual utterance away upon a current stronger and deeper than the individual could have anticipated' (Heaney 1989, 148). Heaney refers to an 'auditory imagination' that 'not only unites for the poet the most ancient and most civilised mentalities' but:

140 *Caoimhe Higgins*

> also unites reader and poet and poem in an experience of enlargement, of getting beyond the confines of the first personal singular, of widening the lens of receptivity until it reaches and is reached by the world beyond the self.
>
> (Heaney 1989, 149)

Regarding this chapter's mention of Ted Hughes, Heaney's management of biography alone is the most significant critical feat, from two neighbouring perspectives. Firstly, and generally speaking, 'biographies have long been a staple in the world of Plath studies' (Brain 2006, 21). Furthermore, the biographies, including her life with Hughes, seem to live in 'a region of cultural near-exhaustion' (Parker 2013, 34). In the arena of literature's infamous couple, it has become almost impossible to discuss the writings of one without the celebrity of the other. Yet, Heaney succeeds in doing so. One could perhaps argue that the cult of personality around Plath had yet to reach its peak in 1986 when these lectures were first delivered. However, no corrections were made to Heaney's essay on Plath when Faber published the study in 1989, so one must accept that his analysis was apt for its time and the times to follow. Heaney's direct refrain from 'depicting [Plath's] life as a soap opera' allows him to sidestep a common 'failure to say anything serious or important about the poetry' (Brain 2006, 25). Secondly, Heaney's feat of biographical management is even more apparent due to the evident and omniscient connection between Sylvia Plath and Ted Hughes and, subsequently, Heaney's friendship and mentorship with Hughes. His resistance to comment on anything other than the poetry and processes that Plath offered, whether under the heading of the auditory imagination or otherwise, demonstrates a critical skill that many have failed to show to both Plath and Hughes.

Returning to Hughes's appearance in this chapter, his name is scattered five times throughout the essay. Heaney refers to him as Plath's husband in the first instance and refuses to award him another title in subsequent mentions, despite his role morphing from husband to editor. For the most part, the direct quotations that Heaney takes from Hughes are not typically those of a spouse as they echo the iterations of an editor, and someone who worked closely with Plath's work. Hughes was responsible for the poetic arrangement and publishing of *Ariel* in 1965 and the *Collected Poems* in 1981 and, for the most part, refrained from publicly commenting on his relationship with Plath, until *Birthday Letters* in 1998. Therefore, one may ask why Heaney labelled Hughes her husband rather than her editor, especially if the focus was on her poetry and not her personal life. Moreover, while the first two or three references to Hughes are specifically suggestive of his domestic life with Plath and, therefore, the husband's title is apt, the latter mentions specifically reference his experience as editor. Yet, Heaney never updates the label. His critical decision, or lack thereof, in marking Hughes as editor in this chapter is odd. One could argue that referring to Hughes as editor instead of husband would have provided more legitimacy to both his and Heaney's claims about her poetry and processes. Why Heaney refused the term editor is a question whose answer remains unclear, but his ability to omit this information and still succeed in providing an objective account of Plath's poetry, with several mentions of Hughes's influence, is an excellent example of critical feat.

Hughes first appears on the fifth page of the analysis as Heaney writes, 'even if her husband had not given us an image of her as the obedient neophyte, we could have deduced it from the procedures of her early verse' (Heaney 1989, 152). Hughes's image of Plath is quoted below:

She wrote her early poems very slowly ... thesaurus open on her knee, in her large, strange handwriting, like a mosaic, where every letter stands separate within the work, a hieroglyph to itself ... Every poem grew complete from its own root, in that laborious inching way, as if she were working out a mathematical problem, chewing her lips, putting a thick dark ring of ink around each word that stirred her on the page of the thesaurus.

(Heaney 1989, 152)

According to Heaney, Hughes's description of Plath is from the late 1950s when she was unknowingly writing her first collection, *The Colossus*. Hughes, living with Plath at the time and fulfilling the husband's role, is not mentioned again until a few pages later when his small biographical note is paraphrased in Heaney's assessment of Plath's poem 'Mussel Hunter at Rock Harbour'. Heaney returns to Hughes for commentary on the verse and to provide evidence to support his own assessment. Heaney argues, 'this is a poem in syllabics, seven syllables to the line, seven lines to the stanza; it inches itself forward as the crabs do' (Heaney 1989, 156). Hughes's welcomed support as husband then inches in again as Heaney reminds the reader that his assessment of her syllabic syntax moving gradually over the page of the poem is just 'as Ted Hughes said her poems did in the beginning, felicity by felicity' (Heaney 1989, 156).

Hughes's third appearance in this chapter seems to fulfil elements of husband and editor, as Heaney focuses on 'the final stage of her artistic achievement' (Heaney 1989, 150). Notably, Heaney admits how Plath's posthumous and most successful poetry 'obviously and notoriously was linked to the developments in her psychological and domestic life', suggesting, or perhaps confirming, that he was aware of the domestic drama that surrounded the two but chose not to include it in the analysis (Heaney 1989, 150). For this third mention of Hughes, who now rests somewhere in the space between husband and editor, Heaney examines Plath's tree-centred poems, specifically focusing on 'Moon and the Yew Tree'. He labels it a poem derived from 'a subject set by Ted Hughes' (Heaney 1989, 161). He then returns to Hughes for an explanation of the poem's conception:

142 *Caoimhe Higgins*

> Early one morning, in the dark, I saw the full moon setting on a large yet that grows in the churchyard, and I suggested she make a poem of it. By midday, she had written it. It depressed me greatly. It's my suspicion that no poem can be a poem that is not a statement from the powers in control of our life, the ultimate suffering and decision in us.
>
> (Heaney 1989, 161)

An earlier quotation from Tracy Brain, taken from Routledge's *Modern Confessional Writing*, stated, 'biographies have long been a staple in the world of Plath studies', and more specifically, biographies which include her life with Hughes (Brain 2006, 21). Heaney diverts from the norm as while he uses elements of Plath's biography, he is not overwhelmed by it, nor is he scared to refer to it. Instead, he handpicks the aspects of her day-to-day life that correspond to her poetry and literary habits, while refusing to mention anything which tethers on the edge of her intimate personal relations. This is especially true of Hughes, who, in this case, was both the controversial husband of the subject, Plath, and at the same time, friend and mentor of the analyst. In the preceding quotation, Heaney clearly states that the poem's idea was Hughes's, which was rather brave of him to do.

Hughes's subsequent mentions in the final chapter of Heaney's *The Government of the Tongue* are those of an editor both in the language that is quoted and the texts from which the commentary is pulled. England's former poet laureate slowly shapeshifts from what an observant husband witnessed at home with his wife, to what an editor collected in the drafts and details of publishing poetry. Moreover, it is a transition so seamlessly done that Heaney does not even refer to it. Hughes morphs from intimate partner to experienced editor with no notion or note from the critic.

Hughes as editor seems to begin when Heaney notes that 'Ted Hughes has written about Sylvia Plath's breakthrough into her deeper self and her poetic fate', before referencing Hughes's edition of her *Collected Poems* within which he 'provides a note to 'Elm', and an earlier draft from which this deeply swayed final version emerged' (Heaney 1989, 160). Hughes's notes, as editor of 'Elm', continue later in the chapter as Heaney resumes his unearthing of the processes behind Plath's poetry and notes:

> It is therefore no surprise to read in Ted Hughes's notes of 1970 that he perceives 'Elm' as the poem which initiates the final phase, that phase whose poems I attempted to characterise earlier as seeming to have sprung into being at the behest of some unforeseen but completely irresistible command.
>
> (Heaney 1989, 163)

Hughes's mention in this chapter is evidence of Heaney's critical skills, specifically in handling and managing biography. In the analyst's eyes, he is not a peer or a poet. He witnesses Plath's poetry and processes, morphing instantly

Different Animals   143

from husband to editor and back to husband again. In the conclusive pages of his essay, Heaney perhaps drifts into the publicity of Plath's persona as he provides a public and poetic context that follows some of Plath's poems, specifically 'Daddy':

> However its violence and vindictiveness can be understood or excused in light of the poet's parental and marital relations, remains, nevertheless, so entangled in biographical circumstances and rampages so permissively in the history of other people's sorrows that it simply overdraws our rights to its sympathies.
>
> (Heaney 1989, 165)

However, he justifies his brief mention of biography before returning to the poetry:

> Sylvia Plath, a poet who grew to a point where she permitted herself identification with the oracle and gave herself over as a vehicle for possession; a poet who sought and found a style of immediate speech, animated by the tones of a voice speaking excitedly and spontaneously; a poet governed by the auditory imagination to the point where her valediction to life consisted of a divesting of herself into words and echoes.
>
> (Heaney 1989, 149)

In his justification for using Plath as his muse for this concluding chapter, Heaney echoes Susan R. Van Dyne's assumption that 'Plath's habits of self-representation suggest she regarded her life as if it were a text that she could invent and rewrite' (Van Dyne 1999, 54). In other words, Plath provided a use for poetry instead of poetry providing a use for Plath. Moreover, as an examination of the public Hughes, Heaney does an impressive job as this is by no means a chapter about Ted Hughes. Heaney successfully examines the poetry of Sylvia Plath while simultaneously highlighting the literary processes that produced it. He gives weight to the biographical factors that influenced Plath's poetry, including Hughes's idea behind 'Moon and the Yew Tree', his hand in editing *Ariel* in 1965 and the *Collected Poems* in 1981, but never allows his influence to overshadow her poetic achievement.

Conclusion

In his foreword to *The School Bag*, which was co-edited with Ted Hughes in 1997, Heaney divulged an editing process that seems undoubtedly similar to the one adopted for his prose analyses: 'time and time again we were forced to decide whether personal affection for something not particularly 'major' could be allowed to outweigh the historical and canonical claims of a more obvious selection' (Hughes and Heaney 1997, xvii). In *Preoccupations* and *The Government of the Tongue*, Heaney manages his affection for Hughes,

144   *Caoimhe Higgins*

and indeed for the other writers that he examines, exceptionally well, by showing commanding skill in the management of biographical influence. In the essays 'Englands of the Mind' and 'The Indefatigable Hooftaps: Sylvia Plath', Heaney portrays Hughes's poetic and public life as two separate instances and only calls on biography if the poetry asks him to do so. This approach in the field of Ted Hughes studies is somewhat of a rarity as it is an area of research where the biographies of Hughes and his romantic partners live in 'a region of cultural near-exhaustion' (Parker 2013, 34).

Perhaps the only instance when Heaney could be considered guilty of blurring the lines between the poetic and public Hughes is in 'On Ted Hughes's 'Littleblood' which first appeared in *The Epic Poise: A Celebration of Ted Hughes* and later in *Finder Keepers*. As was the case for the *Preoccupations* essay, 'Englands of the Mind', Heaney first approaches Hughes from the poem's title:

> the name could belong to oral tradition, to fairy tale, to the world of *A Midsummer Night's Dream*. It could be the cognate of Peaseblossom and Mustardseed, an escape from the conversation of Peter Quince or Robin Starveling.
>
> (Heaney 2003, 407)

He then encounters the public figure of *The Government of the Tongue* and begins his biographical balancing act:

> coming at the end of a book dedicated 'In memory of Assia and Shura', this wisp of a ghost dancer could easily be conflated with the shade of the girl-child who in the meantime has 'Grown so wise grown so terrible/Sucking deaths mouldy tits'.
>
> (Heaney 2003, 408)

Heaney's mention of Assia, Hughes's partner after Plath, and Shura, their young daughter, echoes the biographical management of Plath and Hughes in *The Government of the Tongue*. Heaney uses elements of Hughes's biography, but he is not overwhelmed by it or scared to refer to it. Instead, he handpicks what corresponds to the poetry, demonstrating his skill as a critical analyst and academic researcher, since his prose essays were generally taken from his career as a lecturer. His refusal to provide background on Assia and Shura and their relationship to Hughes may even inadvertently encourage the uninformed reader to attend to their own research on the topic, instead of relying on another critic's assumption. This conscious and careful selection of biography and poetry is fitting when considered against the backdrop of a young, trembling Heaney meeting Ted Hughes for the first time in the 1960s. For Heaney, perhaps demonstrating his skill as a literary critic would have meant more to his mentor than any defence of character. His connection to Hughes is foundational to understanding the extent of his mastery in these prose analyses as by highlighting the content of their letters and mentorship, it gives weight to the affection Heaney pushed aside to perform his critical assessment.

Different Animals   145

Ted Hughes was a regular mention and point of reference in the interviews that were scattered throughout Seamus Heaney's career. When asked about his lecturing posts during an interview with Karl Miller, Heaney recalled Hughes's warning of working in academia for those who consider themselves to be poets; 'as long as you don't change your language, you're safe enough' (Heaney and Miller 2000, 45). When concluding *Writer and Righter*, written for the fourth annual IHRC Human Rights Lecture in 2009, Heaney concluded with a quote that read 'the poet Ted Hughes once said that what distinguishes the work we recognise as poetry from other kinds of literary production is the fact that it arises from what he called "the ultimate suffering and decision" in us (Heaney 2010, 17). That same year, in an interview with *The Observer*, Heaney repeated his quote of suffering in poetry and lamented, 'I always felt safer for Ted's friendship somehow … he was foundational to me. As you know, he transmitted a desire to be more of yourself to yourself'. Notably, the interviewer Robert McCrum later recalled how 'several times in our conversation, Heaney referred to 'Ted' with a deep sense of personal loss' (McCrum 2009).

While the letters, literary analyses and interviews clearly illustrate a career heavily influenced by the poetry and person of Ted Hughes, Heaney was still his own poet. Ingelbien argues that 'Hughes's popularity in the 1960s had created the climate in which Heaney's first two collections were greeted by critical acclaim', suggesting that an ode to the Hughesian influence is due (Ingelbien 1999, 627). However, as his analyses of Hughes's poetry prove, Heaney was acutely aware of his own poetic skill and public persona. He was, in his own words, 'a different kind of animal from Ted' but still 'grateful for the release that reading his work' provided (Heaney 1981, cited in Ingelbien 1999, 627). The last letter addressed to Seamus Heaney in the *Letters of Ted Hughes* is dated the 27th of June 1998, four months before Hughes's death, and is laced with the same support from their first correspondence decades before:

Honour apart, it seems to me a rather wonderful piece, many textured and a whole cat's cradle of subtle counterbalances. A very memorable clarity and deep-toned music too. And one of your very best bits of *Beowulf* … I was/am very grateful that you've written this piece.
(Hughes 2009, 717)

Works Cited

Dyne, Susan R. (1999) 'The Problem of Biography', in *The Cambridge Companion to Sylvia Plath*, edited by Jo Gill, Cambridge: Cambridge University Press, 14–26.

Eliot, T. S. (1933) *The Use of Poetry and the Use of Criticism*, London: Faber & Faber.

Flood, A. (2020). 'Treasure Trove of Unseen Ted Hughes and Seamus Heaney Writing found', *The Guardian* [online] 14 Nov. available at: https://www.theguardian.com/books /2020/nov/14/treasure-trove-of-unseen-hughes-and-heaney-writing-found [Accessed 15 Aug. 2023].

146   Caoimhe Higgins

Brain, Tracy (2009) 'Dangerous Confessions: The Problem of Reading Sylvia Plath Biographically', in *Modern Confessional Writing: New Critical Essays*, edited by Jo Gill, London: Routledge, 11–32.

Hart, Henry (2012) 'Seamus Heaney and Ted Hughes: A Complex Friendship', *The Sewanee Review*, vol. 120, no. 1, 76–90.

Heaney, Seamus (1980) *Preoccupations*, London: Faber.

Heaney, Seamus (1989) *The Government of the Tongue*, London: Faber.

Heaney, Seamus (1989) *The Place of Writing*, Emory Studies in Humanities, No. 1, Atlanta: Scholars Press.

Heaney, Seamus (1991) *Seeing Things*, London: Faber.

Heaney, Seamus (1999) 'A Great Man and A Great Poet', *The Observer* [online] 16 May. Available at https://www.theguardian.com/theobserver/1999/may/16/featuresreview. review2 [Accessed 15 August 2023].

Heaney, Seamus (2003) *Finders Keepers*, London: Faber.

Heaney, Seamus (2010) *Writer & Righter*, Dublin: Irish Human Rights Commission.

Heaney, Seamus (2012) *Seamus Heaney Reads a Poem by Ted Hughes, Plus One of His Own.* [online] www.youtube.com, available at: https://www.youtube. com/watch?v= 8vRTVrdg9GI [Accessed 20 Sept. 2023].

Heaney, Seamus and Karl Miller (2000) *Seamus Heaney in Conversation with Karl Miller*, London: Between the Lines.

Heaney, Seamus (2016) 'Manufacturing Intellect' *Seamus Heaney Interview*, available at https://www.youtube.com/watch?v=WT-dub5v4YA [Accessed 1 Oct. 2023].

Hughes, Ted (1999) *Birthday Letters*, London: Faber.

Hughes, Ted (2009) *Letters of Ted Hughes,* edited by Christopher Reid, London: Faber.

Hughes, Ted (2019) *The Hawk in the Rain*, London: Faber.

Hughes, Ted & Seamus Heaney (1982) *The Rattle Bag: An Anthology of Poetry*, London: Faber & Faber.

Hughes, Ted & Seamus Heaney (1997) *The School Bag*, London: Faber.

Ingelbien, Raphael (1999) 'Mapping the Misreadings: Ted Hughes, Seamus Heaney, and Nationhood', *Contemporary Literature*, vol. 40, no. 4, 627–658.

Longley, Edna (1997) '"Inner Empire" or "Artful Voyeur"? Seamus Heaney's *North*', *New Casebooks: Seamus Heaney*, edited by Michael Allen, London: MacMillan Press Ltd., 30–63.

McCrum, Robert (2009) 'Seamus Heaney: A Life of Rhyme', *The Observer*. [online] 19 July. Available at https://www.theguardian.com/books/2009/jul/19/seamus-heaney-interview [Accessed 23 Sept. 2023].

Morrison, Blake (1982) *Contemporary Writers: Seamus Heaney*, London: Methuen & Co. Ltd.

Parker, James (2013) 'Why Sylvia Plath Haunts American Culture', *The Atlantic Monthly*, https://www.theatlantic.com/magazine/archive/2013/06/why-sylvia-plath-haunts-american-culture/309310/ [Accessed 10 Aug. 2023].

Parker, Michael (1993) *Seamus Heaney: The Making of the Poet*, Dublin: Gill and MacMillan Ltd.

Randall, James (1979) 'An Interview with Seamus Heaney', *Ploughshares*, vol. 5, no. 3, 7–22.

Westminster Abbey (2011) Ted Hughes. *Westminster Abbey*, [online]. Available at https://www.westminster-abbey.org/abbey-commemorations/commemorations/ted-hughes [Accessed 10 Aug. 2023].

8 'Moving in Step'
Seamus Heaney on Patrick Kavanagh

Gary Wade

Introduction

In his review of *Finders Keepers* in *Poetry Review*, Peter McDonald argues that Heaney's critical essays '...offer scores of connections with Heaney's own poetry, assuring us that the critical and the creative functions of this mind are moving in step and towards some wholeness of aesthetic perception and activity' (McDonald 2002, 78). Heaney's first prose collection *Preoccupations* was published in 1980 alongside his *Selected Poems 1965–1975*, eliciting the observation of John Montague that *Preoccupations* effectively provides a 'running commentary' on the *Selected Poems* (Montague 1980). Heaney's first essay on the poetry of Patrick Kavanagh ('From Monaghan to the Grand Canal') appeared in *Preoccupations* and discusses Kavanagh's affection for and impatience with his parish. Published in 1975, it anticipates Heaney's own complex engagement with place towards the end of the 1970s, when he was working on a large poem that would become the subject of *Station Island*, published in 1984. Heaney would revisit Kavanagh in 1985 in an essay ('The Placeless Heaven: Another Look at Kavanagh') collected in *The Government of the Tongue* (1988), this time thinking of place in Kavanagh as luminous space and visionary possibility, just as Heaney was exploring generative absence in *The Haw Lantern* (1987) and visionary impulse in *Seeing Things* (1991). Heaney believed that Kavanagh had been born twice as a poet, the second time marked by a burgeoning creativity in Dublin from 1955 (Heaney 1972, 55) and his two essays largely reflect this early and late Kavanagh, at the same time as they tell us something about a shift in Heaney's own poetry and his 'waiting until I was nearly fifty/To credit marvels' (Heaney 1998, 357). In this essay, then, I reflect both on what Heaney has to say about Kavanagh and what this meant for Heaney's own poetry, how his critical reflections bear fruit in his creative output.

Fosterer

Seamus Heaney first came across several poems by Patrick Kavanagh in *The Oxford Book of Irish Verse*, published in 1958, when Heaney was an

DOI: 10.4324/9781003456148-9

148   *Gary Wade*

undergraduate at Queen's University in Belfast. The anthology included seven of Kavanagh's poems, some of which were important touchstones in ratifying Heaney's experience of growing up on a farm and which he would later discuss in his two critical essays; these included 'Spraying the Potatoes', 'A Christmas Childhood' and 'Epic':

> When I found 'Spraying the Potatoes' in the old *Oxford Book of Irish Verse*, I was excited to find details of a life which I knew intimately – but which I had always considered to be below or beyond books – being presented in a book.
>
> (Heaney 1988, 7)

In 1962, when on teaching practice at St Thomas's Secondary School in Belfast, Heaney met Michael McLaverty, who was headmaster. Born in 1904, the same year as Kavanagh, and in the same county of Monaghan, McLaverty was also an accomplished short story writer, whose stories reacted against the idealisation and sentimentality of rural Irish life (as Kavanagh's writing would) that had been such a strong feature of the Irish Revivalists. McLaverty loaned Heaney *A Soul for Sale*, published in 1947, and which included Kavanagh's poem *The Great Hunger*, the poem which Heaney later confessed would take 'a deeper hold' than the early Monaghan lyrics encountered in *The Oxford Book of Irish Verse* (O'Driscoll 2008, 72). This was an important moment for Heaney, and later, he would come to dedicate his poem 'Fosterage' to McLaverty in his 1975 collection *North*. Only five years after Heaney read *A Soul for Sale*, he was one of three poets who read at the funeral of Kavanagh, who died on 30 November 1967. At the graveside, Heaney read 'A Christmas Childhood', which he had first encountered in the Oxford anthology. Kavanagh wrote 'A Christmas Childhood' in 1940, and while it celebrates the joys of quotidian life on a farm at Christmas, it also reflects on the poet's formation as a writer (a central theme in *Preoccupations*):

> My child picked out the letters
> On the grey stone
> In silver the wonder of a Christmas townland,
> The winking glitter of a frosty dawn.
> (Kavanagh 2005, 39)

The growth of Heaney's own poetic mind is the subject of 'Alphabets', where Kavanagh's 'grey stone' becomes Heaney's gable wall:

> Or like my own wide pre-reflective stare
> All agog at the plasterer on his ladder
> Skimming our gable and writing our name there
> With his trowel point, letter by strange letter.
> (Heaney 1998, 294)

The choice of the poem was perfect. It was not only a valediction, but a verification of a debt owed to a poet who had paved the way for Heaney to credit the local and the ordinary. In 1967, at the age of twenty-eight, Heaney had already published his first collection of poems with Faber and Faber. For Heaney, the slim volume of *Death of a Naturalist* (1966) had been born out of the small farm on which he grew up as a child, and Kavanagh had been instrumental in showing Heaney how the light of imagination could transform the soil of Heaney's childhood and 'set the darkness echoing' (Heaney 1998, 15):

> Kavanagh's genius had achieved singlehanded what I and my grammar-school, arts-degreed generation were badly in need of – a poetry which linked the small farm life which produced us with the slim-volume world we were now supposed to be fit for. He brought us back to what we came from [...] Kavanagh gave you permission to dwell without cultural anxiety among the usual landmarks of your life.
>
> (Heaney 1988, 9)

The usual landmarks of Heaney's life celebrated in *Death of a Naturalist* were already present in 'A Christmas Childhood'. Kavanagh's 'potato-pits' become Heaney's 'potato drills' in his opening poem 'Digging'. Kavanagh remembers 'The tracks of cattle to a drinking place' and Heaney describes how 'Twenty years ago I herded cattle/Into pens ...' ('Ancestral Photograph'). Outside in a cow-house, Kavanagh's mother 'Made the music of milking' just as Heaney's mother '... took first turn, set up rhythms/that slugged and thumped for hours' ('Churning Day'). 'A water-hen screeched in the bog' in Kavanagh's poem; 'The cock would be sounding reveille' in Heaney's 'Dawn Shoot'. The Virgin Mary makes her appearance in the final line of 'A Christmas Childhood', just as poor women pray at her altar in Heaney's 'Poor Women in a City Church'. What these poems of Kavanagh and Heaney attend to is the earthed experience of place and the transforming and transfiguring capacity of poetry to elevate and sanctify the ordinary.

'The Love-Act and Its Pledge': Attachment to Place

In *Preoccupations*, Kavanagh is the subject of Heaney's essay 'From Monaghan to the Grand Canal', a title he borrows from an essay by Kavanagh published in *Studies* in spring 1959 (Quinn 2001, 379). In the essay that follows, 'The Sense of Place', Heaney returns to Kavanagh in the context of other writers, including Heaney himself. Arising out of his discussion of Kavanagh in *Preoccupations*, the theme I want to pick up on in this section is the impulse to transcendence which is located in the quotidian realities of place and time. Heaney observes that Kavanagh's poetry is most successful when it is earthed in the actual and that 'it is only when this ethereal

150   Gary Wade

voice incarnates itself in the imagery of the actual world that its messages of transcendence become credible' (Heaney 1980, 120). He draws attention to early lyrics such as 'Shancoduff', 'A Christmas Childhood' and 'Spraying the Potatoes' as illustrative of poems which sanctify the nature of place and home. I want to argue that the source for this transcendental quality in both Kavanagh and Heaney is to be found in a sacramental view of the world and the loving attention to the *haecceitas* or 'thisness' of a thing, the obverse of which is 'disregard', an important theme in Heaney's later poetry for which he also found a source in Kavanagh.

At the beginning of 'From Monaghan to the Grand Canal' Heaney sets out to 'place' Kavanagh within the English and Irish traditions. The English peasant poet John Clare was writing within an already established poetic tradition and one would have to go back to the eighteenth and nineteenth centuries in the Irish tradition, in the Irish poetry of Brian Merriman and the novels of William Carleton, to find a depiction of the harsh realities of life on a small farm. Heaney argues that much of Kavanagh's 'authority and oddity derive from the fact that he wrested his idiom bare-handed out of a literary nowhere' (Heaney 1980, 116):

> And in expressing that life in *The Great Hunger* and in *Tarry Flynn* Kavanagh forged not so much a conscience as a consciousness for the great majority of his countrymen, crossing the pieties of a rural Catholic sensibility with the *non serviam* of his original personality, raising the inhibited energies of a subculture to the power of a cultural resource.
>
> (Heaney 1980, 116)

This is as much autobiography as it is an observation on Kavanagh's work. Both poets were the products of a rural Catholic sensibility and it was deeply formative of their work. At the heart of Catholic Christianity, and its belief in the incarnation of God, is a deeply sacramental view of the world where the material world is an outward sign of an invisible reality. Both Kavanagh and Heaney grew up in a religious culture shaped by what the historian Emmet Larkin called a 'devotional revolution' brought about by the arrival of Paul Cardinal Cullen from Rome in 1850. A series of devotional exercises, including the rosary, novenas, blessed altars, benediction, devotion to the Sacred Heart, pilgrimages, shrines and retreats, were encouraged to instil a sense of ritual beauty. Larkin writes: '...this was the period when the whole world of the senses was explored in these devotional exercises in the Mass, through music, singing, vestments and incense' (Larkin 1972, 645). In *The Great Hunger*, as Patrick Maguire wonders if he should 'cross-plough that turnip-ground':

> The tension broke. The congregation lifted its head
> As one man and coughed in unison.
> Five hundred hearts were hungry for life –
> Who lives in Christ shall never die the death.

And the candle-lit Altar and the flowers
And the pregnant Tabernacle lifted a moment to Prophecy
Out of the clayey hours.

(Kavanagh 2005, 69)

The same material richness is recalled in Heaney's 'In Illo Tempore', where he describes the altar missal with its 'dangled silky ribbons/of emerald and purple and watery white' and the word 'rubric' as a 'bloodshot sunset' (Heaney 1998, 285).

It is this tactile expression of Catholicism in colour that was to become a focus of the Reformers' iconoclasm during the English Reformation and which Heaney laments in 'Leavings' as he rides down England:

down from Ely's Lady Chapel
the sweet tenor Latin
forever banished,
the sumptuous windows
threshed clear by Thomas Cromwell.

(Heaney 1998, 182)

Heaney credits Kavanagh's crossing of the pieties of a rural Catholic sensibility and the *non serviam* of his personality with 'raising the inhibited energies of a subculture to the power of a cultural resource'. The word 'subculture' frequently occurs in Heaney. Increasingly, he comes to understand Catholicism as a subculture in relation to England. He makes the point light-heartedly in an interview with David Montenegro in 1991: 'The subculture of Catholicism never is reflected in the high art of England, with a few freakish exceptions like Hopkins and Hopkins and Hopkins (*laughs*)' (Montenegro 1991, 181). This sense of belonging to a subculture partly explains his turning to Dante from the poems of *Field Work* (1979) on. Dante allowed Heaney to place his experience of Northern Irish Catholicism in a wider European context and thereby credit it in some way (Glover 1996, 9).

Gerard Manley Hopkins was to become an early influence on Kavanagh together with Edward Thomas and W. B. Yeats (Quinn 2001, 75). When Kavanagh first moved to Dublin in 1939, he stayed with his brother Peter, who taught in a Christian Brothers' School. Occasionally Peter brought his brother into the school to take his class for an hour or so. One pupil recalls how Kavanagh held them 'spellbound' by his reading of *Moby Dick* and the poetry of Hopkins (Quinn 2001, 122). Central to Hopkins's writing of poetry was the notion of *haecceitas*, or 'thisness', the idea that each finite thing has its own particularity or individuation. Hopkins's name for this was 'inscape' and we find a good illustration of what he meant by this in a notable passage in his *Journals* where he describes the inscape of bluebells:

The bluebells in your hand baffle you with their inscape, made to every sense: if you draw your fingers through them they are lodged and struggle/with a shock of wet heads [virgule in original]; the long stalks rub

152   Gary Wade

and click and flatten to a fan on one another like your fingers would when you passed the palms hard across one another making a brittle rub and jostle like the noise of a hurdle strained by leaning against; then there is the faint honey smell and in the mouth the sweet gum when you bite them.

(Hopkins 1959, 209)

The key to understanding the idea of *haecceitas* is the engagement of the senses. In this passage, the wet heads of the bluebells produce 'shock' when *touched*; they *smell* of honey and *taste* of sweet gum, and the *sound* they make when they jostle against each other is like a hurdle leaned against.

At the heart of this sensibility is a sacramental understanding of all material reality, where the innermost mystery of things is conveyed in outward signs. Mystery does not adjure the material, but instead revels in and is revealed in corporeality. In 'The Great Hunger', Kavanagh cautions Patrick Maguire not to turn from 'the five simple doors of sense' (Kavanagh 2005, 72). 'A Christmas Childhood', the poem which Heaney read at Kavanagh's graveside and which he addresses in 'From Monaghan to the Grand Canal', engages not only the sense of hearing, but all five senses in a powerfully descriptive way. The poet *sees* the light between the ricks of hay and straw as 'a hole in Heaven's gable'; he *hears* his father play the melodion and the music of his mother milking cows; he *tastes* (eats) 'the knowledge that grew in clay'; on Christmas morning the 'Mass-going feet/Crunched the wafer-ice on the pot-holes' (*touch*); and towards the end of the poem we can almost *smell* the cut tobacco and the white roses 'pinned/On the Virgin Mary's blouse' (Kavanagh 2005, 39–41). The same attention to corporeality and to the senses is there from the beginning in Heaney in a poem like 'Digging' (Heaney 1998, 3–4) where the pen rests 'Between my finger and my thumb' (*touch*) and his father's spade makes a 'clean rasping sound'. His father *tastes* milk from a bottle 'Corked sloppily with paper', *smells* the 'potato mould' and *hears* the 'squelch and slap/Of soggy peat. It is this tangible, felt sense of things which is at the very heart of a sacramental view of the created world. It involves the whole person as someone sensitive to the sights, smells, tastes and touches of created realities, and responsive to these as outward signs of invisible realities.

It is not only that Kavanagh gave Heaney permission to dwell without cultural anxiety among the usual landmarks of his life, but that something of their imagined life in Kavanagh's remembering of them finds its echo in Heaney's own imagining, especially in his later poetry. In Kavanagh, the inanimate paling-posts of quotidian farming life are brought to life by music:

One side of the potato-pits was white with frost –
How wonderful that was, how wonderful!
And when we put our ears to the paling-post
The music that came out was magical.

(Kavanagh 2005, 39)

'*Moving in Step*' 153

It is not hard to imagine the music of those paling-posts playing in Heaney's imagination when he wrote 'The Rain Stick', the opening poem of *The Spirit Level* (1996):

Upend the rain stick and what happens next
Is a music that you never would have known
To listen for. In a cactus stalk
Downpour, sluice-rush, spillage and backwash
Come flowing through ...
(Heaney 1998, 395)

By the time Heaney was writing on Kavanagh in 'From Monaghan to the Grand Canal', he had published *Death of a Naturalist, Door into the Dark, Wintering Out* and *North*. In discussing these books with Henri Cole in 1997, Heaney said that 'Those books wanted to be texture, to be all consonants, vowels and voicings, they wanted the sheer materiality of words' (Cole 1997, 106). He goes on to say that he was encouraged in this by Philip Hobsbaum, who convened 'The Group' in Belfast in the early 1960s. However, the example was also there in Hopkins and Kavanagh, in two poets who attended to the physicality of language and to the sense of loving attention to the places out of which that language grew. In terms of these early poems of Kavanagh, Heaney thought of his later poem 'Epic' as 'their magnificent coda', which 'represents Kavanagh's comprehension of his early achievement' (Heaney 1980, 120). But the same might also said of one of his Canal Bank Sonnets, 'The Hospital', where Kavanagh celebrates how a bridge, a gate and seat become transfigured by love:

Naming these things is the love-act and its pledge;
For we must record love's mystery without claptrap,
Snatch out of time the passionate transitory.
(Kavanagh 2005, 217)

Once again, the vernacular 'claptrap' ensures a critical distance from the pretentions of the Revivalists, whilst crediting the local voice. But the love-act is found in the naming of the quotidian and in the transfiguring ability of poetry to throw 'some light of imagination in these wet clods' (Kavanagh 2005, 63).

This concentrated attention to the familiar is beautifully illustrated in Heaney's poem 'Mossbawn: Sunlight', which opens his 1975 collection *North* and which is indebted to Kavanagh in its attention to the grounded and the domestic which are transformed by the light of imagination into an act of love. The scene is reminiscent of 'The Milkmaid', by the Dutch painter Johannes Vermeer. In Vermeer's painting, the milkmaid pours milk into an earthenware bowl. She stands by a window in an apron, just as Heaney's aunt Mary prepares the dough 'in a floury apron/by the window'.

154 *Gary Wade*

Vermeer's woman is sturdily built, the light from the window accentuating the folds of her blue apron. Heaney's aunt sits 'broad-lapped' as 'she dusts the board/with a goose's wing'. The poem begins in a 'sunlit absence', the word 'absence' anticipating, by more than a decade, the absence at the heart of 'Clearances'.

The visionary quality of Heaney's later poems, especially those in *Seeing Things*, is already in evidence here, just as the visionary quality of Kavanagh's Canal Bank Sonnets is not entirely absent from his early work. Michael Longley points to an early poem such as 'To the Man After the Harrow' (1940) to show that, even in his early career, Kavanagh 'is producing visionary, transcendental poetry out of his rural experience, its commonplaces and simplicities':

Forget the worm's opinion too
Of hooves and pointed harrow-pins,
For you are driving your horses through
The mist where Genesis begins.
          (Longley 2017, 170–171)

A corollary to the loving attention which Kavanagh and Heaney pay to the routine chores of rural life is acute sensitivity to anything that is overlooked or unloved. In Kavanagh's 'Spraying the Potatoes' the roses 'Were young girls hanging from the sky', but dandelions growing on the headlands show 'Their unloved hearts to everyone'. In 'On Reading a Book of Common Wild Flowers', Kavanagh acknowledges his own neglect: 'O the greater fleabane that grew at the back of the potato-pit./I often trampled through it looking for rabbit burrows!' (Kavanagh 2005, 200). We find the same sense of responsibility to what is neglected in Heaney's poem 'Mint'. The plant is 'almost beneath notice' as it grows at the gable of the house among 'refuse and old bottles'. The poet recalls 'The snip of scissor blades, the light of Sunday/Mornings when the mint was cut and loved'. The neglected plant comes to stand for prisoners who are failed by 'our disregard' (Heaney 1998, 396).

In raising the inhibited energies of the subculture of rural Monaghan to the level of a cultural resource, Kavanagh opened a path for Heaney to name and love the quotidian realities of life on a farm in County Derry, where the earthed experience of the ordinary could be dignified and transfigured in the transforming light of poetry. When Heaney found his footing in his first collections, it was in no small part owed to Patrick Kavanagh whose voice would return thirty years later in *Electric Light* (2001):

On an old recording Patrick Kavanagh states
That there's health and worth in any talk about
The properties of land. Sandy, glarry,
Mossy, heavy, cold, the actual soil
Almost doesn't matter; the main thing is

'Moving in Step'   155

An inner restitution, a purchase come by
By pacing it in words that make you feel
You've found your feet in what 'surefooted' means'.

(Heaney 2001, 14)

'All That Keeps Pleading': The Call to Leave

Kavanagh provided Heaney with a frank and honest depiction of rural life in Ireland which matched Heaney's lived experience of it, and which put the parish at the centre of that experience. Heaney's early instincts that the world of Mossbawn was an *omphalos* (Heaney 1980, 17), which marked the centre of his world, were ratified in his first encounter with Kavanagh's verse in *The Oxford Book of Irish Verse*. However, Kavanagh's attachment to place was not uncomplicated, and if he could delight in the music of paling-posts, he could equally rage at the 'stony grey soil of Monaghan' where 'Dead loves were born to me' (Kavanagh 2005, 39). Those dead loves are at the centre of his long poem *The Great Hunger*, and his autobiographical response to that poem is presented in his novel *Tarry Flynn*:

> *Tarry Flynn* (1948) is his delightful realization of his call to leave, the pivot and centre of Kavanagh's work, an autobiographical fiction full of affection for and impatience with the parish.
>
> (Heaney 1980, 121)

Heaney describes *The Great Hunger* as the obverse of *Tarry Flynn*: 'It is not about growing up and away but about growing down and in' (Heaney 1980, 123). Both Kavanagh and Heaney, of course, left their respective parishes and travelled south to Dublin and Wicklow respectively. In 'From Monaghan to the Grand Canal', Heaney describes how Kavanagh's sonnet sequence 'Temptation in Harvest' 'beautifully and wistfully' describes Kavanagh's move to Dublin in 1939. It was to the sonnet form that Heaney also turned when describing his move to Wicklow in 1972, in his sequence 'Glanmore Sonnets' (*Field Work*, 1979): 'Then I landed in the hedge-school of Glanmore' where 'Vowels ploughed into other, opened ground' (Heaney 1998, 164).

Michael Cavanagh reminds us that Heaney is writing on Kavanagh in the same decade as *Field Work* and that his reading of Kavanagh cannot have failed to have had a bearing on his new home in Wicklow (Cavanagh 2010, 128). When Heaney writes about Kavanagh's call to leave, it is as much about an inner spiritual journey as it is about an outer physical one, and it is equally about Heaney's own inner call to leave, a call heard loudest in his collection *Station Island* (1984), the pivot and centre of Heaney's own work where affection for and impatience with the parish are cinematically on display. His ethical dilemma is between the demands of place and 'all that keeps pleading and pleading' (Heaney 1998, 221) and the commitment of the artist to go his own way.

The poem takes its name from the medieval pilgrimage site located on Lough Derg, in County Donegal. The island is known as 'St Patrick's Purgatory' and

156   *Gary Wade*

has been a place of pilgrimage since the Middle Ages. Pilgrims visit for three days and undergo an intense penitential retreat of fasting, sleep deprivation and intense prayer on 'beds' of stone. Heaney made the pilgrimage several times as a young man (O'Driscoll 2008, 232). In the twelve poems which make up the sequence 'Station Island', Heaney is confronted with ghosts from his past who challenge his adherence to the pieties of his youth. The sequence opens with Simon Sweeney shouting at the poet: 'Stay clear of all processions' (Heaney 1998, 244) and closes with the admonishing voice of James Joyce: 'That subject people stuff is a cod's game,/infantile, like your peasant pilgrimage' (Heaney 1998, 268). In section II of the poem, Heaney meets the ghost of William Carleton, a Catholic convert to Protestantism, whose article 'The Lough Derg Pilgrim', written in 1828, was partly fuelled by the 'mistaken devotion' of this form of popular piety (Hart 1988, 243). Carleton was especially revered by Kavanagh, whose ghost appears in section V of the poem, where he is introduced as 'a third fosterer':

Sure I might have known
once I had made the pad, you'd be after me
sooner or later. Forty-two years on
and you've got no farther!
                    (Heaney 1998, 253)

Kavanagh's poem 'Lough Derg' was written in 1942, after he undertook the pilgrimage as a journalist. However, it was rejected by both Cuala Press and Faber and Faber, and not published in book form until 1978 (Kavanagh 2005, 269–270). Consequently, it is not discussed in Heaney's 'From Monaghan to the Grand Canal'. However, the spiritual aridity which Kavanagh found in some of the pilgrims on Lough Derg is already a theme in *The Great Hunger*.

The parodic opening of *The Great Hunger* – 'Clay is the word and clay is the flesh' – plays on the creative Logos, or Word, whose creative life opens John's Gospel. God's life-giving Logos has been replaced by the poverty of clay and a materialism that Kavanagh explored more fully in the *Lough Derg* poem, where solicitors came to pray for 'cushy jobs' and mothers for their daughters taking 'Final Medicals' (Kavanagh 2005, 90). At the beginning of *The Great Hunger*, the narrator invites us to observe Maguire and his men: 'If we watch them an hour is there anything we can prove/Of life as it is broken-backed over the Book/Of Death?' The pathos of a broken-backed life, shrivelled by hard labour and the absence of love is tenderly evoked in the lines that follow:

Which of these men
Loved the light and the queen
Too long virgin? Yesterday was summer. Who was it promised
marriage to himself
Before apples were hung from the ceilings for Hallowe'en?
                    (Kavanagh 2005, 63)

The sense of time passing and the dying of the light is powerfully evoked in the reduction of summer to a single day. The sense of unfulfilled promise in the form of marriage was a significant factor in the decline and depopulation of rural Ireland and is the backdrop for the frustrations, sexual and otherwise, that permeate *The Great Hunger*. The privations of female love in the absence of a wife are compounded by the prescriptions of female expectations in the person of Maguire's mother: 'And he is not so sure now if his mother was right/When she praised the man who made a field his bride' (Kavanagh 2005, 65). However, Maguire 'knows that his own heart is calling his mother a liar./God's truth is life – even the grotesque shapes of his foulest fire'. Declan Kiberd sums up the poem neatly: 'The title seemed to promise a study of heroic peasants in the nineteenth century, but the text actually delivers a near-nihilistic account of unheroic subsistence farmers in the twentieth' (Kiberd 1995, 478). The poem is Kavanagh's rage against the idealisation of the peasant farmer by the Revivalist poets and travellers who 'touch the roots of the grass and feel renewed/When they grasp the steering wheels again' (Kavanagh 2005, 85). The subject matter of *The Great Hunger* is not the sentimentality of peasant life, but the stunted emotional life of Patrick Maguire. The focus is on the emotional life of a diminished self rather than the parading vanities of a bucolic eclogue. Heaney concludes that Maguire's soul is never born. 'The self he achieves is one dressed to fit the constricting circumstances of home, community and church' (Heaney 1980, 125). It is his own constricted self that Heaney addresses in *Station Island*.

Part of the lie that Kavanagh wishes to expose in telling the story of Patrick Maguire is the replacement of a life-giving spirituality with the materialism of a 'Respectability that knows the price of all things/And mark's God's truth in pounds and pence and farthings' (Kavanagh 2005, 69). It exposes the superficiality and suffocating demands of a religious ethic that was itself as poor as the fields. There are many images in the poem of the sterility of the life endured by Patrick Maguire and his men, but perhaps the most breath-catching and visceral is the image of the dried-out afterbirth of a cow:

> Like the afterbirth of a cow stretched on a branch in the wind
> Life dried in the veins of these women and men:
> The grey and grief and unlove,
> The bones in the back of their hands,
> And the chapel pressing its low ceiling over them.
>
> (Kavanagh 2005, 76)

The claustrophobic sense here of the low chapel ceiling as a metaphor for a life-denying spirituality finds its parallel in Heaney's poem 'In Gallarus Oratory', collected in *Door into the Dark* in 1969. Together with his poem 'The Forge' (Heaney 1998, 19), 'In Gallarus Oratory' provides a door into

158   *Gary Wade*

the dark. The dark concentrated space is reflected in the poem's dimensions, which on the page has the appearance of a sonnet. However, at twelve lines, its shortened form suggests that Heaney may be playing with the proportions of the poem in an effort to reflect the curtailed nature of the oratory itself, which is like 'going into a turfstack,/A core of old dark walled up with stone/A yard thick' (Heaney 1969, 10). The more compressed form of the poem gestures towards the compressed space in which 'You might have dropped, a reduced creature,/To the heart of the globe'. Where the darkness of the forge becomes a generative space for the blacksmith's creativity and craft, the dark of Gallarus Oratory becomes paralysing of those worshippers who seek their God there.

In his essay 'The God in the Tree', collected in *Preoccupations*, Heaney writes about his visit to Gallarus Oratory in 1966: 'I felt the weight of Christianity in all its rebuking aspects, its calls to self-denial and self-abnegation, its humbling of the proud flesh and insolent spirit' (Heaney 1980, 189). It is precisely these rebuking aspects and self-abnegation that Heaney confronts in the self-excoriating poems of *Station Island*, sometimes in a tone of severity, uncharacteristic of Heaney:

'I hate how quick I was to know my place.
I hate where I was born, hate everything
That made me biddable and unforthcoming'.
                                    (Heaney 1998, 263)

Heaney thought of *Tarry Flynn* (1948) in similar terms, as Kavanagh's call to leave. The novel is set in the fictional parish of Dargan in County Cavan in the summer of 1935. It tells the story of Tarry Flynn whose literary aspirations provide a source of escapism from the small-farm mentality he is otherwise tied to. It depicts the suffocating demands of family and parish and the small-town mentality of jealous neighbours and local feuds, the type of feuds wonderfully if sardonically evoked in Kavanagh's poem 'Epic', where locals fight over 'That half a rood of rock, a no-man's land/Surrounded by our pitchfork-armed claims (Kavanagh 2005, 184). The novel opens with Tarry's mother hectoring her son to get to Mass on time, but Tarry 'hated being in time for Mass'. He found spiritual sustenance elsewhere:

The headlands and the hedges were so fresh and wonderful, so gay with the dawn of the world. Tarry never tired looking at these ordinary things as he tired of the Mass and of religion. In a dim way he felt that he was not a Christian. In the god of Poetry he found a god more important to him than Christ. His god had never accepted Christ.
                                    (Kavanagh 2000, 10)

Tarry gives voice here to a recalcitrant strain in Irish culture between the demands of a certain type of legislative Roman Catholicism which emerged in the mid-nineteenth century with the devotional revolution and an older strain of Christianity which sat side by side with a sense of pagan culture. In 'The Poet as a Christian', published in 1978, Heaney drew attention to this dimension of Irish spirituality and to the landscape as sacramental, which provided for 'a marvellous or magical view of the world, a foundation that sustained a diminished structure of lore and superstition and half-pagan, half-Christian thought and practice'. Heaney is both pagan and Christian:

> But I have no doubt that I am also a pagan, and that every poet is: the poet will have to be standing with Oisin against Patrick, he will have to roost in the tree of his instincts with Mad Sweeney while St Moling stands ideologically in the cloister.
>
> (Heaney 2013, 544)

Tarry's 'god of poetry' becomes Heaney's 'god in the tree':

> For example, in the context of monasticism, the god of my title would be the Christian deity, the giver of life, sustainer of nature, creator Father and redeemer Son. But there was another god in the tree, impalpable perhaps but still indigenous, less doctrinally defined than the god of the monasteries but more intuitively apprehended.
>
> (Heaney 1980, 186)

One senses in both Kavanagh and Heaney an attempt to rescue something of the old religion from the creeping imperium of institutional Catholicism. The sense of marginalisation is a theme in both poets and, by way of illustration, might be reduced the single word 'ditches'. Tarry finds the miraculous in 'The nettles, thistles and docks' which 'bloomed wildly at the backs of ditches. Life was very rich' (Kavanagh 2000, 54). If Tarry ventriloquises much of Kavanagh's thought, Sweeney performs the same role for Heaney. Sweeney is 'King of the Ditchbacks' and in the poem of that title the poet is 'a rich young man//leaving everything he had/for a migrant solitude' (Heaney 1998, 241). The third section of *Station Island* is given over to the voice of Sweeney 'the seventh-century Ulster king who was transformed into a bird-man and exiled to the trees by the curse of St Ronan' (Heaney 1984, 123). In Heaney's poem 'Alphabets', language itself is found in ditches:

> The letters of this alphabet were trees.
> The capitals were orchards in full bloom,
> The lines of script like briars coiled in ditches.
>
> (Heaney 1998, 293)

160　*Gary Wade*

In 'From Monaghan to the Grand Canal' Heaney quotes a passage from the final pages of *Tarry Flynn*, where Tarry retreats to his upstairs room to write poetry:

> The net of earthly intrigue could not catch him here. He was on a level with the horizon – and it was a level on which there was laughter. Looking down at his own misfortunes he thought them funny now. From this height he could even see himself losing his temper with the Finnegans and the Carlins and hating his neighbours and he moved the figures on the landscape, made them speak, and was filled with joy in his own power.
>
> (Kavanagh 2000, 178)

Kavanagh is no doubt referencing James Joyce here, and to Stephen's claim in *The Portrait of the Artist as a Young Man* that 'When the soul of a man is born in this country there are nets flung at it to hold it back from flight. You talk to me of nationality, language, religion. I shall try to fly by those nets' (Joyce 1974, 203). When the ghost of Joyce appears in the final poem of the sequence 'Station Island', he advises the poet: 'Let go, let fly, forget./You've listened long enough. Now strike your note' (Heaney 1998, 267–68).

When Heaney moved to Wicklow in 1972, he began working on *Sweeney Astray*, a version of the medieval Irish poem *Buile Shuibhne*. Although he began work on the poem in 1972, it was not until 1979 that he returned to it in earnest. It was eventually published in 1984 together with *Station Island*. Both books assert the artist's freedom against the claims of family, politics and church, just as *Tarry Flynn* had done. *Sweeney Astray* is almost a companion piece to *Station Island*, and Heaney makes an autobiographical reference to it in his poem 'King of the Ditchbacks', which concludes Part One of *Station Island*. Like Tarry Flynn, Heaney retreats to an upper room, this time to live imaginatively with Sweeney:

> I was sure I knew him. The time I'd spent obsessively in that upstairs room bringing myself close to him: each entranced hiatus as I chain-smoked and stared out the dormer into the grassy hillside I was laying myself open.
>
> (Heaney 1998, 239)

In an interview with Fintan O'Toole around the time of the publication of *Sweeney Astray*, Heaney said that 'it was as if the eye-level life of a child was reanimated and it seemed to me that Sweeney in the branches could conduct a lot of that energy out of me into words' (O'Toole 20 November, 12). Tarry's 'level with the horizon' becomes Heaney's 'eye-level life'. Tarry and Sweeney are like sentries whose poetic imagination provides them with a high vantage point from which to survey their respective kingdoms. The distance provided by the scale of imagination transfigures the banal into

'Moving in Step'   161

the comic so that Tarry's hated neighbours become the plaything of the poet and a source of amusement, just as steeplejacks become 'like flies' as Sweeney observes them from a beech tree '... up there at their antics/like flies against the mountain' (Heaney 1998, 271).

In 'On the Road', the final poem of *Station Island*, which brings a book of intense self-scrutiny to a close, Heaney meditates on an image of a drinking deer 'at a dried-up source' and waits for his 'long dumbfounded/spirit' to break cover and 'to raise a dust/in the font of exhaustion'. The idea of *source* is at the heart of his next collection *The Haw Lantern* (1987), but this time as a generative space, where the ground is laid for the visionary poems of *Seeing Things* (1991). By this stage, Heaney had already taken another look at Kavanagh in 1985.

Crediting Marvels: Place as Vision

At the beginning of his essay on Kavanagh in *The Government of the Tongue* (1988), in which he takes 'another look at Kavanagh', Heaney recalls the story of a chestnut tree, planted by his aunt in 1939, the year that Heaney was born. As he grew up and as the tree grew, he came to think of it as co-eval with his own life. It was not only that it was planted in the same year that he was born, but that it came to symbolise his aunt's affection for him. In 1954, when Heaney was boarding at St Columb's College in Derry, his family moved from Mossbawn to The Wood, from one end of the parish to the other. The new owners of the house at Mossbawn cut down all the trees around the house, including the chestnut tree. At first, this was 'deplored', but eventually Heaney came to think of the emptied space as a 'luminous emptiness', where it was not so much a matter of being rooted to a place, but of being unrooted, '...spirited away into some transparent, yet indigenous afterlife ... It was and remains an imagined realm, even if it can be located at an earthly spot, a placeless heaven rather than a heavenly place' (Heaney 1988, 4). He borrows the phrase 'placeless heaven' from Kavanagh's poem 'Auditors In': 'I turn away to where the Self reposes,/The placeless Heaven that's under all our noses' (Kavanagh 2005, 182).

In 'Clearances', the sequence of sonnets in memory of his mother, Heaney uses the image of the chestnut tree as a metaphor for a space cleared, which is:

> Utterly empty, utterly a source
> Where the decked chestnut tree had lost its place
> In our front hedge above the wallflowers.
> (Heaney 1998, 314)

In 'The Placeless Heaven: Another Look at Kavanagh', Heaney borrows the image of the chestnut tree to speak about Kavanagh's early and late poetry. He thinks of Kavanagh's early poetry in terms of the rooted tree and its attachment to a physical place. However, in Kavanagh's later period, in the late

162   Gary Wade

1950s, when he is writing poems such as 'Epic' and the sonnets composed on the banks of the Grand Canal in Dublin, there is a sense of luminous spaces in Kavanagh's work, places now detached from their origin, but which have their own generative life in the poet's mind. By way of illustration, Heaney returns to 'Spraying the Potatoes' – to the 'poet lost to potato-fields' – to show how in early Kavanagh 'self is absorbed by scene' (Heaney 1980, 5), but in a late poem such as 'Canal Bank Walk', scene is the handmaid of the poet's imagination. Heaney quotes the sestet of the sonnet, where Kavanagh asks: 'Feed the gaping need of my senses, give me ad lib/To pray unselfconsciously with overflowing speech' (Heaney 1980, 6). Michael Cavanagh suggests that Kavanagh's 'second life' as a poet 'is no longer governed by reality, but reality by the mind', and he sees this reflected in Heaney's *The Place of Writing*, three essays in honour of Richard Ellmann (Cavanagh 2010, 53).

What Heaney refers to as the 'Canal Bank Sonnets' were published in the late 1950s, by which stage Kavanagh had repudiated *The Great Hunger* for what Quinn called its 'crusading zeal' and 'sociological mission' (Quinn 2001, 182). Kavanagh had recently recovered from an operation for lung cancer in 1955 and in the 'Author's Note' to his 'Collected Poems' (1964), he acknowledges a marked shift in his vision:

> But I lost my messianic compulsion. I sat on the bank of the Grand Canal in the summer of 1955 and let the water lap idly on the shores of my mind. My purpose in life was to have no purpose.
>
> (Kavanagh 2005, 292)

In 'Come Dance with Kitty Stobling', first published in 1958, Kitty Stobling acts as an imagined muse for the poet. Kavanagh imagines a myth which served his purpose, of 'Trees walking across the crests of hills and my rhyme/ Cavorting on mile-high stilts (Kavanagh 2005, 221). Kavanagh's uprooted tree has become pure vision, just as in *The Haw Lantern*, Heaney imagines his mother as a wishing tree: 'I thought of her as the wishing tree that died/ And saw it lifted, root and branch, to heaven ...' (Heaney 1998, 316), or in *Seeing Things*, how the imagined ash plant serves to steady his ailing father: 'As his head goes light with light, his wasting hand/Gropes desperately and finds the phantom limb/Of an ash plant in his grasp, which steadies him' (Heaney 1991, 19).

The poems of *Seeing Things* are replete with the material world giving way to the visionary, the concrete evaporating out of the solid world into the ether of what's imagined. In the title poem of the collection, the poet imagines looking up 'from another boat/Sailing through the air' (Heaney 1998, 339) just as when the monks of Clonmacnoise are at prayer 'A ship appeared above them in the air' (Heaney 1998, 364). In his poem 'The Biretta', Heaney alludes to another boat, this time a small and fragile bronze age boat that was part of the Broighter hoard discovered in County Derry in 1896. He imagines the 'frail' gold work 'Refined beyond the dross into sheer image' (Heaney

'Moving in Step' 163

1991, 27), the perfect metaphor for many of the poems in *Seeing Things*, where matter gives way to vision, and where vision is transfigured into image or poetry. In other words, what is actual and loved becomes transfigured in an afterlife of image, where what was once a heavenly place becomes a placeless heaven.

In a review in *The Literary Review*, Peter Balakian reminds us that *The Haw Lantern* 'reveals Heaney's continuing ability to move in a new direction without relinquishing the core of his sensibility' (Balakian 1988, 501). Some critics saw that new direction in poems which are more visionary (Erlanger 1987, 21) and in which fire and air replace the presiding elements of earth and water in the early work (Tobin 1999, 217). The collection's epigraph for Bernard and Jane McCabe – 'The riverbed, dried up, half-full of leaves./Us, listening to a river in the trees' (Heaney 1998, 291) – lifts Heaney's vision skywards where the tactile and sensuous world gives way to the visionary, so that in the title poem of the collection, breath which 'plumes in the frost' takes on 'the roaming shape of Diogenes' (Heaney 1998, 299). *The Haw Lantern* increasingly becomes a meditation on absence, the word used for the first time in the poem 'Hailstones' as a ball of hail melts in the narrator's hand: 'just as I make this now/out of the melt of the real thing/smarting into its absence (Heaney 1998, 302).

Heaney's choice of 'Clearances' as a title for the sequence of poems in memory of his mother acknowledges, of course, the physical absence of the chestnut tree in his first home, but in its Latin root *'clarus'* ('bright', 'shining', 'brilliant') it also declares something of visionary impulse and the possibility of the restorative power of memory. The space generated by what Philip Larkin called the 'the new absence' (Larkin 1988, 214) is a space into which, or out of which, memory mines the rich core of human love, made whole again in the imaginative life of the poem. In 'Clearances' VII, the penultimate poem of the sequence, this sense of generative space is dramatically conveyed in the final lines, where 'The space we stood around had been emptied/Into to us to keep, it penetrated/Clearances that suddenly stood open' (Heaney 1998, 313). The oxymoronic quality of space being emptied not only plays on empty space, but on the idea that space has something to be emptied of, in other words space as source, a space, therefore, as we have already seen, which is 'Utterly empty, utterly a source'. In *Station Island*, where Heaney wrestled with the pieties of church and community and 'the shackles of the civic', Sweeney/Heaney comes across the image of a drinking deer whose 'nostril flared/at a dried-up source' (Heaney 1998, 288). Sweeney/Heaney long for the spirit to break cover and 'to raise a dust/ in the font of exhaustion'. In *Station Island*, source is a place of aridity; in *The Haw Lantern* it is a place of origin and imaginative energy. However, it is only with the poems of *Seeing Things* that the dust is raised properly and the place of exhaustion becomes a place of extravagant surprise: 'But when the slates came off, extravagant/Sky entered and held surprise wide open' (Heaney 1998, 350).

164   *Gary Wade*

This shift in Heaney's poetry towards the nature of absence and space finds its fullest flowering in the visionary poems of *Seeing Things*, about which Heaney said: 'A great deal of their insouciance arises from their having escaped the shackles of the civic' (Heaney 2002, 125). What I want to argue here is that the turn towards the visionary in Heaney in the late 1980s corresponds with his revisiting Kavanagh in 'The Placeless Heaven' in 1985, and his tracing in Kavanagh of a shift from heavenly places to a placeless heaven, from what is planted and rooted to what is airborne and imagined. In Heaney's treatment of Kavanagh, his critical instincts and his creative output are in step.

In his review of *Seeing Things*, James Wood thought that Heaney had 'regressed' in the first half of the book to his earliest poems and that 'The Pitchfork' (Heaney 1998, 344) was 'as unremarkable a poem as Heaney has ever written' (Wood 1991, 24). And yet a comparison with the pitchfork in Heaney's poem 'The Barn' (Heaney 1998, 7), from *Death of a Naturalist*, suggests otherwise. In 'The Barn', the sheer materiality of Heaney's first collection is everywhere evident in corn described as 'solid as cement' and the 'armoury' of farmyard implements. Entering the barn and adjusting to the darkness 'Slowly bright objects formed' including 'a pitch-fork's prongs'. In other words, as the poet begins to see things in his first collection, they solidify. Now compare the pitchfork of *Seeing Things*:

He would see the shaft of a pitchfork sailing past
Evenly, imperturbably through space,
Its prongs starlit and absolutely soundless.
(Heaney 1991, 23)

Here the material gives way to the visionary. No more is Heaney satisfied to describe merely the *haecceitas* or thisness of a thing but is drawn instead to describe what might be seen or imagined beyond the purely material. He wants not only to see things but to see *beyond* things, beyond the given materiality as he describes it in the title poem of the collection: 'And yet in that utter visibility/The stone's alive with what's invisible' (Heaney 1998, 340).

In 'Canal Bank Walk' Kavanagh entreats the world to 'give me ad lib/ To pray unselfconsciously with overflowing speech' (Kavanagh 2005, 224). There is a sense in the Canal Bank Sonnets of Kavanagh reaching in language for what is abundant and overflowing. In 'The Hospital', which Antoinette Quinn says 'looks forward to his next poetic phase' (Kavanagh 2005, xxvi), 'The Corridor led to a stairway and below/Was the inexhaustible adventure of a gravelled yard' (Kavanagh 2005, 217) and in 'Leaves of Grass' the ground is 'Tumultuous with living, infinite as Cleopatra's variety' (Kavanagh 2005, 218). Returning from New York to Dublin in 1957, Kavanagh announced that he was 'writing verse in a new style' and Quinn describes these poems as 'more colourful and sensuous than usual, and are utterly celebratory' (Kavanagh 2005, xxvii). When Heaney quotes from 'Auditors In' towards

'Moving in Step' 165

the end of 'The Placeless Heaven', he describes Kavanagh as 'afloat above his native domain, airborne in the midst of his own dream place rather than earthbound in a literal field' (Heaney 1988, 13). He goes on to say:

> This then is truly creative writing. It does arise from the spontaneous overflow of powerful feelings, but the overflow is not a reactive response to some stimulus in the world out there. Instead, it is a spurt of abundance from a source within and it spills over to irrigate the world beyond the self.
>
> (Heaney 1988, 13)

This capacity for abundant language in Heaney would become most visible in the poems of *Seeing Things*. In 1990, he published an essay on Robert Frost entitled 'Above the Brim' in the journal *Salmagundi*. In the same edition he also published 'Seeing Things', the title poem of his new collection (Brandes 2008, 355). In the essay, Heaney wrote that Frost's strongest poems were those in which there was 'fullness overflowing', hence the 'brim' of the title (Brodsky/Heaney/Walcott 1997, 83). Heaney also finds sanction for the word 'brim' in Yeats and Larkin. He knew Yeats's 'The Wild Swans at Coole' very well: 'Upon the brimming water among the stones/Are nine-and-fifty swans' (Yeats 1991, 233), and Larkin's 'At Grass', modelled on Yeats's poem: 'Dusk brims the shadows' (Larkin 1988, 29). In both poems 'brim' is used as a verb, not a noun, and Heaney follows suit in 'The Sounds of Rain', where a flood is like 'a named name that overbrims itself' (Heaney 1991, 49). The word is used in other poems in the collection: in 'A Retrospect' (Heaney 1991, 42) 'The skyline was full up to the lip/As if the earth were going to brim over', and the final poem of the 'Settings' sequence concludes with air and ocean 'In apposition with/Omnipresence, equilibrium, brim (Heaney 1998, 373).

In 2002, in an uncollected essay 'Sixth Sense, Seventh Heaven', Heaney comes to reflect on the 'Squarings' sequence of poems in *Seeing Things*. There he discusses Jacques Maritain's *Creative Intuition in Art and Poetry*, published in 1953, where Maritain outlines three stages of the poetic process which he calls Poetic Sense (the emotion of lived experience), Action and Theme (the need to express the emotion) and Harmonic Expression (the writing of the poem). Heaney says that he is most concerned, like Maritain, with the second stage of Action, whereby a poem, which has no will of its own, nonetheless requires expression (Heaney 2002, 116). He goes on to say that for Maritain action is 'hungry for theme' which is 'potentiality discovered within the material' (Heaney 2002, 117). It is this potentiality which Heaney detects in *The Great Hunger*, pushing against the limits of the deadening circumstances: 'The trout played in the pools encouragement/To jump in love though death bait the hook' (Kavanagh 2005, 76).

It is this surplus in the given material which Heaney feels characterises the best of Kavanagh's work. In Heaney's essay 'The Sense of Place', he reminds us of Kavanagh's religious sensibility and his deep childhood piety

166 Gary Wade

which paid attention to 'the small and the familiar' (Heaney 1980, 142). This sensibility remains at the heart of Kavanagh's work, as it does in Heaney's, even if a Catholic sensibility becomes displaced in Heaney so that in his later work the Roman poet Virgil becomes an increasingly important touchstone in dealing with death and the after-image of imagined life. In his beautiful poem 'A Mite-Box', from his final collection *Human Chain* (2010), Heaney recalls going from house to house and collecting alms in a little box which resembled a 'little oratory'. The word 'oratory' takes us back to the oratory at Gallarus, which I discussed in Section III, with its 'core of old dark walled up with stone'. However, now the little oratory provides the opportunity for a placeless heaven. As neighbours donate to the mite-box each donation is recorded by pushing a pin through a card, where the little pin-hole of light is:

> A way for all to see a way to heaven,
> The same as when a pinholed *Camera*
> *Obscura* unblinds the sun eclipsed.
> (Heaney 2010, 19)

Works Cited

Balakian, Peter (1988) 'Seamus Heaney's New Landscapes (Book Review)', *The Literary Review; Madison, N.J., Etc.*, Summer 1988.

Brandes, Rand (2008) *Seamus Heaney: A Bibliography (1959–2003)*, London: Faber and Faber.

Brodsky, Joseph, Seamus Heaney and Derek Walcott (1997) *A Homage to Robert Frost: Essays on Poetry*, London: Faber and Faber.

Cavanagh, Michael (2010) *Professing Poetry: Seamus Heaney's Poetics*, Washington, DC: Catholic University of America Press.

Cole, Henri (1997) 'Seamus Heaney The Art of Poetry LXXV', *The Paris Review*.

Erlanger, Steven (1987) 'How Gracious and Generous Grows Ireland's Poet', *Boston Globe*, 3 July.

Glover, Michael (1996) 'Interview with Seamus Heaney', *Poetry Life*, 1996.

Hart, Henry (1988) 'Ghostly Colloquies: Seamus Heaney's "Station Island"', *Irish University Review* 18 (2): 233–250.

Heaney, Seamus (1966) *Death of a Naturalist*, London: Faber and Faber.

Heaney, Seamus (1969) *Door into the Dark*, London: Faber and Faber.

Heaney, Seamus (1972) 'After the Synge-Song – Seamus Heaney on the Writings of Patrick Kavanagh', *The Listener*, 13 January 1972. Gale NewsVault.

Heaney, Seamus (1980) *Preoccupations: Selected Prose 1968–1978*, London: Faber and Faber.

Heaney, Seamus (1984) *Station Island*, London: Faber and Faber.

Heaney, Seamus (1988) *The Government of the Tongue: The 1986 T.S. Eliot Memorial Lectures and Other Critical Writings*, London; New York: Faber and Faber.

Heaney, Seamus (1991) *Seeing Things*, London; Boston: Faber and Faber.

Heaney, Seamus (1998) *Opened Ground: Poems, 1966–1996*, London: Faber and Faber.

Heaney, Seamus (2001) *Electric Light*, London: Faber and Faber.

Heaney, Seamus (2002) 'Sixth Sense, Seventh Heaven', *Dublin Review* 8 (Autumn): 115–126.

Heaney, Seamus (2006) *District and Circle*, London: Faber and Faber.

Heaney, Seamus (2010) *Human Chain*, London: Faber and Faber.

Heaney, Seamus (2013) 'The Poet as a Christian', *The Furrow* 64 (10): 541–45.

Heaney, Seamus (n.d.) 'MS 49,493/57'. National Library of Ireland.

Hopkins, Gerard Manley (1959) *The Journals and Papers of Gerard Manley Hopkins*, London: Oxford University Press.

Joyce, James (1974) *A Portrait of the Artist as a Young Man*, reprint, Penguin Modern Classics, Harmondsworth, Middlesex: Penguin Books.

Kavanagh, Patrick (2000) *Tarry Flynn*, Penguin Modern Classics, London: Penguin.

Kavanagh, Patrick (2005) *Collected Poems*, edited by Antoinette Quinn, Modern Classics, London: Penguin.

Kiberd, Declan (1995) *Inventing Ireland*, London: Cape.

Larkin, Emmet (1972) 'The Devotional Revolution in Ireland, 1850–75', *The American Historical Review* 77 (3): 625–652. https://doi.org/10.2307/1870344.

Larkin, Philip (1988) *Collected Poems*, edited by Anthony Thwaite, London: The Marvell Press.

Longley, Michael (2017) *Sidelines: Selected Prose, 1962–2015*, London: Enitharmon Press.

McDonald, Peter (2002) 'Appreciating Assets', *Poetry Review* 92 (2): 76–79.

Montague, John (1980) 'Poet's Workshop', *The Guardian*, 27 November 1980.

Montenegro, David (ed.) (1991) *Points of Departure: International Writers on Writing and Politics*, Ann Arbor: University of Michigan Press.

O'Donoghue, Bernard (2019) *Poetry: A Very Short Introduction*, Oxford: OUP Oxford.

O'Driscoll, Dennis (2008) *Stepping Stones: Interviews with Seamus Heaney*, London: Faber and Faber.

O'Toole, Fintan (1983) 'Heaney's Sweeney', *Inside Tribune*, 20 November.

Quinn, Antoinette (2001) *Patrick Kavanagh: A Biography*, Dublin: Gill & Macmillan.

Tobin, Daniel (1999) *Passage to the Center: Imagination and the Sacred in the Poetry of Seamus Heaney*, Irish Literature, History, and Culture, Lexington: University Press of Kentucky.

Wood, James (1991) 'Looking for a Place Where Things Matter', *Guardian*, 30 May 1991.

Yeats, William B. (1991) *Yeats's Poems*. Edited by A. Norman Jeffares, revised edition, reprinted London: Papermac.

9 'The Push of the Whole Man'
Heaney on Robert Lowell

Meg Tyler

In a passage on William Gass's essay on Emerson, Elizabeth Hardwick, in 'The Art of the Essay', points to the distinction Gass makes between an article and essay:

> If the article has a certain sheen and professional polish, it is the polish of 'the scrubbed step' – practical economy and neatness. The essay, in Mr. Gass's view, is a great meadow of style and personal manner, freed from the need for defense except that provided by an individual intelligence and sparkle.
>
> (Andriesse 2022, 3)

I thought of this passage as I began to re-read Heaney's prose and imagined each piece as a 'great meadow of style and personal manner'. Prose about poetry appeared to come easily to Heaney. His lectures and commissioned essays teach us much about his likes, less so about his dislikes. He uses the same ethical care and delicacy in sentences as when he layers and breaks lines on a page. The tone is confiding in the manner of a well-read friend: not presumptuous, not authoritative, but studious of the objects before him. The poem is read as a thing of wonder, of fertility and embedded history. Robert Lowell's legacy benefits from such an eye, eager to examine artifact rather than symptom, ordering principles rather than the unpredictable disorder of the human mind. Both poets feast on deliberate arrangement, setting syllables and images up for confrontation, collusion, or cohesion. Both are champions, in their separate ways, of acoustic volley and volatility.

Even though Lowell confided to Elizabeth Bishop in a 1975 letter that 'without verse ... I found it hard, I was naked without my line ends', his prose about poetry shared a similar quality of buoyancy to Heaney's, although each had different conceptions and representations of vulnerability (Hamilton 2005, 640). Praising Hart Crane's poems in 1961, Lowell wrote: 'all the chaos of his life missed getting sidetracked the way other poets' did, and he was less limited than any other poet of his generation. There was a fullness of experience ... The push of the whole man was there' (Lowell 1961, 262). What Lowell admired was the way Crane harnessed chaos in the

DOI: 10.4324/9781003456148-10

poems, something Lowell himself strived to do. Finding appropriate forms to house this was the challenge. Heaney was fascinated by a similar capacity in Lowell, the transmogrification of raw material into a finished monument.

In *True Friendship*, Christopher Ricks said the difference between Lowell's prose and his poetry has 'nothing to do with the prosaic or the poetical, and everything to with punctuation' (Ricks 2010, 162). Here, Ricks might be thinking about the extended definition of 'punctuation' as supplied by the *OED*: '2b. In reading or speaking: the observance or articulation of appropriate pauses and phrasing, as indicated or as if indicated by punctuation in a text. *Obsolete*'. Heaney's poetry, too, is literally marked differently from his prose. The preoccupations with the texture of language, of the violence of imperialism, of the succor of nature, is in both his prose and in his poems, but the poems have formal precision and shaping, allowing for more noticeable pausing. Heaney never took to writing prose passages within books of poems as did the bolder (older) American, but Heaney also had a less combative relationship with poetic shapes. Lowell found that prose tended 'to be very diffuse' and 'less cut off from life than poetry is' (Giroux 1987, 244). The latter statement might have had something to do with his relationship to novelists, including Elizabeth Hardwick, whose prose was razor sharp in its emotional intelligence.

And both Lowell and Heaney had some sentiments in common. The Irish poet would have liked something Lowell wrote in an essay: 'a Roman poet is much less intellectual than an Englishman, much less abstract. He's nearer nature somehow... he's much more raw and direct than anything in English .... The Roman frankness interests me' (Giroux 1987, 253). In a short 1967 piece on the Russian poet Andrei Voznesensky, Lowell concluded: 'this is a hard time to be a poet, and in each country it is hard in different ways. It is almost impossible, even where this is permitted, to be directly political and remain inspired' (Giroux 1987, 121). This too must have chimed with Heaney, but because he was in a more direct line of fire (criticism from his compatriots), it was better that this American poet gave voice to the claim. In an interview with Frederick Seidel in 1961, of his own production of literary criticism, Lowell offered: 'sometimes I wish I did more, but I'm very anxious in criticism not to do the standard analytical essay. I'd like my essay to be much sloppier and intuitive' (Seidel 1961, 237). I imagine Heaney took courage from Lowell's wish not to follow in the path of his New Critic forebearers. His essays read like the essays of a poet; they are attentive to sound as it mingles with sense.

Many essays about Lowell's poetry cannot help but veer to the side and focus on the writer's madness. Heaney does not. He wrote two prose pieces, the first in 1978 and the second ten years later, that try to take the measure of Lowell's art. These are the ones I will focus on here. Even in his first brief prose piece, 'Full Face: Robert Lowell', a review of the 1978 *Day by Day* for *The Irish Times* (a general audience rather than a literary one), written in the wake of his friend's death, Heaney would rather keep his eye on the

170   *Meg Tyler*

integrity of the poetry than the poetic gossip that has little to teach us about art. Heaney writes of Lowell, that 'there was a nineteenth century sturdiness about the career. He was a master, obstinate and conservative in his belief in the creative spirit, yet contrary and disruptive in his fidelity to his personal intuitions and experiences' (Heaney 1980, 221). This is about as close as we get to a discussion of Lowell's personal missteps. The compounding of vague phrases ('contrary and disruptive in his fidelity to his personal intuitions and experiences') suggests Heaney wanted to evade such discussion. What fascinated Heaney was how much poetry possessed Lowell, became Lowell, emanated from him. Heaney writes of Lowell's 'compulsive' sonnet experiments as an 'attempt to get nearer the quick of life, to cage the minute' (Heaney 1980, 221–222). Lowell was at once a figure of the past ('nineteenth century sturdiness') and someone who lived in the moment, determined to record it. Heaney goes on to say that Lowell was 'not essentially a poet of the present tense: he was a looker before and after, a maker, a plotter, closer to Ben Jonson than to D.H. Lawrence' (Heaney 1980, 222). His movements were methodical, exploratory, deliberately muscular. Free association and drifting were not his operating modes – at least, not until he composed the poems in *Day by Day.*

The review is rich with insights about Lowell's process and achievement. Of the poem as an event, and something that inspires action, Heaney writes: 'the annotations of *Notebook* were always straining away from the speed and particularity of their occasions and pining for the condition of meditation' (Heaney 1980, 222). Here, Heaney hits upon Lowell's drive to exert control over the way the words were taken in by others, whether through constant revision or his own attempts at annotation. *Notebooks 1967–1968* were revised and divided and republished in a variety of forms. As Ernest Hilbert put it, 'the poems in *Notebook 1967–1968* may be understood discretely, as individual poems, or as atoms of a much larger molecule, often referred to by Lowell only as the "long poem"' (Hilbert 2017). Long poems (and lengthy prose, think Proust) allow for a meditativeness to develop that lyric poems always undercut. In the lyric, we step into the stream of dream and then step right out, refreshed if we are lucky.

Intriguingly, Heaney seems less than impressed with the looseness of form in *Day by Day*. He feels that Lowell 'abandoned the arbitrary fourteen-line template to which he had been cutting his cloth' and instead followed 'the movement of the voice' (Heaney 1980, 222). The poems are 'freed but not footless'. Conditioned to hear the blacksmith hammering at the shape in Lowell's poems, Heaney is mildly disappointed: 'we are always being told something interesting or sorrowful even when the manner of telling falls short of whatever we recognize to be his level best' (Heaney 1980, 222). What strikes the ear is the use of that great word of dilution, 'interesting', to describe anything that Lowell wrote. Accustomed to the force of contrariness and disruption in Lowell, Heaney seems momentarily dismayed that the 'manner of telling' in *Day by Day* is more subdued.

'The Push of the Whole Man' 171

We understand why this might be in the next paragraph of the review. Heaney shies away from the confessional mode, Lowell's 'plaints', and returns our attention to Lowell's formal maneuvering and mastery. He refers to the 'agonizing personal pieces', and it is unclear for whom these are agonizing, Heaney or Lowell. Instead, he praises the poems that are transformative of the raw material, 'Ulysses and Circe' and the poem centered on Van Eyck's portrait of the Arnolfini marriage, 'Marriage'. Poetry, for Heaney and for Lowell, is not just about saying things in lines on a page. Poetry requires indirection and transcendence at once. Of 'Marriage', he writes: 'there is a received literary language shimmering behind that writing and its simplicity and amplitude recall Pound's dictum that the natural object is always the adequate symbol' (Heaney 1980, 223). Heaney remarks that the book's 'definitive poems are ones that conduct all this turbulence and love into a fiction or along the suggestions of an image' (Heaney 1980, 222). Looking and saying, it turns out, is not enough. Making and plotting are necessary to poetic achievement, as is indirect direction. Heaney discerns a 'sad, half-resigned autumnal note' in many of the poems (which could be said to hold true for Heaney in his equally unexpected final book, *Human Chain*).

In the next section of the review, he steps away from this observation about the dimming of the light in Lowell and returns to a discussion of Lowell's bravery, compared to Berryman's, as both 'swam away powerfully into the dark swirls of the unconscious and the drift toward death'. The quicksand of the mind could hold both in thrall. However, as Heaney says, 'Lowell resisted that, held fast to conscience and pushed deliberately towards self-mastery' (Heaney 1980, 223). Art and the painstaking efforts it took to make it, saved the man from himself. Aware that reading the last book of a friend will be influenced by both love and sorrowful feeling, Heaney expresses gratitude for the art that Lowell 'could not and would not separate from [the] life' (Heaney 1980, 223–224). The face Lowell reveals here is not 'profiled' or 'braced', but rather, 'close, kindly, anxious, testing' – 'like that of a husband, a father's, a child', a patient's, above all a poet's' (Heaney 1980, 224). This portrait-sketch of Lowell closes with the image of his face turned toward our own. Written within half a year of Lowell's death, we suspect that Heaney was working hard to articulate Lowell's strengths as a poet but did not want to sound too full of flattery. He makes note of the ostensibly weaker poems, when the 'manner of telling falls short' of 'his level best' (Heaney 1980, 224). Space isn't given here to a recounting of which poems constitute that 'level best'; it is, after all a review in a newspaper. But what is here is Heaney's careful if momentary attention, his fascination with the older poet's work and manner. The slight note of dismay about the looser poems in *Day by Day* could simply be from surprise when a familiar poet breaks with the past.

Almost a decade later, Heaney tries again to capture the import of Lowell's work, this time for the different audience of Harvard colleagues and students as part of the 1986 T.S. Eliot Memorial Lecture series. 'Lowell's Command'

172   *Meg Tyler*

opens with a reference to an essay written by Michael Longley, distinguishing between the 'igneous and the sedimentary as modes of composition' (Heaney 1988, 129). Igneous is 'irruptive, unlooked-for and peremptory'; sedimentary is 'steady-keeled, dwelt-upon, graduated'. Lowell's work is seen to possess both, 'a process which begins igneous and ends up sedimentary' (Heaney 1988, 129). We note a shift in how Heaney demarcates the work. Earlier, he was 'a looker before and after, a maker, a plotter'. Now his work is seen to begin in an 'irruptive and unlooked for' manner. Yet an idea he introduces in the earlier piece could be seen to be worked out further in this lecture – that there was 'a stylistic drama being played out all through his work', 'a conflict between his love of literature and his sense of the times, between his predilection for the high rhetorical modes of poetry and the age's preference for the democratic and the demotic' (Heaney 1988, 221). Heaney looks for opposing energies to help describe what makes Lowell's work compelling. However, the metaphors have changed. The contest of rhetorical modes is one strand of his description of Lowell, the comparison of rocks another. What Robert Creeley, quoting Pound, said of verse, that it 'consists of a constant and a variant' has an echo in Heaney's prose about Lowell – and other poets he returns to (Creeley 1989, 413). The obstinacy and disruptiveness in Lowell that he sketches out in the *Irish Times* review has been painted more fully here.

Heaney claims that Lowell 'had a powerful instinct for broaching the molten stuff early but then he would keep returning to work it over with the hot and cold weathers of his revising intelligence' (Heaney 1988, 129). The poem 'is an event', Lowell claimed, 'not the record of an event'. While the labor required to craft a poem is substantive, the poem itself must 'come from some deep impulse, deep inspiration' (Heaney 1988, 129). What is intimated in the earlier review of Lowell's work, that he, like Berryman, 'swam away powerfully into the dark swirls of the unconscious and the drift toward death', is that what begat the poem was this *dark* and deep impulse.

Abandonment also returns to this elaboration. Lowell had earlier been said to abandon the sonnet form. But now, Lowell's 'obsessive subjectivity did not signify an abandonment of the usual life with its attendant moral codes and obligations' (Heaney 1988, 130). Lowell is seen by Heaney to deliberately occupy 'the role of the poet as conscience, one who wakens to a possible etymology of that word as meaning our capacity to know the same thing together' (Heaney 1988, 130). Whether through 'public apostrophe and rebuke', or by 'introspective or confessional example', he brought into view our common knowledge and perhaps even our complicity, our common denial. He may have left behind tired forms (the sonnet) but the need for an alert conscience never tires. That said, Heaney reminds us here that Lowell's choice of form is in a way a 'poet's covenant with his group and his group's language, and that the covenant is based on a mutual understanding that the poetic venture is ultimately serviceable no matter how solipsistic it might at first appear' (Heaney 1988, 130). Poetry serves the public good and

'The Push of the Whole Man' 173

Lowell could be seen as one of its most effective servants. The measurable public efficacy of art is a notion with which Heaney struggled. Art cannot, of course, stop the wheels of a tank from turning, but it has its own form of standing up for what is right. Tellingly, Heaney's implication that Lowell's work helps us remember what we have conveniently and collectively forgotten serves an 'admonitory function' (as could the example of Lowell's life, some might argue).

In choosing the title for this lecture, Heaney spells out the various ways in which Lowell's poetics had command – not simply over the public readership or audience but also a command of the literary past *and* 'the illiterate ear'. I suspect the latter reference is to the biblical overtones, the high rhetoric of Lowell's verse, as if from a preacher on a pulpit, not reliant upon the reading skills of the congregation, but instead upon their ability to take in what comes from above, whether from a human or a divinely inspired voice. Heaney chooses not to elaborate on his use of the phrase 'illiterate ear' but because of his own propensities and interests I suspect he is talking about the way the sounds of syllables, ordered just so, can tap into the primitive in each of us and have a visceral effect. Heaney relates that 'until full middle age', Lowell drew upon his ability to tune his lines and bring them 'to a pitch of tension' by means of 'musical climax, dramatic gesture or ironical plotting' (Heaney 1988, 130) ('those blessed structures, plot and rhyme'). Heaney perceives that Lowell shifted from the 'stand-offish, self-sufficient' poetry of earlier poems to a 'more face-to-face contact with his reader and his reader's world' (Heaney 1988, 130). The 'full face' of Lowell is given more dimension by Heaney's brushstrokes.

Imitative of his Puritan predecessors like Jonathan Edwards, Lowell relies upon high rhetoric and the force of revelation to deliver impact on the page. Particularly insightful is Heaney's remark that Lowell was 'always seeking to outfox if not to overwhelm the logic of argument by the force of image or oracle' (Heaney 1988, 131). Images and oracles are two entirely different things but both can be used as a means to an end. Moving is his account of the effect of reading such concluding lines:

> Closing lines like these would tremble in the center of the ear like an arrow in a target and set the waves of suggestion rippling. A sense of something utterly completed vied with a sense of something startled into scope and freedom. The reader was permitted the sensation of a whole meaning simultaneously clicking shut and breaking open, a momentary illusion that the fulfillments which were being experienced in the ear spelled out meaning and fulfillments available in the world.
>
> (Heaney 1988, 131)

This is Heaney at his readerly best, when he teaches us how he hears a poem. What captures his interest is the effect that Lowell achieves by successfully employing the 'stretched safety net of poetic form itself' (Heaney 1988, 131).

174 *Meg Tyler*

In his description of *Life Studies*, Heaney uses terms like 'hard', 'intelligent', 'well-braced' to describe Lowell, not unlike in the earlier review, but now we also have a more expansive rendering of the power of *Life Studies* which melds 'the unnerving business of autobiography with a certain air of courtesy'. These poems derive strength from their decorum, technical mastery and a 'drive towards impersonality' (Heaney 1988, 131). Heaney avoids the psychoanalytical reading many have used as a lens to understand Lowell. He emphasizes instead the public good that Lowell's structures serve: 'his poetic art, however self-willed it might on occasion be, could never escape from an innate demand that it should not just be a self-indulgence' (Heaney 1988, 132). Heaney believed that there had to be 'something surgical in the incisions he made, something professional and public-spirited in the exposure', which reveals a deeper purpose to the work than the earlier 'stand-offish' poems could achieve (Heaney 1988, 132). An echo of the earlier review is heard again in his claim that Lowell 'strove to outstrip the level best of his peers by swerves that were all his own: doctrinal, ancestral, political' (Heaney 1988, 132).

Intriguingly, Heaney sees Lowell's act of conscientious objection as the great signifier of his life's work, when 'doctrine, ancestry, and politics fused themselves in one commanding stroke and Lowell succeeded in uniting the aesthetic instinct with the obligation to witness morally and significantly in the realm of public action' (Heaney 1988, 133). Heaney lends a heroic air to Lowell's decision: 'the refusal to enlist burst up from some deep magma and had a sort of igneous personal scald to it' (Heaney 1988, 133). A pattern of witnessing and exploring that takes place in many Heaney poems, from picking out an image and turning its symbolic weight over in his mind's eye, appears here in the prose too. The comparison of Lowell's production to igneous rocks, formed by lava, has greater resonance than the references to Lowell's 'commanding stroke'.

The igneous and sedimentary nature of Lowell's oeuvre is connected to Lowell's command in that both refer to what stays, is durable and forceful. Heaney's repeated emphasis on poetry not just as art but as lasting public monument helps us to see perhaps how he wanted his own work to be taken in, as an act of public service in addition to being a piece of craftsmanship. The sentences in his prose have a potential charge similar to that in the poetic line. Prose relies no less on the explosive energy of images; what differs is that in poetry they are set out for display, visually and aurally. What Heaney admired in Lowell was his command of the formal elements in a poem that could contain the eruptive force of his content. Lowell's voice not only had command but was also commanded by the past and present urgencies. It is reasonable to think that Heaney saw himself as working with similarly volatile material: the history of conflict, embedded in language and landscape. Heaney's choice of the word 'command' as title also points to another less direct connection between the Irish poet and the American. Deriving from the Latin *mandare* (*manus* hand + *dare* to give), the word 'command' suggests 'to give into any one's hand or charge'. This is a sense retained by the

'The Push of the Whole Man' 175

ancient compound *commendāre* (to commend). Late Latin offers *commandāre* (*com-* intensive + *mandāre* to commit), meaning 'to give in charge, enjoin'. To command, then, is to hand over and also to commend. Lowell gave into Heaney's 'hand' a license to pursue a particular poetic path that honored both artfulness and political urgency. Heaney mentions that both Yeats and Lowell inhaled 'a sense of public responsibility for their country, their culture and the future of both' (Heaney 1988, 134).

To make emphatic this connection between private art-making and public value, midway through the essay, the direction takes a slight turn. Heaney leaves behind Lowell's poetry for a spell and turns to other models of poets as public spokespeople. Most of us do not particularly associate Lowell with selflessness, or pair him with Osip Mandelstam. Heaney is aware of the crudeness of the comparison ('an exaggeration and an insolence') but draws attention to the 'collision between individual moral conscience and the demands of the historical moment' (Heaney 1988, 134). For Lowell, his refusal to enlist

> permitted him to feel that the discharge of violent energy from the cauldron of his nature had a positive witnessing function, that by forging a poetic sound which echoed the resolute hammering within his nature, he was forging a conscience for our times.
>
> (Heaney 1988, 135)

Perhaps in Heaney was also lodged the memory of some language in an essay that Christopher Ricks wrote about Lowell in 1971. In 'The War of Words: The Poetry of Robert Lowell', Ricks claimed that 'violence was Lowell's essential subject, terrible in its variety (of time, of place, of motive, of nature) and terrible in not changing' (Ricks 1984, 256). Heaney, unlike Ricks, perceives a constructive use made of this violence, like lava forming into rock, a 'conscience for our times' was forged.

Next Heaney looks at a passage in 'The Quaker Graveyard in Nantucket' with its 'sovereign diction' and implacability. He recognizes that the 'monotone of majesty' in such a poem as this could well bring about its own demise by silencing the human note: 'somehow the thing would have to be toned down or else the command established would quickly devolve into cacophony, into something unmodulated and monomaniacal' (Heaney 1988, 137). And change is what Lowell did. Heaney cites Anna Swir's words that the first task of a poet is 'to create one's own style', and the second to destroy it (Heaney 1988, 138). Lowell, according to Heaney achieved this twice.

After the 'dominant music of Lowell's poetic prime', comes a Lowell who persists in writing public poems but 'they do not address the world in order to correct it', once again enacting variant and constraint (Heaney 1988, 140). Heaney juxtaposes the new and less assertive voice of 'Waking Early Sunday Morning', and 'For the Union Dead' with his previous 'ruling passion for sounding victorious' (Heaney 1988, 141). Oddly, Heaney devotes

176   *Meg Tyler*

only one paragraph to the three books, *History, The Dolphin* and *For Lizzie and Harriet*. He acknowledges the strong lines within, and the 'good artistic intentions', but he finds that confronting the triptych is akin to confronting 'a phalanx. I feel driven off the field of my reader's freedom by the massive riveted façade, the armoured tread, the unconceding density of it all' (Heaney 1988, 141). No mention is made of the way Lowell has inserted Lizzy's words, supposedly verbatim, into the poems, and the sense of betrayal that that gesture awakened. Heaney skirts around the too personal.

What he claims gives him pause, rather, is the defiant and defensive formal choice of repeating shapes. Is he remembering what Lowell once said, years earlier, after they met at the Kilkenny festival in 1975 and exchanged sonnets? 'I was very conscious of how correctly iambic [my Glanmore poems] were in comparison to his own much lumpier ingots, and indeed he implied in a letter to me that they could do with a bit of knocking about' (O'Driscoll 2008, 216). Whatever the case, Heaney does not want to dwell on these three books and turns his gaze instead to the accomplishment of *Day by Day*, which by now Heaney has had a decade to digest.

He begins by describing its felt effect: 'is of moving from a works-floor ringing with the occasional treble beauty of that busy crowbar to a room full of canvases by, say, Bonnard' (Heaney 1988, 141). This seems different from his earlier account of the poems not all being equal to Lowell's 'level best'. Continuing, he reports that 'the voice comes from pillow level rather than from a podium' (Heaney 1988, 142). The poems are 'as tousled, amiably importunate and comfortably unpredictable as lovers weaving through warm rooms at the end of a slightly erotic, slightly drunken party' (Heaney 1988, 142). The poems are both persistent and unpredictable, signifying a shift in style, but their tone is never 'insinuatingly personal' (Heaney 1988, 142). The unmentioned emotional assault of the poems from *The Dolphin* might be in his mind here as a point of comparison. These poems are ones of 'dramatic personal utterance' but also 'impersonal and oracular' (Heaney 1988, 142), the personal lifting to the transcendent. The imagery has been tempered down, as has been the tone: 'we have come far indeed from the kind of command this poet sought and exercised in the early work, where truth was piledriven by metre and condensed allusions' (Heaney 1988, 143). Insightfully expressed, Heaney hears a tone that is not 'forced or forcing, the voice of the poem does not come down upon you but rises towards its own surface' (Heaney 1988, 143). Command has shifted ground, perhaps toward something resembling commending.

Of the virtue of the book's best poems, Heaney writes

> is the feeling of being at the eye of an agitation, in an emotional calm that is completely impersonal, a condition evenly distanced from the infinite indifference on the minus side of the graph, and the infinite serenity of the other extreme.
>
> (Heaney 1988, 145)

Day by Day 'wakens rather than fixes' (Heaney 1988, 146). For Heaney, the poems here are 'pre-eminently events rather than the record of events' (Heaney 1988, 146). No more flexing of the 'literary muscle', no more emphatic tone; 'Lowell's command finally came to reside in this self-denial, this readiness not to commandeer the poetic event but to let his insights speak their own riddling truths' (Heaney 1988, 147). A far cry for his underestimation of the book's worth in his earlier review, Heaney senses the unproclaimed 'wisdom' of these poems. Lowell has let go the need for command in these freely associative poems; we see a similar movement in Heaney's final book, *Human Chain*, toward poems that have formal shapes but ones that seem less committed to a particular type of form.

The rhetorical and even the rhythmic movement of a Heaney essay is not dissimilar to that of a Heaney poem. He often starts with an image that taps into a feeling he has, and he registers in the poem the image's resonance, whatever ripples out from it. Heaney's early observation of Lowell's concluding images, similes, or references to oracles, created a kind of settlement in Heaney's thinking, one that expanded over the course of a decade and enabled him to write this more comprehensive piece (no doubt the pressure of the deadline helped too). The prose allows him greater space to describe the sensation of reading and absorbing Lowell, of appreciating the impact of the poems on his own sensibility. Heaney was always alert to the way a poem lands in the ear (or a poet in the heart and mind).

Along with thematic inter-stitching, the prose paragraphs have a texture and density to them not unlike the poems. Heaney's interest in the history and largesse of words reverberates here. As in the poetry, Heaney relies upon repetition, repeating a word to illustrate how it takes on a slightly different meaning in each new context, as we see with 'command' in the 1988 lecture. The 'great meadow' of his prose is teacherly but not abrasively didactic (Andriesse 2022, 3). Even when collected in paragraphs, his work brings to mind the tactility of language. The touching measures that Heaney takes of the work of his friend Robert Lowell are generous, loyal and insightful. They choose to focus on craft and achievement rather than on the lasting consequence of fracture. I would like to close with some prose from Elizabeth Hardwick, Lowell's brilliant and ebullient if long-suffering former wife, whose (altered) words had been inserted into the material of his poems. As she writes in an 'occasional' piece for *Mademoiselle* in 1973:

> Nevertheless, I have seen freedom, happiness, and goodness come, finally, from what had seemed to be the wreckage of personal existence, from alterations violently resisted, from unhappiness that fell as a devastating blow. No one would wish misery surmounted as the way to peace. It is merely important to remember that it can sometimes happen.

(Andriesse 2022, 213)

178 *Meg Tyler*

Heaney might well agree that framing helps us perceive that darkness is born of light, strife will be followed by peace, from command can grow camaraderie. He would recognize that Lowell's polished if dogged creative efforts are a monument to 'misery surmounted'.

Works Cited

Andriesse, Alex (ed.) (2022) *The Uncollected Essays: Elizabeth Hardwick*, New York Review of Books.

Creeley, Robert (1989) *The Collected Essays of Robert Creeley*, Berkeley: University of California Press.

Giroux, Robert (ed.) (1987) *Robert Lowell: Collected Prose*, New York: Farrar, Straus & Giroux.

Hamilton, Saskia (ed.) (2005) *The Letters of Robert Lowell*, New York: Farrar, Straus & Giroux.

Heaney, Seamus (1988) *The Government of the Tongue: 1986 T.S. Eliot Memorial Lectures*, London: Faber and Faber.

Heaney, Seamus (1980) *Preoccupations: Selected Prose 1968–1978*, New York: Farrar, Straus & Giroux

Hilbert, Ernest (2017) 'Our Monotonous Sublime: Robert Lowell's Notebook Poems', *Literary Matters* 10:1 (Fall 2017) https://www.literarymatters. org/10-1-our-monotonous-sublime-robert-lowells-notebook-poems/.

O'Driscoll, Dennis (2008) *Stepping Stones: Interviews with Seamus Heaney*, New York: Farrar, Straus & Giroux.

Ricks, Christopher (2010) *True Friendship: Geoffrey Hill, Anthony Hecht, and Robert Lowell Under the Sign of Eliot and Pound*, New Haven, CT: Yale University Press.

Ricks, Christopher (1984) *The Force of Poetry*, Oxford: Oxford University Press.

Seidel, Frederick (1961) Robert Lowell: The Art of Poetry #3, interviewed by Frederick Seidel, *The Paris Review*, issue 25, Winter/Spring https://www.theparisreview. org/inter views/4664/the-art-of-poetry-no-3-robert-lowell.

10 Seamus Heaney's Wordsworthian Prose Assessments of Brian Friel's Drama

Richard Rankin Russell

L is for letter, the first one Brian wrote to me after *Death* of a Naturalist was published in 1966, a gesture that was generous, typical and of immense significance for me. It was an admission to the guild of makers, permission to draw up a stool to the edge of the magic circle, and as such an honor to be cherished and a standard to be lived up to ever since.

Seamus Heaney, *Spelling It Out* (Heaney 2009, n.p.)

Seamus Heaney's prose has not always been given the acclaim it deserves, particularly in contrast with his much better-known poetry. Eugene O'Brien points out in only one of two monographs devoted to his prose that 'Generally, he is seen as a poet who gives occasional lectures, writes occasional pieces and gives interviews' (O'Brien 2016, 39). But we are gradually realizing how Heaney's prose has become a major contribution to our understanding of literature's power and purpose. For instance, his ability to get to the heart of a given poem springs from his own deep commitment to poetry, and his lifelong obligation to teach others the deep mysteries of poetry. His Nobel Prize address, *Crediting Poetry*, remains one of the foremost defenses of poetry in the last century, as does one of his Oxford lectures, 'The Redress of Poetry'. His deep debt to writers as diverse as Patrick Kavanagh, Hopkins, Keats, Wordsworth, Plath and even George Herbert emerges throughout his prose.

The tenor of Heaney's literary criticism is usually celebratory, although counter-examples come to mind, such as his (correct) rejection of Philip Larkin's 'Aubade' as 'the definitive post-Christian English poem, over against Yeats's 'The Cold Heaven' (Heaney 1995a, 156), despite praising Larkin in two earlier essays where he felt the English poet's propensity for transcendence was still operative ('Englands of the Mind' and 'The Main of Light'). Neil Corcoran locates this general critical enthusiasm in Heaney's aesthetic to that of Wordsworth, observing that 'the permeability of Heaney's critical consciousness to Wordsworth makes his basic conceptions of poetry essentially late Romantic ones, however much they may have been put through a Modernist or, in some respects, a post-modernist filter' (Corcoran 1998, 229). He notes further that 'Approbation, celebration and self-identification, rather

DOI: 10.4324/9781003456148-11

180   *Richard Rankin Russell*

than irony, temper and measure, are the characteristic motives and moods of his criticism' (Corcoran 1998, 229). Yet, Heaney was selective in choosing his exemplary writers, seemingly following the longstanding rule of book reviewing: if a book is sufficiently bad, it will die of its own faults, and there is no need to savage it in print. On the other hand, there are lesser-known writers out there to whom the public's attention should be devoted, and these authors are worth devoting one's literary criticism to in order to recover them and clearly present their virtues. Hence, Heaney's devotion to not only better-known poets such as those listed above, but also to Theodore Roethke, George Sefaris, Norman MacCaig, Hugh MacDiarmid and others.

Both then, for the sheer pleasure he found in others' words and in recovering those words he thought should be acknowledged and highlighted, there is an air of delighted discovery and sheer pleasure in Heaney's prose criticism that is missing in much literary criticism today that is instead often dedicated to what Paul Ricoeur has termed the 'hermeneutics of suspicion'.[1] In this regard, Heaney has recalled 'not being taught the idiom of suspicion in the university', musing further, 'Literary study had not yet been politicized, the aesthetic and the moral were the endorsed categories, the humanist wager was still in place' (Heaney 1997, 12). Moreover, he goes on to speak approvingly of how 'The critic's act was then one of empathy, and critical endeavor was based upon an anticipation which to some extent paralleled the writer's anticipation'. What he valued throughout his career as a literary critic was 'Artistic success and the celebration of it, an orientation of the spirit towards enjoyment of the transformations and raptures of awakened language' (Heaney 1997, 12). Unlike some professional literary critics, Heaney does not presume to know more than the literary work he reads and analyzes; rather, he submits himself to its imaginative power and is often transformed in the process. If his best essays 'are themselves rapt exercises in the articulation of the pleasure given to a fine reader by what Wordsworth is quoted as naming "the grand elementary principle of pleasure"', they also risk simplification, as Corcoran argues his reading of Marlowe's poem 'Hero and Leander' does by neglecting that poem's 'entanglement in issues of gender and sexuality' (Corcoran 1998, 215). For Heaney, this risk seems worth taking since readers who might know Marlowe better for his dramas such as *Dr. Faustus* might then be led into the poetry after reading this essay, which was first given publicly as one of his lectures while Heaney was Oxford Professor of Poetry from 1989 to 1994. And presumably, such readers can determine for themselves such issues as Corcoran identifies. The process, however, likely does not work in reverse given our current hyper-politicized climate: if Heaney were to succumb to Ricoeur's 'hermeneutic of suspicion', readers might *only* read the poem reductively for issues of sexuality and gender and have little or no pleasure in it.

And yet it would be a mistake to characterize Heaney's prose as sheerly aesthetic and not attuned to ethical issues. Indeed, he often weds aesthetics and ethics, particularly when he is writing of political and cultural issues. As I note in my introduction to Heaney's work, his 'remarkable literary criticism

Seamus Heaney's Assessments of Brian Friel's Drama 181

constitutes a body of work that makes the most serious apologia for lyric poetry in the second half of the twentieth century', and further, his defense of poetry 'has been so well made and articulate that it stakes a substantive claim to the best kind of ethical poetry criticism' (Russell 2016a, 233). Ethics and aesthetics are marvelously married in Heaney's best criticism, and his poetic antennae were remarkably well tuned to this marriage. As Corcoran remarks about this aspect of Heaney's literary criticism, 'it carries ... a strong ethical as well as aesthetic charge' (Corcoran 1998, 211). Perhaps Heaney's supreme formulation of the relationship between ethics and aesthetics in his prose occurs in the last sentence of his Nobel Lecture, *Crediting Poetry*, where, after meditating upon the famous stanza of Yeats's 'Meditations in Time of Civil War', where the speaker bids the honey bees to come build in the empty house of the starling, Heaney yokes the form of poetry to its ethical dimension:

> The form of the poem, in other words, is crucial to poetry's power to do the thing which always is and always will be to poetry's credit: the power to persuade that vulnerable part of our consciousness of its rightness in spite of the evidence of wrongness all around it, the power to remind us that we are hunters and gatherers of values, that our very solitudes and distresses are creditable, in so far as they too are an earnest of our veritable human being.
>
> (Heaney 1995b, 29)

Thus, an essential part of poetry's aesthetic appeal—its form on the page—highlights, even spotlights the issues it chooses to focus upon, here, in the case of Yeats brooding upon the Irish civil war and its destruction by asking a symbol of sweetness to build in an empty bird's nest. This passage also exemplifies the relationship between Heaney's theory of poetry as an interior art illuminated by publicly delivered prose in his largest and most important venue ever, as a recipient of the Nobel Prize for Literature.

In the other book dedicated to Heaney's prose, *Professing Poetry: Seamus Heaney Poetics*, Michael Cavanagh argues that because 'Heaney often characterizes poetry as a nondiscursive, nondidactic art, as something that issues from a private contact with the world', his prose 'has come into being as the ground of his expression'. Prose, for Heaney, 'would be poetry's public face, its public relations agent' (Cavanagh 2009, 11). Because of Heaney's deep commitment to the poem as an inspired, interior event that arrives unexpectedly, he came to view the process of composing poetry as amorphous and ambiguous and has employed his prose in an attempt to explicate this mysterious process in more direct terms often offered in public lectures.

For those who know his work, Heaney's prose criticism became an indelible part of his poetic program, yet his prose criticism on other genres is largely unknown and if known, largely unremarked upon. Of these other genres, drama had long captured Heaney's imagination, going back to his acting as a teenager in his local area of Northern Ireland and his interest in playwrights such as Marlowe and Shakespeare as a college student. In 1983,

182   *Richard Rankin Russell*

for example, Heaney remembered acting as a schoolboy in dramas about the 1798 rebellion:

> Far from the elegances of Oscar Wilde and the profundities of Shakespeare, I was acting with the Bellaghy Dramatic Society in plays about 1798, now playing a United Irishman, a blacksmith forging pikes on a real anvil fetched from Devlin's forge at Hillhead, now playing Robert Emmet in a one-act melodrama and having my performance hailed in the crowded columns of the *Mid-Ulster Mail*.
>
> (Heaney 1983, 7)

And during his first year at Queen's University, in 1957, Heaney was listening to lectures by Professor Terence Spencer on Marlowe's *Tamburlaine*. Significantly for appreciating the incantatory power of many passages in Friel's drama, a point to which I shall return later, Heaney argues in his essay on 'Hero and Leander' that in *Tamburlaine* 'the reader or audience is in thrall to the poetic equivalent of a dynamo-hum, a kind of potent undermusic. It is a sound which both exhilarates and empowers, as if the words are at one and the same time being set free and held on course along some high flight-path' (Heaney 1995a, 29). Heaney's own acting continued into his career after Queen's as well. As I have argued in *Seamus Heaney's Regions* (Russell 2014, 283), 'in the early 1960s, he developed his fascination with drama further during his teaching days at St. Joseph's Training College, Belfast, when he led a group of first-year teachers-in-training on Easter putting on the Passion section from the medieval Chester cycle of mystery plays' (Heaney 1965, 58–60). By the late 1960s, Heaney was contributing radio scripts for the Schools department of BBC Northern Ireland Radio. In 1970, he published a short play about 1798, *Munro*, which was broadcast by BBC Northern Ireland, and the next year, BBC Northern Ireland broadcast his radio play about the Troubles, *Everyman*, which was modeled, to some degree, on the medieval morality play of the same name.[2] Throughout his early life, then, Heaney not only was interested in drama, he acted in dramas and studied them—and most important, perceived continuities between the type of interior, captivating music he was cultivating in his own poetry and that of drama. Dramatic conceptions lie behind some of his greatest poems, such as 'Casualty'.[3] And much later in his career, he turned to crafting Northern-Irish inflected renderings of two great Greek dramas: *The Cure at Troy*, his 'version' of Sophocles' *Philoctetes* (1991), and *The Burial at Thebes*, his 'version' of Sophocles' *Antigone* (2004). But the short fiction and especially drama of Brian Friel became Heaney's touchstone for drama, and his prose engagements with it were early, ongoing, and significant. They are still underappreciated for apprehending Heaney's prose criticism in other genres and for critical assessments of Friel specifically.

Heaney long admired Friel, a fellow graduate of St Columb's College secondary school in Derry City, who, like himself, was reared Catholic in

Seamus Heaney's Assessments of Brian Friel's Drama   183

divided Northern Ireland and who moved to the Republic of Ireland early in the 'Troubles'. As Marilynn Richtarik has pointed out, when Friel sent Heaney a draft of his play *Volunteers* in 1974, 'it had a galvanizing effect on Heaney', who was struck that they were both exploring archaeology; Heaney ended up putting together his bog poems and Viking Dublin poems plus his autobiographical poems into what became his landmark volume *North*, published in 1975.[4] Friel eventually dedicated that drama to Heaney. That same year Heaney read and suggested changes to a draft of Friel's play *Faith Healer*, and, in 1979, he would send Friel a draft of *Station Island*, which he eventually dedicated to the playwright upon its publication in 1984 (Richtarik 2021, 189). Friel's recently published recollections about his rehearsing of *Faith Healer* in New York during February of 1979 show phone calls to and from Heaney and visits to and from Heaney, who was teaching at Harvard that year.[5] And Heaney would dedicate the loving later poem, 'A Call', collected in *The Spirit Level* (1991) to Friel. Yet in the public mind—and even in much academic discourse—Friel and Heaney's relationship was largely confined to their work together on the Field Day Theatre Company, particularly after Heaney joined the board of directors in the early 1980s.[6] But Heaney had long been a student of both Friel's short fiction and drama and his stance as a Catholic nationalist (but not ideologue) toward the conflict in the North, and thus, this essay delineates how Heaney engaged with Friel's drama repeatedly in his prose. For instance, in 'Digging Deeper: Brian Friel's "*Volunteers*"', published in the *Times Literary Supplement* in 1975, Heaney assesses Friel's play *Volunteers* wherein he perceptively analyzes the role of the republican internees who are excavating a Viking site near Dublin. For Heaney, *Volunteers* represents a new kind of Frielian drama that was exemplary to Heaney in crafting his own thoughtful poetry: 'a kind [of drama] that involves an alienation effect but eschews didactic address' (Heaney 1975, 215). He recognizes Friel's desire to 'shock' his audiences, that 'an expert, hurt and shocking laughter is the only adequate response to a calloused condition', and realizes too that Friel was trying 'to create, despite resistance, the taste by which he is to be enjoyed' (Heaney 1975, 216).

Feeling increasingly alienated himself from Northern Irish Catholics while he and his family lived first in County Wicklow in the early to mid-1970s, then in County Dublin from 1976 on, Heaney took some of his artistic bearings from Friel's public dramatic examinations of those fictionalized characters from Northern Ireland torn among allegiances—to family, friends, country and to varying selves. By 1980, in his *Times Literary Supplement* review of the Dublin Theatre Festival's production of *Translations* starring Stephen Rea, Heaney would argue, 'Brian Friel has by now produced a more significant body of work than any other playwright in Ireland, and it is time, that he was, as it were, translated' (Heaney 1980b, 1199). Here, Heaney is challenging other critics to seriously undertake critical appreciations of Friel—and, just as important, challenging himself to do so as well.

184   *Richard Rankin Russell*

In the years that followed, Heaney did just that. His critical 'translations' of Friel's work include an analysis of his masterpiece, *Faith Healer* (1979) in his third Richard Ellmann lecture of 1989 (ostensibly about Yeats), along with discussions of the still underappreciated short fiction, *Faith Healer*, his better-known and often-anthologized *Translations* (1980), and his most commercially successful play, *Dancing at Lughnasa* (1990) in his 1993 essay, 'For Liberation: The Use of Memory in Brian Friel', his most sustained engagement with the arc of Friel's career. And Friel continued to engage Heaney's critical and creative attention right through the last decade of the poet's life. In 2008, Heaney delivered a public address for Friel at the McGill Summer School honoring the playwright, published the next year by Gallery Press as *Spelling It Out* as part of the Friel 80th birthday celebrations in Ireland. *Spelling It Out* is a prose volume replete with associations Heaney drew out from each letter of Friel's name. The first 'I' in the playwright's name (in 'Brian') gets to the heart of Friel's exemplary aesthetic for Heaney: '*I* is for integrity, the quality which distinguishes Brian as man and as artist', and it is 'also for Ireland, to which he is both chronicler and soul doctor, towards which he feels both responsibility and detachment'. Heaney finally argues in this 'entry' for that first letter 'I' that '*I* is also for intimacy, for the inner self, the mysterious source and lining of being, that which is both articulate and inarticulate in all of us, and which underwriters the poetry of Brian Friel's theatre' (Heaney 2009, n.p.). In what is likely his last publication addressing Friel's brilliance, Heaney wrote the program note to the 2011 Gate Theatre production of the playwright's 1994 play, *Molly Sweeney*, wherein he memorably (and accurately) claimed, 'Just to say the names of certain plays is to be reminded of how deeply Friel's work has become embedded in the common consciousness of Ireland: *Philadelphia, Here I Come!, Faith Healer, Translations, Dancing at Lughnasa*' (Heaney 2011, n.p.).

Heaney's engagement with Friel as a young, then mature, then aging poet proved essential to his own craftsmanship and development of his own considerable aesthetic integrity. This essay charts how Heaney's often Wordsworthian prose engagements with Friel's drama and artistic persona reveal his deep debt to Friel as the only other Irish writer of his era with a comparable reach and status who (largely) successfully kept faith with his truthful art, particularly in terms of its ability to conjure up an abiding love of his home ground, its mesmeric qualities and its ability to evoke powerful memories.

Heaney has written in the interviews that comprise *Stepping Stones* of his early interest in Friel, going back to the older writer's first book of short fiction, *The Saucer of Larks*, which he bought

> soon after it came out and I believe the first Friel story I read was the title story. Then a couple of years later I drove with Marie to the German cemetery in Glencree in County Wicklow because it had figured in that story.
>
> (Heaney 2008, 177)

Seamus Heaney's Assessments of Brian Friel's Drama 185

Famously a writer of specific places, Heaney was thus drawn to Friel's example of paying attention to small and intimate places. As he expounded, 'The great thing about him is *his total grip on the home ground* and his attentiveness to it, and at the same time his sense of intellectual and artistic responsibility drawn from the farthest horizons' (Heaney 2008,177; my emphasis). Notice, though, that Heaney immediately links Friel's intimate knowledge of home ground to responsibilities 'drawn from the farthest horizons'. Friel had likely acquired that cosmopolitan, rich and well-developed sense of 'intellectual and artistic responsibility', according to Heaney, from his 'constant awareness of Chekhov and O'Neill, to name only two of the dramatists he would invoke. You could feel the inner devotion and couldn't help knowing that he had a calling as a writer and that equally he had a determination not to let the calling bloat into celebrity (Heaney 2008, 178). For those 'farthest horizons' also drew upon the early Broadway success of Friel's 1964 breakthrough play, *Philadelphia, Here I Come!*, which emerged from his tutelage under Northern Irish playwright Tyrone Guthrie in Minneapolis. Heaney sagely notes that Friel

> stayed clear of a lot of the razzmatazz of show business, probably because he got a lot of success early on and had had his fill of the "luvvy" scene. After *Philadelphia*, he came back from Broadway, built himself a house that was both a family home and a writer's bunker, and began his long campaign of staying put.
>
> (Heaney 2008, 178)

But as Friel stayed put, Heaney ranged more and more abroad,[7] particularly as he grew more famous after his move to the Republic of Ireland in 1972, yet he often engaged with and was inspired by Friel's work, particularly his drama.

I adduced Neil Corcoran's conception of Heaney's criticism as essentially Wordsworthian earlier, and understanding Heaney's conception of Wordsworth remains crucial to his appreciation of Friel's art. In his introduction to his selected edition of poems by Wordsworth, Heaney makes clear his immense respect for him, noting that 'his achievement' is

> the largest and most securely founded in the canon of native English poetry since Milton. He is an indispensable figure in the evolution of modern writing, a finder and keeper of the self-as-subject, a theorist and apologist whose *Preface to Lyrical Ballads* (1802) remains definitive.
>
> (Heaney 2001, vii)

Whether or not one agrees with Heaney's assessment of Wordsworth's place in English poetry, he clearly looked to him time and again as he assessed more contemporary writers, including those from his own native province of Northern Ireland such as Friel.[8]

186   *Richard Rankin Russell*

We can detect obliquely this interest in Friel through Heaney's reading of Wordsworth in 'Feeling into Words', a crucial poetic statement, which opens with a quotation from *The Prelude* about Wordsworth's 'hiding places of my power' (Heaney 1980a, 41). Heaney had already been reading Danish archaeologist P.V. Glob's book, *The Bog People* (English translation, 1969) and writing the so-called 'bog poems', and he thus was already interested in poetry as a type of excavation, as archaeology. Friel's sending him in 1974 a draft of *Volunteers*, treating the archaeological excavation by republican prisoners, certainly affirmed this urge. Thus, we can discern his appreciation of Friel's play about 'digging' lurking behind his reading of Wordsworth here:

> Implicit in those lines is a view of poetry which I think is implicit in the few poems I have written that give me any right to speak: poetry as divination, poetry as revelation of the self to the self ... poems as elements of continuity, with the aura and authenticity of archaeological finds, where the buried shard has an importance that is not diminished by the importance of the buried city; poetry as a dig, a dig for finds that end up being plants.
>
> (Heaney 1980a, 41).

Already, we can see Heaney reaching toward an early analysis of Friel's drama through his long immersion in Wordsworth poems of subterranean power.

A decade later, in his Pete Laver Memorial Lecture, *Place and Displacement: Recent Poetry of Northern Ireland*, delivered at Grasmere, the Wordsworth house and museum, on August 2, 1984, Heaney did more than merely 'name-check' Wordsworth; instead, he made clear his sense of 'place and displacement' was foundational to his own poetry and to his criticism of other Northern Irish poets such as Derek Mahon, Paul Muldoon and Michael Longley. Drawing on Jung's theories of psychological development in the face of conflict for Wordsworth's simultaneous devotion to the ideals of the French Revolution and his sense of place, Heaney argues that 'The good place where Wordsworth's nurture happened and to which his habitual feelings are most naturally attuned has become, for the revolutionary poet, the wrong place'. Thus, he

> is displaced from his own affections by a vision of the good that is located elsewhere. His political, utopian aspirations deracinate him from the beloved actuality of his surroundings so that his instinctive being and his appetitive intelligence are knocked out of alignment.
>
> (Heaney 1985, 3)

There may have never been a greater writer of place until both Friel and Heaney came along; yet both were similarly displaced like Wordsworth from their home ground by their 'political, utopian aspirations'.

Eavan Boland captures this sense of place and displacement in her 1973 interview with Friel when she notes that:

> Friel's emphasis on the chasm between the mind that suffers and the man who creates proves two things: one of them is simply that he has read Eliot's influential essay, which draws that distinction; secondly, that he is a prey to the confusion that an essentially private, scrupulously honest artist must feel living next door to a public, uproariously violent situation.
>
> (Friel 1973, 58–59)

We shall return to Eliot and his essay, 'Tradition and the Individual Talent', which was another lens, along with Eliot's 'Little Gidding' through which Heaney also learned to read Friel's work, but here, notice Boland's accurate perception that the conflict in Northern Ireland had by that point in 1973 sufficiently disrupted Friel's interior creative process, making him 'prey to the confusion' by 'living next door' to the conflict in County Donegal, where he had moved in 1967 from Londonderry/Derry City.

Heaney has amply testified in various essays, interviews and even poems to how he felt displaced from Northern Ireland by the violence at the time, finally choosing to leave the province, where he and Marie and their growing family were living in Belfast, in 1972, for the safety of Glanmore Cottage in County Wicklow, and his prose on Friel makes clear he sensed that same displacement as part of the older writer's dilemma too. In 'For Liberation: Brian Friel and the Use of Memory', for example, he asks, quoting from Friel's dramas *Translations* and *Making History*, respectively, 'how does the fully conscious human life find its bearings in order to navigate between what Hugh O'Donnell calls "privacies" and what Mabel Bagenal calls "the overall thing"?' (Heaney 1993, 230). Heaney's Friel, like Wordsworth, successfully negotiated between the necessary artistic commitment to the interior life and the demands of the outside world, 'the command to participate intelligently in the public world of historical process' (Heaney 1993, 230).

Despite his being attuned to the outer world of fact and politics, Wordsworth also epitomized for Heaney's sense of Friel's similar surrender to his inspirational inner voice and the way in which Friel's best work, often musically, hypnotizes his audience into breaking down the fourth wall of the theatre, among other aspects of the English Lake poet. In his lecture, 'The Makings of a Music: Reflections on Wordsworth and Yeats', Heaney argues that Wordsworth's ability to surrender himself and 'be carried by' the 'initial rhythmic suggestiveness, to become somnambulist after its invitations' of the 'given line, the phrase or cadence which haunts the ear and the eager parts of the mind', results in a music 'not unlike Wordsworth's, hypnotic, swimming with the current of its form rather than against it' (Heaney 1980a, 61). Friel has always been sensitive to the musicality of his own prose and sought to

188   *Richard Rankin Russell*

enchant audiences through it. In his 1999 essay, 'Seven Notes for a Festival Programme', he pointed out that 'words are at the very core of it all' for his dramatic writing, observing further that unlike in other genres, 'The playwright's words aren't written for solitary engagement—they are written for public utterance. They are used as the story-teller uses them, to hold an audience in his embrace and within that vocal sound' (Friel 1999, 173). Elaborating on his conception of the musicality of his word-hoard as a dramatist, Friel further claims, that 'unlike the words of the novelist or poet, the playwright's words are scored for a very different context ... And it is with this score that the playwright and the actor privately plot to work their public spell' (Friel 1999, 173). This view of the artist as strong enchanter through mesmeric language appealed enormously to Heaney, and he saw it in other exemplary writers as well, including Yeats, the 'Poet-Mage'.

Heaney has extensively praised Friel's language, his word-hoard, what he terms 'the wordy element in which his gift exists and exults even as it aspires beyond words' (Heaney 2009, n.p.). Offering the highest praise, Heaney believed that

> No contemporary playwright has a greater lexical range or relish than Friel, no cast of characters is more endowed with original speech. There is fecundity and felicity and at the same time a forensic vigilance in everything he writes, a Shakespearean rough magic which does not preclude Beckettian fine-tuning.
>
> (Heaney 2009, n.p.)

Employing a musical metaphor, he avers that

> There is in Friel's language, what Robert Frost calls "the wonder of supply", the more-than-enoughness which distinguishes the great ones, a scale that runs from the demotic to the rhapsodic, as capable of mocking wit as elegiac wisdom or lyric fantasy.
>
> (Heaney 2009, n.p)

Friel's employment of the right words aptly rendered for their context captivated Heaney as he admired both the great range and the precision of his vocabulary.

Animated by music to the extent that Simon Kress argues it is the 'preverbal prime mover' in his work (Kress 2021, 157), Heaney consistently affirmed this inspired, mesmeric notion of poetry and drama throughout his career. In his 1974 interview in the *Guardian*, for instance, he privileged 'the poem as a centre which attracts energies and allows energies to pass through it while still remaining a perfect whole, *the poem as an entrancement*, ideally, rather than the poem as a message' (Heaney 1974, 47; my emphasis). Other examples of his championing of poetry as incantation abound, including Heaney's opening of his essay, 'The Impact of Translation' with the text of Czesław Miłosz's

Seamus Heaney's Assessments of Brian Friel's Drama   189

poem entitled 'Incantation', which he terms 'a spell' (Heaney 1988, 36; 37). Writing as a translator of the Anglo-Saxon epic *Beowulf* in 1999, Heaney returned to the notion of inspired music, musing that while

> It is one thing to find lexical meanings for the words and to have some feel for how the metre might go ... it is quite another thing to find the tuning fork that will give you the note and pitch for the overall music of the work.
>
> (Heaney 1999, xxvi)

And in his 2002 address to the Royal College of Physicians in Dublin, Heaney cited his own poem about inspiration, 'The Given Note', about a fiddler who 'had gone alone into the island/And brought back the whole thing', taking it 'Out of wind off mid-Atlantic'. After discussing the notion of inspiration, including among Jesus' disciples when the Holy Spirit descended upon them at the first Pentecost after Christ had ascended to heaven in Acts 2, Heaney also recalls 'William Wordsworth's invocation of the blowing breeze as a sort of angelic messenger (at the start of his autobiographical magnum opus, *The Prelude*' (Heaney, 2002, 6; 7). Heaney thus links Biblical inspiration and Romantic poetry, and he brought this view to his reading of Friel, who fits well his definition of an inspired artist, one whose 'intelligence and cognitive faculties are never more alive than during those moments when he appears to be off in a world of his own, absorbed in the creative trance, preoccupied with the dream-work' (Heaney 2002, 8). Two years before his untimely death, in his program note for the Dublin Gate Theatre's production of *Molly Sweeney*, Heaney still was arguing for Friel's drama as one of enchantment, observing, '*Molly Sweeney* is beautifully written, in beguiling cadences, reminiscent of the mixture of actuality and entrancement that characterizes *Dancing at Lughnasa*' (Heaney 2011, n.p.). For earlier examples of this theatre of entrancement, we might call to mind Friel's protagonists Frank Hardy and Michael Munday from *Faith Healer* and *Dancing at Lughnasa*, respectively, who step forward from the wings, themselves wordsmiths and artists of the highest order, who enchant themselves and their onstage and theater audiences.

In congruence with his statement in 'The Makings of a Music' about Hazlitt's recollection of hearing Wordsworth read his poetry in June of 1798 that 'Wordsworth's chaunt acted as a spell upon the hearer, whether that hearer were Hazlitt or Wordsworth himself. It enchaunted' (Heaney 1980a, 65), Heaney found that incantatory music in Friel's major plays as well, perhaps nowhere more than in *Faith Healer*. That play memorably opens with the title character trying to enchant us and himself with his 'opening incantation' that runs through a litany of Welsh town names (Friel 1996a, 331). As he interrupts himself, he muses, 'All those dying Welsh villages' and his eyes open. Then he reveals reasons for this recitation: 'I'd get so tense before a performance, d'you know what I used to do? As we drove

190 *Richard Rankin Russell*

along those narrow, winding roads I'd recite the names to myself just for the mesmerism, the sedation, of the incantation —' (Friel 1996a, 332). And yet we quickly find ourselves enchanted too, caught up in the slipstream of Frank's verbal incantations, a Frielian music pitched so adroitly that we sit entranced through four monologues. And when Frank offers himself as a sacrifice to his killers in the conclusion, Friel's magic continues, as Heaney points out:

> the conclusion of *Faith Healer* has the radiance of myth, it carries its protagonist and its audience into a realm beyond expectation, and it carries the drama back to that original point where it once participated in the sacred, where sacrifice was witnessed and the world renewed by that sacrifice.
>
> (Heaney 1993, 237)

I have shown elsewhere how Friel employs repetition of particular words and phrases at the end of this play to establish a haunting sense of timelessness that catapults us into the scene and also enchants us so that we weirdly desire Frank's sacrificial death and community with his killers and thus, by extension, imagine the possibility of forgiveness and peace in Northern Ireland (Russell 2022, 171; 175–178; 185–192).

Almost a decade after *Faith Healer*'s initial productions in 1979, Heaney devoted a significant part of his third Richard Ellmann lecture at Emory University, 'Empty Shell and Cornucopia: Variations on a Theme from Ellmann', to discussing the drama of Yeats, Friel and Beckett, and his remarks about Frank Hardy illustrate his ongoing critical insight into Friel's penchant for inspiration through mesmerism, even when facing the possibility of failure unto death. Heaney argues that Frank Hardy is 'swayed between intimations of himself as a charlatan and fleeting convictions about the marvel of his gift' (Heaney 1989, 63). Then quoting in full the last passages of the play when Frank walks to meet his brutal, would-be killers, Heaney suggests the stark truth of Frank's homecoming: 'a blank and hostile stare, the malignity of those he would embrace concentrated back upon him as the antithesis of the benignity he would exercise upon them' (Heaney 1989, 65). Frank has previously healed the farmer Donal's bent finger, yet he always knows when he cannot heal someone, and thus, he walks to his certain death here at the end of this powerful drama, nonetheless seeking the community of those he would embrace, as he stares

> into that space which opens between hope and reality, into an effulgence that most of us prefer to close our eyes to, the light of imagination which invites us to sacrifice our actual situation to a vision of our possibilities which is doomed to fail.
>
> (Heaney 1989, 65)

Seamus Heaney's Assessments of Brian Friel's Drama 191

Gazing into the 'light of imagination' was at times inspiring for Friel and at others disabling and infertile, as any perusal of his many diaries he wrote while composing his plays over the years. Heaney even points out that when Frank announces that he is 'renouncing chance' in the play's conclusion he 'means that the fulfillments that came involuntarily as the result of the unpredictable but departed efficacy of his faith-healing gift are no longer to be either hoped for or credited'. And thus, 'Here, Frank's creator, the artist Brian Friel, is expressing in terms of the faith-healing parable *his* awareness for the necessity in the mature artist of a preparedness for a *via negativa*' (Heaney 1989, 66–67). Yet I think by extension, Heaney suggests that Friel held that gaze at the 'light of imagination' for many decades for our own benefit, often bringing back the tune to us like Heaney's fiddler from the Blasket Islands in 'The Given Note': 'what distinguished him was his ability to carry it through, to make a job of it and bring it back whole' (Heaney 2002, 8). Even if Frank Hardy is torn apart for the sake of his art, which finally Friel extrapolates from to suggest the faint glimmerings of a possibility of healing eventually taking place in Northern Ireland, Friel was able to achieve a vision of wholeness through his mesmeric art throughout his career, a wholeness that resembles Heaney's first criterion for poetry and for art generally: 'it is first and foremost a whole thing, a hale thing, a thing formally and feelingly sound, right within itself, a thing to which the ultimate response—if not always the immediate response—is "yes"' (Heaney 2002, 8).

Frank Hardy's continuing iteration of not only those incantatory Welsh (and Scottish) town names, combined with his ongoing narration of the moments leading up to his death, suggest another aspect of Friel's drama that was attractive to Heaney beyond this conception of mesmerism—memory— which he read through T. S. Eliot's and Wordsworth's conceptions of memory. As Heaney points out in his major essay on Friel, while 'All of the characters in *Faith Healer* speak out of a kind of afterlife, a kind of post-fatal depression, as it were', Frank alone 'is capable of turning the workings of memory into "the use of memory", and revealing how the world can be "renewed, transfigured, in another pattern", which is the ancient pattern of tragic art itself' (Heaney 1993, 237). Heaney, of course, is citing famous lines from Eliot's concluding passage of 'The Four Quartets': 'Little Gidding'. He opens 'For Liberation: Brian Friel and the Use of Memory' by citing a passage from 'Little Gidding' and observing that Eliot's conception of memory is akin to Aristotelian catharsis, 'that momentary release from confusion which comes from seeing a drama complete itself in accordance with its own inner necessities rather than in accordance with the spectator's wishes' (Heaney 1993, 229). Moreover, he posits that 'The satisfaction which art gives resides in this sense of rightness which is wholly independent of the happiness of the characters, and separate from what the audience would wish for itself' (Heaney 1993, 229). This language of artistic completion, 'aesthetic rightness', we might term it, anticipates the full-throated apologia for poetry's

192   *Richard Rankin Russell*

wholeness Heaney would propound later in 'The Whole Thing: On the Good of Poetry'. In that lecture, Heaney would affirm poetry's sufficiency in and of itself, as we have seen, and in his reading of his own poem, 'The Given Note', there, he holds that 'at a primal level, the good of poetry resides in just such a sensation of rightness, a sensation you might characterize by saying, "It did me good to hear it"' (Heaney 2002, 7). For Heaney,

> What an audience experiences at the final curtain of Brian Friel's *Faith Healer* or *Translations* is just such an experience of rightness; even though things have manifestly gone wrong for the people on the stage, the people in the stalls go away happy because of something completely rendered, a single meaning precipitated from a whole swirl of different elements.
>
> (Heaney 1993, 229)

Crucially, the artist figure in Friel's plays such as Frank Hardy or Michael Munday must be the one in whom these various memories inhere, who then issues forth an artistic vision of wholeness that mesmerically catches us up into its own truth, even if that truth is a fiction for those in the play (including the storyteller/artist figure) who might have experienced terrible hardships. Understanding this conception of artistic wholeness and rightness is crucial for understanding Heaney's final contention about *Faith Healer* that 'The tragic emotion subsumes all kinds of loss and disappointment into itself, and there is a sense in which *Faith Healer* is a play of triumph and affirmation'. That triumph and affirmation occurs because

> The performer in Frank Hardy comes to his rescue at the very end so that he takes his destiny into his own hands even as he hands himself over to the deadly custody of the dangermen at first light. There is a shine off the writing in this finale, a cathartic brilliance.
>
> (Heaney 1993, 237)[9]

Heaney became the best poet of childhood since Wordsworth, and his intense and vivid memories of his South Derry rearing found confirmation in Wordsworth's similarly memorable accounts of his Lake District boyhood in his autobiographical poem *The Prelude* and many lyric poems. In Heaney's early autobiographical essay, 'Mossbawn', he muses that

> All children want to crouch in their secret nests. I loved the fork of a beech tree at the head of our lane, the close thicket of a boxwood hedge in the front of the house, the soft collapsing pile of hay in a back corner of the byre, but especially I spent time in the throat of an old willow tree at the end of the farmyard.
>
> (Heaney 1980a, 18)

Seamus Heaney's Assessments of Brian Friel's Drama   193

Recalling that 'once you squeezed through it, you were at the heart of a different life, looking out on the familiar yard as if it were suddenly behind a pane of strangeness' (Heaney 1980a, 18). This sort of Romantic identification with the landscape is indebted to Wordsworth's and Coleridge's conception of poetry and the environment in their introduction to the *Lyrical Ballads*. In his penetrating reading of Friel's career, Heaney approvingly cites his short stories, alluding to their famous phrase about how their imagination enabled them to render the ordinary extraordinary, noting that:

> What they do is to trace what William Wordsworth called, in a memorable phrase, the primary laws of our nature, and they do it by the methods which Wordsworth said he employed in composing the *Lyrical Ballads*. Like the poet, Friel also chooses incidents from common life, incidents which allow him to focus upon their psychological import for the characters; and then, by throwing over them a certain colouring of imagination, he proceeds to trace, truly though not ostentatiously, those primary laws—in particular, the laws of love and all their complicated relations to the operations of memory.
>
> (Heaney 1993, 231).

In this reading, Friel is also Wordsworthian in his reclamation of the ordinary and rendering it extraordinary and Other through his imaginative recreation of those landscapes. One of Heaney's favorite Friel stories, 'The Saucer of Larks', features a number of Wordsworthian passages, such as the one where Friel describes the 'saucer of green grass bordered by yellow sand dunes... [where] the promontory itself ended in a high, blunt hill which broke the Atlantic wind' (Friel 1996b, 112). As the two Irish policemen and the German who has come to recover the remains of a World War Two German soldier in County Donegal enter into the life of the place, they

> became aware of the silence and then, no sooner were they hushed by it, than they heard the larks, not a couple or a dozen or a score, but hundreds of them, all invisible against the blue heat of the sky, an umbrella of music over this tiny world below.
>
> (Friel 1996b, 113)

This Frielian music renders the ordinary world Other, beyond our ken, wondrous and affirmed Heaney's own desire to represent his region in such ways.

Other moments of wonder at his childhood landscape are recounted in these opening pages of 'Mossbawn', but they are counterpoised with other moments of fear, such as when he remarks walking up the Sandy Loaning, a 'sandy pathway' near his home, which eventually 'gave way to scraggy marshland', where he heard 'Scuffles in old leaves [that] made you nervous and you dared yourself always to pass the badger's set [sic] ... Around that

194 *Richard Rankin Russell*

badger's hole, there hung a field of dangerous force. This was the realm of bogeys' (Heaney 1980a, 18). At this moment, readers cannot help but recall the mature Wordsworth's recollection of being 'Fostered alike by beauty and by fear' in Book I of *The Prelude* as he experienced both the wonder at the joys of the passing seasons and anxious apprehension at the 'Low breathings coming after me, and sounds/Of undistinguishable motion, steps/Almost as silent as the turf they trod' (Wordsworth 2004, 194).

As 'Mossbawn' proceeds, Heaney recalls the local 'names of its fields and townlands, in their mixture of Scots and Irish and English etymologies ... Broagh, The Long Rigs, Bell's Hill, Brian's Field, the Round Meadow, the Demesne; each name was a kind of love made to each acre' (Heaney 1980a, 20). He then immediately cites Wordsworth, noting 'saying the names like this distances the places, turns them into what Wordsworth once called a prospect of the mind. They lie deep, like some script indelibly written into the nervous system' (Heaney 1980a, 20). In 'Feeling into Words', Heaney offers other Wordsworthian prospects of the mind in his remembered litany of 'the beautiful sprung rhythms of the old BBC weather forecast: Dogger, Rockall, Malin, Shetland, Faroes, Finisterre', after which he mentions the 'gorgeous and inane phraseology of the catechism', and then concludes with 'the litany of the Blessed Virgin that was part of the enforced poetry in our household: Tower of Gold, Ark of the Covenant, Gate of Heaven, Morning Star, Health of the Sick, Refuge of Sinners, Comforter of the Afflicted' (Heaney 1980a, 45).

Wordsworth's exemplary notion of prospects of the mind made Heaney realize the worth of his home place, and in turn, the worth of Friel's commitment to his home ground. One of Friel's exemplary stories for Heaney because of the operation of Wordsworthian memory is 'Among the Ruins', about a man named Joe who returns to his home ground in Donegal to see the remnants of his childhood home. While there, Joe startles his son who is playing an imaginary game, and he berates himself for even coming back on the drive home, thinking 'Because the past is a mirage—a soft illusion into which one steps in order to escape the present' (Friel 1996b, 106). Heaney points out the protagonist's marked disillusionment:

> he himself is let down by the gap between the aura of the place in his recollections and the plain, small factuality of its topographical existence; and during the course of the visit, his disappointment at all this was only banished by a panic that his son Peter had been lost in the field.
> (Heaney 1993, 233)

And yet, as Joe drives on, he realizes how happy the child had been there. Heaney quotes most of the last two paragraphs on the story, including Joe's vow to remember what will be a fleeting memory of happiness for his son: 'The fact that Peter would never remember it was of no importance; it was his own possession now, his own happiness, this knowledge of a child's private

Seamus Heaney's Assessments of Brian Friel's Drama 195

joy' (Friel 1996b, 108; Heaney 1993, 233). Friel privileges the preservation through words such a moment, which is compounded by Joe's realization that

> his own father must have stumbled on him, and must have recognized himself in his son. And his father before that, and his father before that. Generations of fathers stretching back and back, all finding magic and sustenance in the brief, quickly destroyed happiness of their children.
>
> (Friel 1996b, 108–109)

Thus, 'The past did have meaning. It was neither reality nor dreams, neither today's patchy oaks nor the great woods of his boyhood. It was simply continuance, life repeating itself and surviving' (Friel 1996b, 109).

But this process is far from simple and inherently imaginative, as Heaney recognizes:

> This conclusion enacts that process of rumination and internalization of knowledge which I had in mind when I spoke of intelligence being at work upon psychic matter, and it is a process, of course, which is repeated every time a writer carries through successfully a work of imaginative composition.
>
> (Heaney 1993, 234)

Already, we see in this story marks of what would become the mature, Frielian drama that unites the two aspects of Friel Heaney apprehended through his early immersion in Wordsworth: *memory through mesmerism*. Friel himself signals how the process starts in a passage that immediately precedes the lines Heaney cites and employs 'mesmerism' as a way in which memory is activated: 'Silence filled the car. Through the mesmerism of motor, fleeing hedges, shadows flying from the headlights, three words swam into Joe's head. "Donging the tower"' (Friel 1993, 108). Lulled by the sound of the engine and the hedges and shadows, Joe's mind travels back to that afternoon, which in turn enables him to project the series of ancestors in his family line who surely must have witnessed similar scenes of childhood happiness in their offspring. Moreover, Friel enchants us as readers even as we read the last sentences through mesmeric repetition: '*It was neither* reality nor dreams, *neither* today's patchy oaks nor the great woods of his boyhood. *It was* ...'. Metafictionally, the story is hypnotically inviting us back into the world of the story we have just read, recreating it in our memory, perhaps adding a layer of family memories of our own.

Heaney complicates his reading of Friel's use of memory in this story and more generally in his dramas by recourse to Jung's *Memories, Dreams, Reflections*, particularly Jung's emphasis on truth-telling, which arises from the individual's unconscious and its desire to 'tell my personal myth. I can only make direct statements, only 'tell stories'. Whether or not the stories are 'true' is not the problem. The only question is whether what I tell is my fable,

196   *Richard Rankin Russell*

my truth' (quoted in Heaney 1993, 234). Rather than embracing a postmodernist denial of truth claims, Heaney, following Jung and implicitly, I think, Wordsworth, argues for a Friel committed to telling imaginative truth:

> He is insisting rather that the individual consciousness take the measure of reality in a first-hand, unmediated encounter, that the panaceas and alibis and stereotypes offered by convention be avoided and the impact of the real be received directly and registered in an authentic voice.
>
> (Heaney 1993, 235)

The authentic, mesmerizing, truth-telling voice is steeped in love and memory for Friel, Heaney recognizes.

In his 2009 Friel tribute, *Spelling It Out*, Heaney meditates upon the 'r' in Friel's last name in terms of reverie, which transcends even language ultimately. 'R' he says there, 'is for reverie, for the repose the spirit seeks in song and music, for the rhythm that prolongs the moment of contemplation, that carries beyond language' (Heaney 2009, n.p.). That 'moment of contemplation' beyond language induced by reverie occurs repeatedly in Friel, perhaps nowhere more clearly than in his 1990 drama, *Dancing at Lughnasa*, particularly in the closing monologue by Michael, the narrator. *Dancing at Lughnasa*, which concerns itself with the conflict between truth and myth in 1936 Donegal, a magical, mad summer that the narrator Michael turns back to much later in life to make sense of his father's return, two of his aunts' emigration, his Uncle Jack's return from the mission fields, and his mother's and sisters' incessant dancing that marks their loneliness and lost opportunities with men. If one were just examining a documentary record of that hard and hot summer, one would see a tale of grinding poverty, exclusion for the sisters from the life of the village, and a possible rape of one sister, Rose, by local man Danny Bradley.

Heaney, however, points out that 'it is because of the authenticity of the transition from narrative presentation to reverie and narcotic dream-life at the end of *Dancing at Lughnasa* that we can respect Michael's entrancement as an adequate response to "the evidence"' (Heaney 1993, 235). And while Friel's narrator Michael never shies away from those realities, which he gives us in flash-forward devices that recall those of Muriel Spark in *The Prime of Miss Jean Brodie* (1961), he becomes a Frielian artist toward the end, re-enchanting himself and us to a child-like state of wonder and awe as he imaginatively remembers and recreates that summer, particularly the sisters' dancing. As Heaney argues so insightfully,

> at the end of *Lughnasa* the fiction of transition into the eternal world of dance, the tír-na-nóg of memory itself, is acceptable precisely because it has been demonstrated to be a personal truth. It is Michael's own fable, constructed in face of but not in avoidance of the evidence ...
>
> (Heaney 1993, 235)

Seamus Heaney's Assessments of Brian Friel's Drama   197

He cites part of this long, hypnotic passage (Heaney 1993, 235), which I excerpt in part here from Friel's play to draw attention to the incantatory, repetitive dream music of Michael's last monologue, which somehow lifts off from language itself and carries us into that long-ago past, caught up in the central image of dancing:

> And what is so strange about that memory is that everybody seems to be floating on those sweet sounds, moving rhythmically, languorously, in complete isolation; responding more to the mood of the music than to its beat. When I remember it, I think of it as dancing. Dancing with eyes half closed because to open them would break the spell. Dancing as if language had surrendered to movement—as if this ritual, this wordless ceremony, was now the way to speak, to whisper private and sacred things, to be in touch with some otherness. Dancing as if the very heart of life and all its hopes might be found in those assuaging notes and those hushed rhythms and in those silent and hypnotic movements. Dancing as if language no longer existed because words were no longer necessary.
>
> (Friel 1990, 71).

For Heaney, such Frielian fable-making is not escapist but artistic and authentic, deeply personal even as it mesmerizes us into marveling at the sounds and dancing of that summer, which together become a sacred site of reimagined and re-presented memory.

Heaney takes a similar approach to Friel in one of his last prose assessments of his drama, from *Spelling It Out*: 'I is also for intimacy, for the inner self, the mysterious source and lining of being, that which is both articulate and inarticulate in all of us, and which underwrites the poetry of Brian Friel's theatre.' He thus reads Friel's drama as essentially poetic and private in its origins, a 'mysterious source and lining of being', from which the playwright publicly stages his rough magic. Through learning from Wordsworth's example, Seamus Heaney wrote literary criticism that affirmed the validity of Brian Friel's home ground, confirmed the mesmerizing music of his drama and illuminated the storehouse of memories therein staged. In Heaney's prose about Friel, these qualities finally merge, leading to a theatre of memory wherein incantatory narratives about particular places are staged that whirl us up into worlds of wonder.

Notes

1 Ricoeur links 'hermeneutics' and 'suspicion' together in longer phrases and sentences throughout his *Freud and Philosophy*. I offer a model of restorative, regenerative criticism in the coda inspired in part by Ricouer to my recent study, *James Joyce and Samaritan Hospitality: Postcritical and Postsecular Reading in Dubliners and Ulysses*,198–211.

198 *Richard Rankin Russell*

2 For the definitive discussion of these plays and Heaney's other radio work at the time, see my chapter, 'Recording Bigotry and Imagining a New Province: Heaney and BBC Northern Ireland Radio, 1968–73', in my *Seamus Heaney's Regions*, 66–100.

3 See, for instance, my essay, 'Heaney's Yeats', 203–208, about how essentially dramatic conceptions influenced by Yeats's conception of tragedy lie behind one of Heaney's greatest poems, 'Casualty' (Russell 2016b).

4 Marilynn Richtarik, 'Field Day' (2021), 189. It is important to note, however, that Richtarik takes Heaney's account of *North*'s origins straight from his own remarks in *Stepping Stones* (2009, 177, 179) that glibly suggest he put the volume together in a weekend after getting the draft of *Volunteers* from Friel. Instead, as I have shown in *Seamus Heaney's Regions* (2014, 187–197) that volume had a much longer gestation than either Heaney or Richtarik suggest and originally included a whole suite of prose poems, many of which were collected in the scarce volume of prose poetry, *Stations*, also published in 1975.

5 See Friel, *Rehearsal Diary (Faith Healer, 1979)*, [2022], *passim*.

6 See for instance the outstanding monograph by Richtarik on Field Day, *Acting between the Lines: The Field Day Theatre Company and Irish Cultural Politics, 1980–1984*.

7 As he mused in *Stepping Stones*, their paths were opposed: 'His was to a large extent centripetal and mine centrifugal' (178).

8 See, for instance, Matthew Campbell's reading in 'Wordsworth and Romanticism' (2021) of Heaney's assessment of Sylvia Plath's achievement through his recourse to the boy of Winander story in Book Five of *The Prelude*, 69–70.

9 Heaney goes on to discuss at length immediately after this analysis of *Faith Healer* the 'unmitigated' disappointment in the conclusion of *Translations* (1980), which is 'amplified very resourcefully and deliberately by the dramatist's play upon the audience's own literary and historical memory' ('For Liberation', 238).

Works Cited

Campbell, Matthew (2021) 'Wordsworth and Romanticism', in *Seamus Heaney in Context*, edited by Geraldine Higgins, Cambridge: Cambridge University Press: 61–72.

Cavanagh, Michael (2009) *Professing Poetry: Seamus Heaney's Poetics*, Washington, DC: Catholic University Press.

Corcoran, Neil (1998) *The Poetry of Seamus Heaney: A Critical Study*, London: Faber and Faber.

Friel, Brian (1990) *Dancing at Lughnasa*, London: Faber and Faber.

Friel, Brian (1996a) Brian Friel: Plays 1: Philadelphia, Here I Come! The Freedom of the City. Living Quarters. Aristocrats. Faith Healer. Translations, London: Faber and Faber.

Friel, Brian (1996b) *Selected Stories*, Loughcrew, Ireland: Gallery Press.

Friel, Brian (1999) 'In Interview with Eavan Boland (1973)', in *Brian Friel: Essays, Diaries, Interviews: 1964–1999*, edited by Christopher Murray, London: Faber and Faber: 57–62.

Friel, Brian (1999) 'Seven Notes for a Festival Programme [1999]', *Brian Friel: Essays, Diaries, Interviews: 1964–1999*, edited by Christopher Murray, London: Faber and Faber: 173–180.

Friel, Brian (2022) *Rehearsal Diary (Faith Healer, 1979)*, edited by Peter Fallon, Loughcrew, Ireland: Gallery Press.

Heaney, Seamus (1965)'A Chester Pageant', *Use of English*, 17, no. 1: 58–60.

Heaney, Seamus (1977) 'The Irish Quest', *The Guardian*, Nov. 2, 1974, reprinted in *Seamus Heaney*, edited by Edward Broadbridge, Copenhagen: Skoleradioen: 46–48.

Heaney, Seamus (1980a) *Preoccupations: Selected Prose 1968–1978*, London: Faber and Faber.

Heaney, Seamus (1980b) 'English and Irish', Review of Brian Friel's *Translations* at the Dublin Theatre Festival, *Times Literary Supplement*, 24 October: 1199.

Heaney, Seamus (1983) *Among Schoolchildren*, John Malone Memorial Lecture, Queen's University, Belfast, June 9, 1983, Belfast: John Malone Memorial Committee.

Heaney, Seamus (1985) *Place and Displacement: Recent Poetry of Northern Ireland*, Peter Laver Memorial Lecture delivered at Grasmere, August 2, 1984, Kendal, UK: Frank Peters Printers on behalf of the Trustees of Dove Cottage.

Heaney, Seamus (1988) *The Government of the Tongue: Selected Prose, 1978–1988*, New York: Noonday: 36–44.

Heaney, Seamus (1989) 'Cornucopia and Empty Shell: Variations on a Theme from Ellmann', *The Place of Writing*, Atlanta: Scholars Press for Emory University: 54–72.

Heaney, Seamus (1993) 'For Liberation: Brian Friel and the Use of Memory', *The Achievement of Brian Friel*, edited by Alan Peacock, Gerrards Cross, UK: Colin Smythe: 229–240.

Heaney, Seamus (1995a) *The Redress of Poetry: Oxford Lectures*, New York: Farrar, Straus, Giroux.

Heaney, Seamus (1995b) *Crediting Poetry: The Nobel Lecture*, Loughcrew, Ireland: Gallery Press.

Heaney, Seamus (1997) 'Further Language', *Studies in the Literary Imagination*: special issue on 'The Schoolroom in Modern Irish Literature and Culture', vol. 30, no. 2: 7–16.

Heaney, Seamus (1999) 'Introduction', *Beowulf*, translated by Seamus Heaney, London: Faber and Faber: Ix–xxx.

Heaney, Seamus (2001) 'Introduction', in *William Wordsworth: Poems Selected by Seamus Heaney*, London: Faber and Faber; originally published, New York: Ecco Press, 1988.

Heaney, Seamus (2002) 'The Whole Thing: On the Good of Poetry', *The Recorder: A Journal of the American Irish Historical Society*: 5–20.

Heaney, Seamus (2008) *Stepping Stones: Interviews with Seamus Heaney*, Conducted by Dennis O'Driscoll, New York: Farrar, Straus, Giroux.

Heaney, Seamus (2009) *Spelling It Out*, Loughcrew, Ireland: Gallery Press.

Heaney, Seamus (2011) 'Vision', Program for Gate Theatre Production of Brian Friel's *Molly Sweeney*, Dublin: Summer.

Kress, Simon (2021) 'Music', in *Seamus Heaney in Context*, edited by Geraldine Higgins, Cambridge: Cambridge University Press: 157–164.

O'Brien, Eugene (2016) *Seamus Heaney as Aesthetic Thinker: A Study of the Prose*, Syracuse: Syracuse University Press.

Richtarik, Marilynn (1994) *Acting between the Lines: The Field Day Theatre Company and Irish Cultural Politics, 1980–1984*, Oxford: Oxford University Press.

Richtarik, Marilynn (2021) 'Field Day', in *Seamus Heaney in Context*, edited by Geraldine Higgins, Cambridge: Cambridge University Press: 188–197.

Ricoeur, Paul (1970) *Freud and Philosophy: An Essay on Interpretation*, New Haven, CT: Yale University Press.

Russell, Richard Rankin (2014) *Seamus Heaney's Regions*, Notre Dame: University of Notre Dame University Press.

Russell, Richard Rankin (2016b) 'Heaney's Yeats', *Literary Imagination* vol. 18, no. 2: 1–22.

Russell, Richard Rankin (2016a) *Seamus Heaney: An Introduction*, Edinburgh: Edinburgh University Press.

Russell, Richard Rankin (2022) *Modernity, Community, and Place in Brian Friel's Drama*, 2nd revised edition, Syracuse: Syracuse University Press.

Russell, Richard Rankin (2023) *James Joyce and Samaritan Hospitality: Postcritical and Postsecular Reading in Dubliners and Ulysses*, Edinburgh: Edinburgh University Press.

Wordsworth, William (2004) *Selected Poems*, edited by Stephen Gill, New York: Penguin.

Index

Abbey Theatre 107
Adams, G. B. 76, 88
aesthetic 2, 4, 10–12, 23, 26–28, 32, 52–53, 56, 60, 110, 112, 114–118, 123–126, 147, 174, 179, 180–181, 184, 191
alterity 19, 24, 29–31, 41, 43, 56, 58, 61, 66, 74, 92, 97, 99, 101, 125, 132, 140, 144, 161, 176, 180–181
Alvarez, Al. 130; *The New Poetry* 130, 139
America xi, 11, 32, 48, 69–70, 106, 127, 166
Anahorish 10, 37, 40, 54, 62
Andrews, Elmer 67–68, 84; *The Poetry of Seamus Heaney All the Realms of Whisper* 87
Anglophone xi
Apollo 39
aporia 20
art 3, 4, 6, 7, 9, 11, 13, 23, 28–29, 38, 58, 60–61, 64–66, 74, 85, 94–95, 101, 107, 113–114, 116, 120, 125–127, 133–134, 141, 149, 151, 169–176, 178, 181, 183–187, 191–192, 197
association 4, 22, 24, 53, 83, 94, 101, 170, 177
Atherton, Cassandra: *Prose Poetry* 56, 58–59, 70
attachment 155, 161
Auden, W. H. 3, 87, 90, 112, 133, 138–139
Austen, Jane: *Sense and Sensibility* 81, 87

Balakian, Peter 163
Ballylee 29, 46, 106
Barańczak, Stanislaw: *Laments* 2
barbarian 10–11, 31

bawn 43, 45, 47
beauty 25, 91, 102, 115, 121, 125, 127, 150, 166, 176, 194
Beckett, Samuel 121, 190
being 119
Belfast xi, 2, 33, 38, 51, 54, 60, 62–63, 68–69, 71, 88, 91, 105, 107, 130, 137, 148, 153, 182, 187, 199
Bellaghy 5, 68, 96–97, 99, 182
Bennett, Sarah 69
Berkeley x, 2, 45, 53, 66–67, 178
Bernstein, Charles 21, 32
binary 25, 29, 68
binary oppositions 25
Bishop, Elizabeth 3, 9, 168
Blake, William 67, 70, 132, 146
Blasket Islands 191
body 8, 25, 44, 98, 101
bog 16, 40, 43–44, 51, 60, 64–65, 68, 104, 133, 149, 183, 186
Booth, James 120, 126–128
Boothby, Richard 17, 32
border 3, 7, 9, 42, 54, 68
borderline 123
Bradley, Catherine 17–18, 24; sampler 17–18, 24
Bradley, Thomas (ed): *Seeking the Kingdom St Columb's College, 1879–2004* 50
Brain, Tracy 140, 142, 146
Brandes, Rand 23, 32, 87, 166
Britain x, 18
British ix, x, xi, 6, 18, 29–31, 41–42, 45, 60, 62, 66, 69, 76, 82, 87, 128
Brodsky, Joseph 10, 20, 28, 32, 106, 165–166
Brown, John 111
Browne, Sir Thomas 29; *The Garden of Cyrus* 29

202   *Index*

Buile Shuibhne 160
burial 103

canny 35
Caoineadh Art Uí Laoghaire 104
Carleton, William 150, 156
Carrickfergus Castle 29
Castledawson 16, 68
Catholicism xii, 30, 32, 36, 38, 41, 45,
    49, 51, 54–55, 60–62, 105, 117, 123,
    127, 150–151, 156, 158–159, 166,
    182–183, 198
Cavafy, Constantine P. 19
Cavanagh, Michael 1, 123, 155, 162;
    *Professing Poetry Seamus Heaney's
    Poetics* 30, 32, 89, 123–124, 127,
    166, 181, 198
Celtic 71, 72
Chekov, Anton 138
chestnut tree 25, 122, 161–163
Christian 10, 11, 31, 37–38, 49, 105,
    110, 119–120, 123, 125, 127, 151,
    158–159, 167, 179
civil war 181
civilization 80, 92
Clare, John 3, 72, 78, 80, 87, 127, 150
classical 74, 102, 106
classical tradition 74, 102, 106
Cole, Henri 22–23, 32, 153, 166;
    'Interview with Seamus Heaney'
    22–23, 153
concept 12, 16, 54, 63, 67, 110–114,
    121–126, 138
connections 4–10, 12, 16–21, 25, 30,
    32, 48, 54, 68, 72–73, 78, 81, 89, 95,
    97–98, 100–104, 126, 140, 144, 147,
    174, 175
consciousness 10, 16, 17, 30, 35, 41,
    53–56, 59–60, 64–66, 95, 106, 112,
    118, 120–121, 125, 150, 179, 181,
    184, 196
constellation 9
context 6, 9, 12, 15–16, 25, 27–29, 31–
    32, 61, 66, 79, 95, 98, 101–103, 110,
    116, 122–123, 126–127, 133–134,
    143, 149, 151, 159, 177, 188
Corcoran, Neil 29, 32, 67, 69, 82–83,
    87, 88, 179–181, 185, 198; *Poets of
    Modern Ireland* 32; *The Poetry of
    Seamus Heaney* 82–83, 180, 181
County Derry xii, 5, 50–51, 54, 66, 72,
    75, 130, 154, 161–162, 182, 187,
    192
County Donegal 155, 187, 193
Creeley, Robert 172, 178

Critchley, Simon 17, 32; *Things Merely
    Are* 32
critical distance 11, 153
criticism 2, 89
critique 1, 3, 8, 10, 12, 117, 123, 127
Crowe Ransom, John 137
Culler, Jonathan: *Critical Rhythm* 19,
    33
Cullingford, Elizabeth Butler 96, 108
culture 2–3, 5–11, 13–14, 23, 27–28,
    30–31, 51, 54, 66, 68, 71–72, 94,
    102, 104–106, 123, 140, 144, 146,
    149–154, 158–159, 175, 180
Curtis, Tony 69–70, 88, 120, 127

Dante Alighieri 5, 10–11, 27–28, 31,
    33, 37, 41, 106, 151
deconstruction 12, 22, 132
Deleuze, Gilles 16, 30, 33; *Dialogues*
    33; *A Thousand Plateaus Capitalism
    and Schizophrenia* 30, 33
Delphi 4, 39, 75
democratic 172
Dennison, John 123, 125, 127
Derrida, Jacques 15, 33; *la navette*
    15; *Negotiations Interventions and
    Interviews* 33, 120; shuttle 15, 21
Derry xii, 5, 50–51, 54, 66, 72, 75, 130,
    154, 161–162, 182, 187, 192
desire 3–4, 45, 64, 68, 73–74, 84, 116,
    121, 133, 136, 145, 183, 190, 193,
    195
deterritorialization 30
Devlin, Barney (blacksmith) 32, 84
Devlin, Brendan P. 11, 14, 32, 41, 43,
    49, 84, 182
Devlin, Marie (wife) 43
diachronic 119
diagram 29, 80
dialectic 10, 18, 30
diamond shape 29
Dickinson, Emily 14, 33; *The Complete
    Poems of Emily Dickinson* 14
discourse 1, 3, 18, 22, 25, 56–57, 60,
    121, 183
displacement 18, 49, 79, 166, 186, 187
dúchas 103
dwelling 29, 126

Eastern Europe x, 10–11, 28, 31, 106,
    111, 116
Eliot, T. S. 1, 3, 7, 13, 33, 37, 43, 49,
    81, 88–93, 106, 108, 132–133, 138,
    139, 145, 166, 171, 178, 187, 191;
    auditory imagination 21, 7–6, 83,

Index 203

85, 91–92, 96, 132–140, 143; *Four Quartets* 49, 191; *Selected Prose of T.S Eliot* 91, 92; *The Use of Poetry and the Use of Criticism* 145; *The Waste Land* 7, 91
Ellmann, Richard 2, 162, 184, 190, 199
Emory University 2, 46, 49, 69, 146, 190, 199
emotion 7, 15, 16, 35, 40, 46, 48, 81, 113, 119–120, 122, 127, 157, 165, 169, 176, 192
England 1, ix, x, xi, xiii, 2, 16, 18, 21, 23, 29–35, 42, 44, 48, 62–63, 71, 73–83, 87–88, 91, 94, 105–106, 113, 133–136, 142, 150–151, 169, 179, 185–187, 194, 199
English lyric 71, 73, 7-, 82–83, 87
enjambment 22, 82
epiphany 37, 48
epistemology 14, 18, 22, 26
Erlanger, Steven 166
ethics 2, 7, 10–12, 27–28, 52, 111, 113, 115–116, 155, 168, 180–181
etymology 8, 15, 61, 77, 79, 124, 172, 194
Europe 1, x, 2, 9–10, 13, 28, 31, 33, 106, 116
European 1, x, 2, 9–13, 28–33, 100, 102, 106, 111, 116, 151
Eurydice 101
experience 8, 11, 16, 32, 35–36, 39, 43, 48–49, 52, 55, 57, 66, 75, 78, 87, 93, 106, 112–113, 116–119, 127, 130, 137–138, 140, 148–149, 151, 154–155, 165, 168, 192
expression 35, 44, 59, 116, 151, 165, 181

Farndale, Nigel: *Interview with Seamus Heaney* 111
figurative 37, 80, 115
Fitzpatrick, Maurice: *The Boys of St Columb's* 49
flag 42, 103
Flood, Alison 131, 145
Foster, John Wilson 30, 33, 67, 69, 117, 128; *The Achievement of Seamus Heaney* 33
Foster, Roy: *On Seamus Heaney* 30, 33, 67, 69, 117, 128
France 64, 70, 82, 186
freedom 22–23, 60, 68, 73, 116, 136–137, 160, 173, 176–177
French 64, 186
French Revolution 186

Freud, Sigmund 11, 16, 19, 22, 32–33, 35–38, 44, 46, 49, 197, 200; *Heimlich* 11, 22, 35–37, 39–40, 45–49; *The Interpretation of Dreams* 16; *Sachvorstellungen* 16–17, 19–21, 24; *Unheimlich* 11, 22, 35–37, 39–43, 46–49; *Vorstellung* 16; *Wortvorstellungen* 16–17, 19–21
Friel, Brian 1, viii, xi, 13, 179, 182–200; 'Among the Ruins' 194–195; *Brian Friel Plays 1* 189–190; *Dancing at Lughnasa* 184, 189, 196–198; *Faith Healer* 183–184, 189–192, 198; 'In Interview with Eavan Boland' 188; *Molly Sweeney* 184, 189, 199; *Philadelphia, Here I Come!* 184–185, 198; *The Saucer of Larks* 184, 193; *Selected Stories* 193–195; 'Seven Notes for a Festival Programme' 188; *Translations* 34, 183, 184, 187, 192, 198–199; *Volunteers* 183, 186, 198
frontier 3, 22, 29–30, 58
frontier of writing 3
Frost, Robert ix, 9, 20, 32, 39, 49, 139, 165–166, 188; *The Poetry of Robert Frost* 49
fusions 21, 35

Gawain and the Green Knight 21
genre 1–2, 21, 57, 68
Germanic 10, 31, 72–74, 76–85
Ginsberg, Allen 9
Giroux, Robert 128, 178
Glanmore 11, 45–48, 55, 68, 155, 176, 187
Glaser, Ben: *Critical Rhythm* 19, 33
Glob, P. V.: *The Bog People Iron-Age Man Preserved* 40, 44, 50, 68–69, 186
Glover, Michael 151, 166
God Save the Queen 18
grammar 74, 149
Greece x, 2, 4, 9–10, 18, 31, 39, 93, 182
Greek 4
Group, The 153
Guardian, The 131, 145, 167, 188, 199
Guattari, Félix 30, 33; *A Thousand Plateaus Capitalism and Schizophrenia* 30, 33

haecceity 20–26, 29–32, 150–152, 164
Haffenden, John: *Viewpoints Poets in Conversation* 38, 50, 81, 87
Hamilton, Saskia 168, 178
Hammond, David 98

204   *Index*

Hardwick, Elizabeth 168–169, 177–178
Hart, Henry ix, 11, 35, 53–54,
    66–69, 131, 146, 156, 166, 168;
    Seamus Heaney Poet of Contrary
    Progressions ix, 53–54, 66, 68, 69
Harvard x, xi, 2, 47–48, 88, 171, 183
Heaney, Margaret (mother) 122
Heaney, Mary (aunt) 153
Heaney, Seamus: 'After the Synge-Song'
    147; *Among Schoolchildren* 2, 17,
    24, 30, 33, 88, 199; Antigone 102–
    103, 105, 108, 182; *Anything Can*
    Happen 94; *Beowulf* 2, 10, 20–21,
    24, 33, 88, 131, 145, 189, 199; *The*
    Burial at Thebes 102–105, 182; 'A
    Chester Pagent' 182; craft x, 53,
    75, 83–87, 89, 104, 139, 158, 172,
    177; *Crediting Poetry* 1–3, 9, 13,
    18, 22, 33, 39, 100, 108, 179, 181,
    199; Creon 105; *The Cure at Troy*
    A Version of Sophocles' 'Philoctetes'
    182; *Death of a Naturalist* 17, 35,
    44, 57, 66, 69, 77, 87, 149, 153,
    164, 166, 179; *District and Circle*
    68, 70, 167; *Door into the Dark* 14,
    33, 66, 69, 87, 153, 157–158, 166;
    'Eclogues In Extremis' xi; *Electric*
    Light 50, 154, 166; *Field Work* 53,
    60, 67, 78, 82–83, 86, 88–89, 151,
    155; *Finders Keepers* 1, 12, 21,
    33, 69, 89, 91–92, 108, 132, 135,
    146–147; Glanmore 11, 45–48, 55,
    68, 155, 176, 187; *Glanmore Sonnets*
    155; *The Government of the Tongue*
    1, 7–8, 11–13, 27–28, 33, 40, 46, 48,
    74, 77–78, 88–89, 112, 116, 128,
    130, 132, 138–143, 144–149, 161,
    165–166, 172–178, 179, 189, 199;
    'A Great Man and A Great Poet'
    179, 184, 188, 196; Haw Haw 63;
    The Haw Lantern 13, 15, 22–23,
    33, 67–69, 73, 76, 88, 122, 128,
    147, 161–163; *Human Chain* 28, 97,
    101, 104, 145, 166, 167, 171, 177;
    'Introduction', *William Butler Yeats:*
    Poems selected by Seamus Heaney
    107; 'The Jayne Lecture Title Deeds
    Translating a Classic' 102–105;
    Laments 2; *The Letters of Seamus*
    Heaney 99, 108, 146; *The Midnight*
    Verdict 187, 190–197; Mossbawn
    1–5, 9–11, 13, 16, 31, 33, 36–49, 71,
    75, 79–80, 93, 96–99, 108, 133–137,
    153, 155, 161, 192, 193–194;
    'Mossbawn Via Mantua: Ireland

    in / and Europe – Cross-Currents
    and Exchanges' 9–10, 31, 135, 137;
    North 47, 51–56, 60–69, 81–88,
    104, 116, 127, 136, 146, 148, 153,
    183, 198; *omphalos* 4–6, 10, 30, 36,
    38–39, 75, 93, 137, 155; 'On the
    Staying Power of Pastoral' 135, 144;
    Opened Ground 50, 62, 67, 69, 166;
    Oxford Lectures 1, 6–7, 22, 29–30,
    88–89, 128, 181, 199; Philocetes
    182; *Place and Displacement Recent*
    Poetry of Northern Ireland 1, 9,
    18, 33, 89, 186, 199; *The Place of*
    Writing 1, 46–47, 50, 89, 106, 108,
    146, 162, 199; placeless heaven 161,
    163–164, 166; *A Poem and Essay*
    94, 107; 'The Poet as a Christian'
    159; *Preoccupations* 1–13, 16, 21,
    23, 33, 36, 39–40, 49–53, 57, 60,
    66–69, 71–80, 84–90, 93, 95–98,
    102, 104–106, 108, 113–114, 128,
    132–139, 143–144, 146–149, 150,
    153, 155, 157–159, 162, 166, 170–
    171, 178, 183, 186–189, 192–193,
    194, 199; quincunx 11, 28–31; *The*
    Rattle Bag 130, 146; *The Redress of*
    Poetry 1, 2, 5–7, 9, 11, 13, 22, 28,
    31, 33, 58, 60–61, 69, 72, 87–89,
    101–102, 108, 110–112, 116–120,
    124–125, 128, 179, 182, 199; *res*
    xi, 83, 95; 'Retitling Antigone' 103;
    'Review of Brian Friel's *Translations*'
    183; *The School Bag* 130, 143,
    146; *Seeing Things* 13, 41, 50, 104,
    107, 123, 126, 128, 132, 146–147,
    154, 161–166; 'Sixth Sense, Seventh
    Heaven' 15, 22, 68, 91–92, 164–165,
    189, 191–192; slant 14, 27, 30, 32;
    Spelling It Out 179, 184, 188, 196–
    197, 199; *The Spirit Level* 101–102,
    153, 154, 183; *Station Island* 31, 60,
    68–69, 104, 131, 147, 151, 155–163,
    166, 183; *Stations* 39, 51–56, 61–69,
    71, 198; *Stepping Stones Interviews*
    with Seamus Heaney 14, 17, 24, 33,
    40, 45–48, 50, 70, 88, 95, 98–99,
    109, 128, 167, 178, 184, 198, 199;
    Sweeney Astray 160; technique x, 56,
    75, 83–85; *Thebes via Toomebridge*
    Retitling Antigone 9, 102, 108;
    The Tollund Man 44–45, 48; 'The
    Unacknowledged Legislator's Dream'
    52, 64, 66, 68; *William Wordsworth*
    Poems Selected by Seamus Heaney
    43, 155, 185; *Wintering Out* 62, 66,

69, 78, 87, 131, 147, 153; *Writer and Righter* 28, 33, 145, 166
Herbert, Zbigniew 31, 116, 120, 125, 179
Hetherington, Paul: *Prose Poetry* 56, 58–59, 70
Hewitt, John 132
Hilbert, Ernest 170, 178
Hill, Geoffrey ix, 65, 66, 70, 113, 115, 128, 130, 133, 137, 178, 194; *Mercian Hymns* ix, 65–66, 70, 113, 115, 128, 130, 133, 137, 178, 194
Hirsch, Edward: *The Essential Poet's Glossary* 58, 70
history 3, 7, 10, 58, 67, 71, 78–79, 112–113, 133, 138, 143, 175, 187, 198
Hobsbaum, Philip 130, 153
home 12–13, 22, 35–49, 54, 63, 68, 98–99, 106, 122, 142, 150, 155, 157, 163, 184–186, 193–194, 197
Hopkins, Gerard Manley 3, 8, 12, 20, 28, 41, 49, 73–75, 79–81, 84–92, 93–96, 106, 108, 132–133, 151–153, 167, 179; *Gerard Manley Hopkins Selected Prose* 93; *The Journals and Papers of Gerard Manley Hopkins* 152
Horace 10
Hufstader, Jonathan: *Tongue of Water, Teeth of Stones* 66, 70
Hughes, Francis 102
Hughes, Ted 1, x, 12–13, 20–21, 23, 28, 38, 50, 76, 81, 91, 102, 113, 115, 130–146; *Birthday Letters* x, 131, 140, 146; *The Hawk in the Rain* 136, 146; *Letters of Ted Hughes* 130, 145–146; *Lupercal* 38, 130, 134, 137; *The Rattle Bag* 130, 146; *The School Bag* 130, 143, 146; *Wodwo* 21, 23, 133–134, 137–138
human 9, 111, 118, 181
Hume, John 6
hunger strikes 102
hybridity 68
Hyperborean 10–11

Ibsen, Henrik 93; *A Doll's House* 93
ideation 5, 10, 26–29, 31, 46, 48–49, 84–85, 94, 105, 107, 111–112, 117, 121, 125–126, 132–134, 137, 138–139, 142–143, 151–152, 161, 163, 172
identity 1–2, 4–11, 15–16, 18, 28–29, 49, 54, 102, 104–105

ideology 9–10, 14–15, 18, 28, 30–31, 120, 159
image 7, 11, 15, 18–20, 22, 25–26, 31, 43–44, 58, 76–77, 79–80, 86, 91, 94–96, 98, 101–103, 108, 119, 122, 124–125, 132, 134–135, 141, 150, 157, 161–163, 166, 171, 173–174, 176–177, 197
imagination 5–6, 9–10, 14, 19, 21, 26, 27–28, 30, 32, 36, 39, 46, 58–59, 72–79, 83, 85, 91–92, 96–98, 100, 111–118, 121–122, 124, 132–136, 138–140, 143, 149, 152–153, 160–162, 164, 166, 168, 181, 190–191, 193
imagination, auditory 21, 72–76, 83, 85, 91–92, 96, 132–140, 143
Incertus 52
individual 4, 6, 10, 20, 28, 58, 68, 90, 112, 139, 168, 170, 175, 195–196
Ingelbien, Raphael 124, 128, 132, 145–146
inheritance 30, 77, 79
instinct 6, 27, 28, 54, 72, 155, 159, 164, 172, 174, 186
intellectual 9, 19, 31, 40, 71, 116, 169, 185
interanimation 30
interpretation 19, 90, 94, 118, 120, 133
Ireland ix, x, xi, 1–11, 13, 15–19, 23, 28, 29–33, 36, 42, 45, 50–55, 60, 62–68, 70–82, 86–89, 94, 97–109, 116, 127–128, 146–148, 150–151, 155, 157–160, 166–169, 172, 174, 181–187, 190–194, 198, 199
Ireland, Northern xi, 1, 3, 5–6, 11, 13, 16, 18, 28, 33, 36, 42, 51, 54, 60, 62–64, 66–68, 71, 73, 79, 82, 87–89, 97, 116, 181–187, 190–191, 198–199
Ireland, Republic of 45, 54, 67–68, 183, 185
Irishness 10–11, 29–31, 131
irrational 114, 120

Jackaman, Rob 79, 86, 88; *Broken English/Breaking English* 79, 86, 88
Joyce, James xi, 9, 11, 29–30, 33, 56, 63, 96, 156, 160, 167, 197, 200; *Dubliners* xi, 29, 33, 197, 200; *A Portrait of the Artist as a Young Man* 160
judgement 110
Jung, Carl 186, 195–196
justice 112

206 *Index*

Kaplan, Louise J.: *Cultures of Fetishism* 19, 33
Kavanagh, Patrick 1, viii, 5, 12–13, 20, 28, 73–78, 81, 88, 91, 106, 132–133, 138–139, 147–167, 179; *Collected Poems* 148, 151–158, 161–162, 164–165; *Collected Pruse* 88; *The Great Hunger* 148, 150, 152, 155–157, 162, 165; *Patrick Maguire* 150, 152, 157; *A Soul for Sale* 148; *Tarry Flynn* 150, 155–160, 167
Keats, John 73, 84–88, 106, 113, 179; 'Letter to John Taylor' 73, 84–88, 106, 113, 179
Keenan, Rosie 99
Kennedy Andrews, Elmer: *The Poetry of Seamus Heaney* 69, 87, 198
Kennelly, Brendan x
Kerrigan, John: 'Ulster Ovids' 77, 88
Kiberd, Declan 157, 167; *Inventing Ireland* 167
Kinahan, Frank: 'An Interview with Seamus Heaney' 82, 86, 88
knowledge 1, 8, 11, 15, 19, 22, 25–26, 49, 58, 77, 108, 126, 132, 152, 172, 185, 194–195
Kress, Simon B. 98, 109, 188, 199; 'Music' 98, 188

Lacan, Jacques 17, 32–33; *The Four Fundamental Concepts of Psycho-Analysis* 33
landscape 3, 6, 19, 75, 113, 134, 138, 159–160, 174, 193
language 7–8, 10–26, 29–32, 35, 51–52, 56–57, 61–63, 66, 71–86, 91–98, 100–105, 113–114, 123–127, 134, 137, 139, 142, 145, 153, 159, 160, 164–165, 169, 171–172, 174–175, 177, 180, 188, 191, 196–197
Larkin, Emmet 150
Larkin, Eva 122, 127
Larkin, Philip 1, vii, x, 12, 110, 113–128, 133, 163, 165, 167, 179; *Book Reviews 1952–1985* 115, 128; *Complete Poems* 33, 119, 128; *Further Requirements Interviews, Broadcasts, Statements and The Less Deceived* 115; *Letters Home 1936–1977* 127, 128; *Letters to Monica* 114, 128; *Selected Letters of Philip Larkin* 114, 128
Latin x, xii, 8, 15, 57, 73, 77–78, 151, 163, 174–175
Latinate 72–73, 76–77, 79–80, 82

Laverty, Christopher: *Seamus Heaney and American Poetry* 66–67, 70
law 113
Lawrence, D. H. 37–38, 106, 170
Leech, Geoffrey N.: *A Linguistic Guide to English Poetry* 80, 88
linguistic 12, 15, 19, 23–26, 56, 63, 71–72, 76, 79–87, 95, 98, 113, 134
literary theory x, 121
literature x, xi, 1–9, 12–13, 28–32, 39, 49, 57, 67, 72–76, 80, 85, 102, 104, 106–108, 110, 113, 117, 121, 123, 125–126, 131–136, 139, 140, 142, 143, 144, 145, 150, 158, 169, 171–173, 177, 179, 180–181, 197, 198
local 4, 5, 6, 8, 11, 51–52, 63, 66, 77–78, 84, 97, 105, 130, 149, 153, 158, 181, 194, 196
location 17, 108
London Magazine 136–137
Londonderry 41–42, 187
Longley, Edna xi, 47, 50, 80, 83, 88, 115, 126, 133, 138, 146, 154, 167, 172, 186; 'North "Inner Emigré" or "Artful Voyeur"'? 80, 83
Longley, Michael xi, 47, 50, 154, 172, 186
Lowell, Robert viii, ix, xi, 9, 13, 92, 106, 128, 132–133, 138, 168–178; *Day by Day* 13, 169–171, 176, 177; *The Dolphin* 176; *History* 33, 108, 167, 176, 187; *Life Studies* 174; *For Lizzie and Harriet* 176; *Notebooks 1967–1968* 176
lyric 1, 11, 20, 27, 52, 56–59, 67, 71, 73, 76–77, 82–83, 86–87, 98, 110, 116, 126, 148, 150, 170, 181, 188, 192

MacCaig, Norman 180
MacDiarmid, Hugh 180
Mackay Brown, George 47
MacNeice, Louis 11, 29, 30
Madden, F. J. M. (ed): *Seeking the Kingdom St Columb's College, 1879–2004* 50
Magherafelt 42, 96
Mahon, Derek x, 186
Mandelstam, Osip 10, 27, 106, 111, 116, 138, 175
Mantua 1, 2, 9, 11, 13, 31, 33
Maritain, Jacques 165; *Creative Intuition in Art and Poetry* 165
materialism 4, 8, 11, 16, 18, 20, 22–23, 42, 54–56, 59, 64–66, 82, 111, 130,

136–137, 150–153, 156–157, 162, 164–165, 169, 171, 174, 177
materiality 16, 22, 153, 164
McCafferty, Kevin 79, 88; '[H]ushed and *Lulled* Full Chimes for *Pushed and Pulled*' 79, 88
McCarthy, Thomas 102; *The Last Geraldine Officer* 102
McGahern, John 100
McLaverty, Michael 148
meaning 4, 6, 8, 11–12, 15, 18–19, 21, 22, 24, 28, 30, 35–36, 63, 77–78, 90–94, 101, 107, 110, 111, 115–116, 125, 137, 139, 172–177, 189, 192, 195
Merriman, Brian 102, 150; *The Midnight Court* 102
metaphor 5, 9–10, 17, 19, 22, 24, 28, 52, 57, 86, 96, 97, 110–111, 117, 123, 157, 161, 163, 188
metonymy 41
Miller, Karl 145–146
Mills, Georgina: *Strawberry Fare* 50
Miłosz, Czesław 31, 81, 88, 111, 116–118, 120–121, 188; *The Witness of Poetry* 88
Milton, John 4, 38, 92, 115, 185
mind 6–11, 16, 18, 20–21, 30, 32, 36–39, 47, 49, 58, 65, 94–97, 99, 102, 104–105, 115, 120–122, 134, 147–148, 162, 168, 171, 174, 176–177, 179, 183, 187, 189, 194–195
Monroe, Jonathan: *A Poverty of Objects* 57, 70
Montague, John 5, 76, 88, 147, 167; *Poisoned Lands* 88
Monteith, Charles 78
Montenegro, David 151, 167
Morrison, Blake 67, 70, 130, 132, 146; *Seamus Heaney* 67, 70, 130, 132, 146
Muir, Edwin 92
Muldoon, Paul 186
music 4, 6–12, 14, 25, 27, 58–59, 61, 71, 72, 74, 82, 89–108, 133, 135, 145, 149–155, 175, 182, 187–197
myth 14, 16, 17, 30, 38, 162, 190, 195, 196

naming 71, 102, 153, 180
Nazi 63
negotiation 1, 10, 12, 15–18, 21, 24, 30–31, 71–72, 76, 94, 120–121, 127, 187
neighbourly 81–82

Nobel Prize 1, 8, 39, 99–100, 131, 179, 181, 199
Noel-Tod, Jeremy: *The Penguin Book of the Prose Poem* 58, 70
Norman 80, 134–135, 167, 180
Northern Ireland xi, 1, 3, 5–6, 11, 13, 16, 18, 28, 30, 33, 36, 42, 51–54, 60, 62–68, 70–73, 79, 82, 87–89, 97, 102–103, 116, 151, 181–187, 190–191, 198–199

O'Brien, Eugene: *Seamus Heaney as Aesthetic Thinker A Study of the Prose* x, 28, 34, 89, 109, 199
O'Donoghue, Bernard: *The Cambridge Companion to Seamus Heaney* 87, 128; *Seamus Heaney and the Language of Poetry* 88
O'Driscoll, Denis: *Stepping Stones Interviews with Seamus Heaney* 14, 17, 24, 33, 40, 45–48, 50, 70, 88, 95, 98–99, 109, 128, 167, 178, 184, 198, 199
O'Neill, Hugh 79
Observer, The 145–146
Old English 73–74, 78
omphalos 4–6, 10, 30, 36, 38–39, 75, 93, 137, 155
organic 24–25, 27
Orkney 47–48
Orpheus 101–102
Other, the 19, 24, 29–31, 41, 43, 56, 58, 61, 66, 74, 92, 97, 99, 101, 125, 132, 140, 144, 161, 176, 180–181
Oxford Lectures 1, 12, 71, 88–89, 128, 199
Oxford University x, 3, 6, 49, 108, 127–128, 131, 167, 178, 199

paradigm 101
Parker, Michael 34, 88, 146; *Seamus Heaney The Making of the Poet* 34, 88, 146
Parnet, Claire: *Dialogues* 33
personal 3–8, 10, 13, 46, 48, 62, 64, 94, 101, 117, 120, 122, 130, 132, 140, 142–145, 168, 170–171, 174, 176–177, 195–197
perspective x, 10–15, 19–20, 27, 30, 32, 39, 79, 101, 111, 113, 115–116, 121, 130–135, 138, 140
Petrarchan 115
philosophy 110, 117, 120
phonetic 21
Plath, Sylvia 132, 138–146, 179, 198

208 Index

pleasure xiii, 25, 37, 72, 92, 108, 113, 180
plurality 28–30
poetic 1–10, 12–14, 17, 19, 20–30, 36–39, 41, 44, 46, 49, 53–67, 71–73, 77, 79, 84, 86, 89–93, 96–108, 111–118, 120–126, 130, 132–136, 138–148, 150, 160, 164–165, 169–177, 181–182, 186, 197
poetic language 62
poetic thinking 13–14, 20, 23, 25, 28, 30
poetic vision 115
politics 1, 2, 6, 10–11, 15–18, 28–29, 31, 45, 48, 51–54, 60–67, 98–99, 103, 106–107, 111–112, 114, 116–117, 126, 160, 169, 174–175, 180, 186–187
Pope, Alexander 97, 118
Pound, Ezra 138, 171–172, 178
prose x, xi, xiii, 1–17, 22, 28, 38–39, 49, 52–68, 71, 87, 89–96, 99, 101–108, 111, 113, 123, 132, 136–137, 143–144, 147, 168–172, 174, 177, 179, 180–187, 197–198
prose poems 12, 52–58, 61–62, 64–68, 198
Protestants 41, 68
psyche 38, 105
psychoanalytic theory x, 16, 19, 35, 174
pump 4–6, 10, 38–39, 93

quincunx 11, 28–31
Quinn, Justin 149, 151, 162, 164, 167
Quinn, Antoinette 164, 167

radio 8, 63, 100, 182, 198
Randall, James 67, 69, 83, 88, 130, 137, 146; 'Interview with Seamus Heaney' 67, 83, 130, 137
rational 119–120, 127
real 6, 17–18, 20–23, 31, 58, 60–61, 65, 84, 90, 124, 163, 174, 194, 196
reason 3, 23, 28, 65, 117, 119–120, 122, 124, 127, 133
referential 5, 31, 55, 65, 80, 100, 110, 137–138, 140, 142, 145, 160, 172–173
relationship 3–4, 10–13, 16, 19, 24–26, 28, 35, 43, 54, 59–60, 63, 66, 71, 73, 77–79, 82, 85, 90–91, 110, 115–116, 126, 131, 138–144, 151, 169, 181, 183, 193

religion xii, 38, 45, 48, 51, 67, 105–106, 111, 114, 119–120, 123–127, 134, 150, 157–160, 165
representation 11, 16, 58, 61, 68, 143
repression 11, 31, 35–36, 38
revolution 150, 159
rhetoric 25, 63, 80, 172, 177
rhyme 7–8, 21–22, 24, 61, 75–76, 90, 92–93, 96–98, 102, 107, 113–114, 162, 173
rhythm 10, 22, 53, 56, 59, 74, 84, 92–98, 100–101, 114, 133, 139, 177, 187, 196
Richtarik, Marilynn 183, 198–199
Ricks, Christopher 169, 175, 178
Ricoeur, Paul 180, 197, 200
Riffaterre, Michael 57, 70
ripples 40, 177
Roethke, Theodore 9, 106, 180
Rome xii, 10–11, 31, 38, 123, 134, 150, 158, 166, 169
roots 110, 157
Rottenberg, Elizabeth 15, 33; *Negotiations Interventions and Interviews* 33, 120
Russell, Richard Rankin xi, 13, 52–53, 66–68, 70, 104, 109, 179, 181–182, 190, 198, 200; *Modernity, Community, and Place in Brian Friel's Drama* xi, 200; *Seamus Heaney An Introduction* xi, 70, 181, 200; *Seamus Heaney's Regions* xi, 52, 66, 68, 70, 109, 182, 198, 200

sampler 17–18, 24
Samuel Taylor Coleridge 32
Saxon 85, 105, 189
Scotland 47, 76, 81–82, 191
Scullions 45
Sefaris, George 180
Seidel, Frederick 169, 178
self 7, 15, 21, 25, 27, 41, 43, 47–48, 53, 55–61, 64–68, 82, 106–107, 116, 122, 136–137, 140, 142–143, 157–158, 161–162, 165, 171, 173–174, 177, 179, 184–186, 197
sense 5–9, 12, 15–19, 20–29, 30, 32, 36–39, 41–44, 47–48, 52–53, 61–63, 65, 71, 75, 77, 83–89, 91, 95, 98–99, 103, 105, 107, 113, 120, 124–125, 132–133, 145, 150–154, 157, 159, 162–164, 169, 172–176, 185–187, 190–192, 196

Index 209

Shakespeare, William 47, 79, 88, 92, 95, 106, 134, 181, 182; *The Merchant of Venice* 81, 88; *Timon of Athens* 95
Shelley, Percy Bysshe: *Shelley's Poetry and Prose* 65, 70
SHP-EU: Seamus Heaney Papers, Emory University 38, 45, 47, 49, 50
shuttle 15, 21
shuttling 18
signified 18
signifier(s) 15, 17, 121, 174, 176
Simon, Jules 17, 32, 98, 109, 156, 188, 199
singular 4, 13, 41, 119, 140
slant 14, 27, 30, 32
Smith, Stan 106
societal 2, 138
somatic 16
Sonzogni, Marco 19, 20, 34; *The Translations of Seamus Heaney* 34
Sophocles 182; *Antigone* 102–108, 182
sound 5, 8, 10, 19, 28, 32, 57, 59, 61–62, 66, 71, 76–78, 85, 93–96, 101, 103, 105, 108, 119, 132, 152, 169, 171, 175, 182, 188, 191, 195
space 3–9, 10–12, 15, 17–21, 23–27, 30, 39, 46, 53, 94, 101, 122, 133, 141, 147, 158, 161–164, 177, 190
spatial 10–11, 15–24
Spenser, Edmund 11, 29–30
Stanfield, Paul Scott 86, 88
stanza 22, 24–27, 83, 86, 102, 119, 135, 141, 181
St. Columb's 11, 37, 41–43, 48, 50, 54, 99, 105
stepping stone 52, 76
Stevens, Wallace ix, 17, 32, 46, 50, 58, 70, 112, 123; *Necessary Angel* 50
Stevenson, Anne 67, 70
Strachey, James: *The Interpretation of Dreams* 16
structure 21–29, 30–32, 46, 51–56, 59, 68, 72, 96, 102, 104, 159, 173, 174
Sweeney 156, 159–161, 163, 167, 184, 189, 199
Swir, Ana 7, 175
symbol 11, 18, 23, 26–30, 32, 39–40, 45, 46, 85, 101, 127, 171, 174, 181
synecdoche 9–10, 14, 38, 90, 105
syntax 6–8, 21, 59, 106–107, 134–135, 138, 141

Terdiman, Richard: *Discourse/ Counter-Discourse* 57, 70
text 1, 9–10, 15, 17, 22, 27, 51, 53–56, 62, 67, 89, 105, 110, 142–143, 157, 169, 188
thingness 21–26, 29
thinking 1–6, 8–18, 20–31, 45, 52, 56, 58–59, 74–75, 78, 89, 91–96, 98–101, 110, 111, 115, 121, 125, 127, 131, 133, 147, 153, 158–164, 168–169, 177, 180, 194
Thomas, Dylan 3, 101, 133, 138
threshold 124
Times Literary Supplement 117, 183, 199
Tobin, Daniel 30, 34, 163, 167; *Passage to the Center Imagination and the Sacred in the Poetry of Seamus Heaney* 34, 167
Toome 16
tradition 6, 10–11, 18, 28–32, 38, 51, 54, 56, 66–67, 73–80, 83, 86, 98, 100, 105, 117, 133, 144, 150
transcendence 14, 18, 26, 112–113, 120–126, 149–150, 154, 171, 176, 179
transformation 20, 56, 58, 63, 66, 71, 118, 149
translation 2, 10, 11, 19–20, 31, 103–104, 186
tribal 10
trope 11, 22, 95
Troubles, the 6, 12, 51, 54, 60–68, 82, 103, 182–183
truth 6, 13–14, 28, 49, 101, 115, 119–121, 125, 157, 176, 184, 190, 192, 195–196
tuning fork 7, 94–96, 102–103, 164, 189, 192

Ulster 18, 30, 42, 45, 63, 73–79, 88, 159, 182
Ulster linen 18
uncanny 11, 35–40, 42, 44, 46–49
unconscious 3, 7–8, 10, 15–17, 20, 27, 35, 38–39, 54, 64, 94, 104, 108, 171–172, 195
Unionism 42
universal 4, 8, 20, 79
utterance 55, 80, 90, 105, 139, 176, 188

Van Dyne, Susan R. 143
Vendler, Helen 127, 129

210 *Index*

vernacular 72, 75, 77–78, 114, 153
Viking(s) 10, 31, 60, 81–83, 86, 105, 183
violence 12, 18, 28, 46, 51, 54, 60–61, 64, 66, 82, 143, 169, 175, 187
Virgil 10, 101, 106, 166; *Aeneid* 106
visceral 64, 130, 157, 173
vocable 134
voice 3–4, 16–17, 24, 28, 30, 39, 49, 52, 56, 59, 61, 71–78, 85, 87, 94, 98, 107, 113–114, 126, 131, 136, 139, 143, 150, 153–159, 169–170, 173–176, 187–188, 196
Voznesensky, Andrei 169

Wales 32, 74, 127, 189, 191
Ward, Joe (neighbour) 84
Weil, Simone 12, 110–118, 120–121, 126, 128–129; *Gravity and Grace* 110–111
Wevill, Assia Esther 144
Wheatley, David 123, 125
White, Harry 94; *Music and the Irish Literary Imagination* 94
Whitman, Walt 56

Wilde, Oscar 12, 182
William of Orange 29, 62
Wilson, Ross 33
Wood, James 164
Wood, The (Heaney's home) 161
Woolf, Virginia 56
Wordsworth, William 5, 7, 12, 32, 36–39, 44–45, 50, 54, 57, 70–73, 84, 88, 92, 94–96, 106, 116, 179–180, 185–189, 191–200; *Lyrical Ballads* 32, 185, 193; *The Prelude* 54, 186, 189, 192, 194, 198; *Selected Poems and Prefaces* 50, 70
worldview 27, 36, 123
Wormald, Mark 131

Yeats, William Butler 1, 3, 5, 7, 10–12, 24–30, 34, 46–47, 73, 85, 88, 92–93, 94–96, 105–109, 113–120, 125–126, 128, 139, 151, 165, 167, 175, 179, 181, 184, 187–190, 198, 200; *Autobiographies* 93; *The Collected Poems of W. B. Yeats* 34; *Yeats's Poems* 165

Printed in the USA
CPSIA information can be obtained
at www.ICGtesting.com
LVHW020817170924
791295LV00004B/335